WHERE WILL I BE?

.

WHERE WILL I BE?

In Search of Sokolov

Barbara Truman

YOUCAXTON
PUBLICATIONS

ISBN 978-1-914424-80-9
Published by YouCaxton Publications 2022

YouCaxton Publications
www.youcaxton.co.uk

For my late, much missed parents,
whose love of music I was so fortunate to inherit.

Contents

Introduction   ix

1. SPAIN & PORTUGAL   1

2. ITALY   20

3. MONACO   43

4. FRANCE   47

5. SWITZERLAND   71

6. AUSTRIA   94

7. POLAND   107

8. CZECH REPUBLIC   119

9. FINLAND   122

10. SWEDEN   147

11. NORWAY   159

12. DENMARK   166

13. NETHERLANDS   169

14. BELGIUM   184

15. LUXEMBOURG   188

16. UNITED KINGDOM   194

17. GERMANY   198

ACKNOWLEDGEMENTS   291

Introduction

THE GERMANS HAVE a word, *fernweh*, which roughly translates into English as 'farsickness', and for much of my adult life until the age of fifty-three I experienced a longing to be elsewhere, doing something new and as yet unknown, living a different life altogether. At times it was almost a physical pain, more often a heaviness of heart, especially when on a summer's day I heard the distant drone of an aircraft up in the blue or glimpsed the etchings of vapour trails.

But my life was to change direction completely one balmy June evening in 1997 when I went along to a recital at the BBC's Pebble Mill Studio in Birmingham: part of a weekly series of live broadcasts featuring world class pianists. On this particular evening, the artist was unknown to me: an imperious looking Russian by the name of Grigory Sokolov, who strode into the small arena, directed his gaze somewhere above the heads of the audience as if they were of no consequence, performed a smart manoeuvre combining a perfunctory bow with a sideways swoop onto his seat and incorporated a deft upward flick of his coat tails as he descended. There followed no sacred moment of concentration, no flexing of fingers or adjustment of cuffs, no preparatory contemplation of the keyboard. Instead, as his backside hit the piano stool, his hands leapt simultaneously into action and an audible gasp of astonishment swept through the studio.

My front row seat provided an unimpeded view of Sokolov's miraculous finger and foot work as he delivered eight meticulously wrought Preludes and Fugues by J S Bach and four atmospheric Chopin Polonaises. It was a masterclass in precision, power and poetry, as if during a long period of preparation he had lifted each note from the score, held it in his hands and considered it lovingly. I sensed right away that I was witnessing something very significant indeed, and the experience had such a profound effect upon me that I was reluctant to leave my seat at the end of the evening, instead taking the opportunity to regard the inner workings of the piano, as if I needed to offer my thanks for the part it had played in this momentous experience. Thus I was last to leave the studio, and in the corridor outside stood the producer of the programme, Jeremy Hayes, who took one look at my thunderstruck expression, grinned at me and said, "He's rather good, isn't he? Would you like to meet him?" I hesitated for a moment, fearing Sokolov's aloof demeanour might tarnish the magnificence of what I'd just heard, but decided he may as well be given the benefit of the doubt.

Joining a line of admirers waiting to pay their respects, I noticed that Sokolov was speaking quite good English and listening intently to whatever was said to him, answering each question, however trivial, with patience and generosity, all the while maintaining unwavering eye contact. He greeted every compliment with a broad smile and humble thanks, betraying not the slightest hint of artifice, as if it had never occurred to him that he was in any way special. When my turn came, I was unprepared and could think of little to say, and I was much too shy to shake his hand. My initial impression of him had been so wrong; he was far from being pompous or remote, and the combination of his gentle countenance and endearing modesty, the intensity of his pianism, his extraordinary articulation and stupefying technique, proved fatal. As a consequence I left the studio determined to learn more about him, unaware that I'd just taken my first steps along the road to Damascus. I'd grown up listening to piano music, my mother having played and both my parents sharing a love of the Russian composers, so it seemed fitting that I should have discovered this treasure.

Within weeks, the BBC Proms listings announced that during August Sokolov would be performing a concerto with the Scottish Symphony Orchestra, so naturally I took the train down to London for the event. However, the Albert Hall experience was a far cry from the intimacy of the Pebble Mill Studio; this time my seat was at the back of beyond, seemingly miles away from the platform, the piano a tiny miniature. But as Sokolov's heroic performance of Tchaikovsky's 1st Piano Concerto unfolded I was once again captivated, and I spent the homeward journey planning my next move.

A phone call to Sokolov's London agents generated a few photographs and reviews of performances in far flung places, as well as the date of his next engagement in the British Isles: a solo recital in Dublin in December. The trip to London had been no big deal, but

Dublin was a different matter, involving either a winter sea crossing or a flight, and for me flying was not an option. Coerced by an ill-chosen and manipulative first husband eleven years my senior, I'd emigrated to Australia at the age of twenty-one under the ten pound assisted passage scheme. It was my first experience of flying, and the twenty-nine hour journey, which I endured with mounting fear and misery, comprised six consecutive flights, starting from Heathrow and travelling via Rome, Tehran, New Delhi, Bangkok, Singapore, ending at Sydney's Mascot Airport, where I stumbled down the aircraft steps, vowing never to fly again. A year later I returned to England by sea, and in the subsequent thirty-two years I refused to fly anywhere and suffered frequent nightmares in which I was involved in a variety of appalling airborne catastrophes. It was a deeply entrenched phobia, but the prospect of a ferry journey to Dublin in December was almost as frightening. I agonised for days, until my compulsion to be at that concert finally transcended the fear, and I decided that for Sokolov I would take to the skies again.

On the dreaded day of lift-off I awoke feeling physically sick, and at Birmingham Airport I sat in the departure lounge as if awaiting the hour of my execution. At boarding time, despite a compelling urge to run in the opposite direction, I trailed dutifully behind the other passengers along a corridor and out onto the tarmac, where what looked like a propeller-driven Dinky toy was perched, patiently waiting to transform every nightmare I'd ever had into one terrifying reality. At that moment I wanted to turn back the clock to a time before I'd taken leave of my senses and contemplated such a foolish escapade, but time soon revealed that my life was to be spared. The journey to Ireland was stressful, but I had the good fortune to be sitting beside a friendly overweight businessman, whose considerable bulk provided a comforting cushion, as if I were leaning against the arm of a familiar old sofa. Breakfast also provided a welcome diversion, and in less than an hour we were preparing to land. I hated the bumpy descent through the cloud cover and the excruciating moments before touchdown, but felt an overwhelming sense of elation as the aircraft finally wobbled to a standstill. After thanking my neighbour for his support, I wasn't sure who to thank next: God, Sokolov or Aer Lingus.

My first night in Ireland was spent with friends at their cottage in the Wicklow Mountains, and I lay awake worrying that having risked so much I may not even be allowed to speak to Sokolov after the recital. Transferring to a small guest house in Dublin the next day, I prepared for my evening at the National Concert Hall in a flurry of anticipation tinged with anxiety. At the recital I sat next to an elderly gentleman who'd been a professional pianist in his time. At the interval he remarked on the lack of connection between artist and audience, labelling Sokolov a 'cold fish'. The first half of the programme had been devoted to Rameau, but by the end of the second half, during which Sokolov produced towering performances of sonatas by Beethoven and Brahms, the music had spoken and my neighbour had changed his tune.

As I shuffled nervously out of the auditorium I noticed a long queue in a side corridor, indicating that others had a similar desire to meet the man. Unlike in Birmingham, I spent the waiting time trying to decide what to say, but as I drew closer I lost my nerve and merely blurted out that I'd overcome a thirty-two year fear of flying in order to travel from Birmingham to Dublin expressly to hear him. He looked impressed and beamed from ear to ear, telling me that although it would be many months before he returned to the UK, he would be performing at Jersey Arts Centre in two days' time. I would have given anything to be moving on to Jersey myself, but told him I was expected back at the office.

At the guest house I lay awake for the third consecutive night, longing to be free to follow Sokolov to Jersey, but acknowledging that there were too many obstacles in my path. By dawn, however, I'd convinced myself that if I could just get back to Birmingham sooner rather than later, I might somehow be able to make it all happen. My return flight wasn't until mid-afternoon, so I needed to establish whether I could switch to an earlier one. Seething with agitation, I galloped downstairs with a view to asking if I could use the proprietor's telephone, but he was waiting in the dining room with a welcoming smile and a chair pulled back for me to sit myself down and enjoy one of his hearty Irish breakfasts. My world must have tilted on its axis overnight, for despite having adhered to a strict vegetarian diet for the previous sixteen years, I found myself ordering a gigantic fry-up, calmly guiding bacon rashers, fried eggs and sausages into my mouth with no consideration for my unsuspecting digestive system. Some sort of exceptional fortification seemed necessary to sustain me through the oncoming challenge, but I drew the line at black pudding. It was a shameful lapse upon which I chose not to dwell for too long as there were far more pressing matters to be addressed.

When I explained that I had no mobile phone but needed to make an urgent call, or possibly several, the proprietor ushered me into what was little more than a cupboard containing a fax machine, a telephone and a pile of directories. I quickly discovered that there was no possibility of an earlier flight home, so the next step was to contact Jersey Arts Centre in the hope of securing a ticket for the recital. I mentioned that I was calling from Dublin and had been so enthralled by Sokolov's performance there that I'd decided to repeat the experience in Jersey. Luckily, one or two seats remained unsold, and soon everything else began to fall into place. Making a careful note of the duration of each call, I rang my office and begged for two days' additional leave, called the tourist office in St. Helier to arrange accommodation and booked a flight from Birmingham to Jersey the following afternoon. The eye-watering air fare stopped me in my tracks, but not for long. I'd imagined it might be similar to the eighty pound flight to Dublin, but only business class seats were available and one of those was going to cost me a whopping two hundred and forty pounds. Spending that amount of money on anything else would have necessitated the most careful consideration, but I wasn't prepared to fall at the final hurdle. With all the arrangements in place, I sat down with the proprietor to work out how much I owed him, collected my air ticket from a city centre travel agent and headed back to Dublin Airport with a singing heart.

I arrived at the airport in a state bordering on delirium. I'd never been tempted by drugs, but could well imagine this might be how they made you feel. My rash decision to spend such a colossal sum on one concert, let alone commit myself to more flying, seemed to make perfect sense. I felt more alive than I could ever remember, and my feeling of euphoria rendered me incapable of sitting still for more than five minutes. Restless and impatient to begin my next adventure, I began wandering through the airport's shopping aisles, finally reaching the outermost departure lounge, where who should be pacing back and forth, hands clasped behind his back, but

Sokolov. I was unsure whether to approach him in a public place, but was bursting to tell him I'd made plans to go to Jersey. If he had any qualms that I might be about to embark upon a stalking campaign, he kept them well hidden and looked genuinely pleased. We talked about his discography and he expressed a dislike of recording studios and a strong preference for the spontaneity of live recordings. My flight was called and I ventured to ask if I could say hello to him after the recital. "Yes, of course", he said, "I will be easy to find", and as I walked away he followed up with a cheery, "See you tomorrow!" which rang in my ears all the way home.

Sleep eluded me yet again that night, and by morning I felt paralysed with weariness and almost too ill to move. I seriously considered not going to Jersey after all, but finally hauled myself out of bed, tottered round the block to clear my head, and prepared to leave home again. It wasn't until I'd checked in at Birmingham Airport and been handed a complimentary newspaper that I remembered I was travelling business class. I'd eaten nothing since my breakfast bonanza in Dublin the previous day, but the cornucopia of free drinks and snacks on offer in the first class lounge was wasted on me; all I could manage were a few sips of water. The aircraft waiting to whisk me across to the Channel Islands was a flimsy forty-eight seater, and we were buffeted by strong winds and squally bursts of rain as we gained altitude in the gathering dusk. The route was via Guernsey, which looked no bigger than a postage stamp floating on a dark, boiling sea, and I wondered how we could possibly land on such a minuscule target. The ten minute hop from Guernsey to Jersey was a bumpy one, and I counted every second.

In St. Helier, at the Jersey Arts Centre box office a note attached to my ticket told me that I would be Mr Sokolov's guest that evening, and accordingly he'd requested my card payment be refunded. As I struggled to process this prized piece of information, the lady who'd taken my original telephone booking introduced herself, told me how pleased everyone was that I'd made the journey, that I'd been mentioned on local radio and that a car had been organised to take me back to the airport the next day. The Director of the Arts Centre then came sailing across the foyer to shake my hand, assuring me that as soon as the performance was over, he would escort me to Mr

Sokolov's dressing room. For the first time in my life I had an inkling of how it might feel to be a VIP.

At our short meeting afterwards, Sokolov was interested in discussing travel related topics, asking me about my journey. Anxious not to outstay my welcome, I thanked him for providing my concert ticket, expressed the hope that I might hear him somewhere in Europe before too long, and took my leave. Back at my hotel I literally jumped for joy before falling into an exhausted sleep. By lunchtime the next day I was airborne again, this time propelled by jet engines, and as I contemplated the sunlit cloudscape outside my window I sensed that a new and thrilling chapter in my life had just begun.

Without access to the internet, it was necessary to research Sokolov's forthcoming engagements via the telephone. I called his recording company in Paris, who directed me to his management agents in Verona, and they told me the next concert would be in February, in Bordeaux. My phone call to the Grand Theatre Bordeaux was a convoluted affair, as I struggled in my antiquated schoolgirl French to request a seat with a view of the keyboard, but not too far over to the left. All I could do was hope for the best. A travel agent found me an early morning direct flight from Heathrow, which necessitated travelling to the airport by overnight coach. We pulled out of Birmingham Bus Station at three in the morning and began our tedious journey, stopping at numerous pick-up points along the way and arriving at Heathrow at six. A mixture of excitement, desperate tiredness and a renewed fear of flying overtook me as I boarded my BA flight some hours later. Compared with the aircraft on which I'd flown to Dublin and Jersey, this was a big brute, and my face must have said it all. A young woman sitting across the aisle asked if I was nervous, and as we gathered speed along the runway she reached across and took my hand, holding it tightly as we left the ground. She kept me talking throughout the flight and helped me to find the airport coach into the city. I had no idea where the concert hall was situated but, as if by magic, the coach stopped there en route. I was dropped off in a huge square, one side of which was dominated by the imposing classical facade of the Grand Theatre, displaying across its frontage just one reassuring word in giant letters: SOKOLOV.

I found a small hotel in a side street close to the theatre, whose rooms were unappealing but affordable. Seized with a desire to explore the immediate vicinity and spend as little time as possible in the hotel's dreary surroundings, I wandered the boulevards for an hour or so but finally surrendered to fatigue and returned to my room. Instead of sleeping, I lay prostrate, compiling a mental list of all the ways in which the evening might prove disappointing. A few hours later I was inside the theatre, admiring one of the loveliest interiors I'd ever seen. It had an elaborately decorated ceiling, gilt and crystal chandeliers, elegant blue velvet seats and a stunning *trompe l'oeil* backdrop, in front of which the piano stood waiting. Although my seat was close to the platform, I noticed one of the balconies was empty apart from two people, and at the interval I asked an attendant if I might be allowed to sit up there, imagining the panoramic view it would provide. After consulting her superior she told me that the couple sitting up there were the Mayor of Bordeaux and his wife. The loge next to theirs was normally reserved for their personal guests, but I was welcome to occupy it for the second half. Positioned directly above the stage, it provided a marvellous vantage point from which to luxuriate in the music, drink in the atmosphere and beauty of the auditorium and imagine that Sokolov was playing expressly for my benefit.

Afterwards I walked along a floodlit colonnade at the side of the building and climbed a flight of steps to gain access to Sokolov's dressing room. As I knocked on the door I felt a stab of apprehension, but he smiled in immediate recognition and introduced me to his agent, his recording manager and his wife, explaining that I was the lady he'd already told them about, who'd flown for the first time in thirty-two years to hear him in Dublin. I was flattered that he'd remembered the details and delighted when he asked his agent to let me have his schedule of engagements. When he also offered to help me with concert tickets whenever it was possible my night was complete. Later, I realised what an enormous risk I'd taken in flying to Bordeaux without firstly checking with Sokolov's agent. The possibility of a last minute cancellation had never occurred to me.

Within less than a fortnight I was gazing out of yet another aircraft at the cluster of islands surrounding the city of Stockholm, the deep blue of the Baltic Sea giving way to paler shades of turquoise, each of the islands fringed with ice. It was my first trip to any Scandinavian country and I remember walking along the waterfront later that day, as huge blocks of ice clunked together in the harbour, marvelling that I was in Sweden of all places. Whichever country I visited in subsequent years, I could never quite believe I was actually there; it was as if I'd played no part in the planning at all, but merely been planted there by some external force.

At the Berwaldhallen that evening I was handed a ticket marked 'Sokolov's Guest' which gave me inordinate pleasure, and on being ushered into the front row of the balcony and told my seat was frequently occupied by Swedish royalty, I felt exultant. A magisterial performance of Rachmaninoff's Piano Concerto No.3 brought the entire audience to its feet as an almighty tidal wave of cheering filled the hall. Sokolov stood back modestly, allowing the conductor and orchestra to take their share of the acclaim before stepping forward to receive his own. Some months later I was given a recording of that night's performance, which still brings back all the excitement of those early times when I first stepped into Sokolov's realm. It was a night to remember, as were each of the hundreds of nights I would spend in the future listening to his unique artistry. Every trip was a fresh adventure, every concert a profound emotional experience.

I heard Sokolov perform with orchestras on many occasions in the UK, Germany, Italy, Monaco, Sweden and Finland, until 2005 when he ceased to be involved with orchestral concerts in order to concentrate on solo recitals. There's a special kind of grandeur about a piano concerto, and witnessing Sokolov in collaboration with his favourite conductors was always a joy. Those complex and beautiful pieces of music normally lasted no longer than forty-five minutes, sometimes considerably less, and such fleeting episodes of what I thought of as 'exquisite agony' contained far too much emotion for my liking, and not nearly enough Sokolov. The orchestral concerts often took place on two consecutive evenings, usually on Thursday and Friday, so I got a second bite of the cherry, but in order to qualify for an economy class flight it was necessary to stay over on Saturday night as well, which caused me unimaginable anguish. The extra day enabled me to explore some wonderful cities, but all I really wanted to do at the end of a concert was return to my room, pack my bag and catch the earliest available flight home. In retrospect, I should have relished such opportunities, but I always awoke on those Saturday mornings with a sinking feeling, realising that Sokolov was winging his way to the next engagement and I'd been left behind.

During a twenty-three year period following my epiphany at Pebble Mill, I attended over five hundred of Sokolov's performances, visiting an amazing variety of music venues, from Europe's most prestigious concert halls, sumptuous opera houses and theatres to historic castles and churches, town halls, music conservatories, university lecture halls, chamber music salons, museums, even schools, converted factories, and most unusually, a sheep shelter in Lower Saxony. Many of the smaller churches were especially atmospheric: in Finland some of them overlooked the sea, others were in picturesque medieval German locations and ancient Italian hill towns; one of my favourites was perched on a wooded hillside in Switzerland, entirely concealed by trees but for its slender cream-coloured spire and little bell tower.

Airport departure lounges became my natural habitat and mainland Europe my second home. I received countless acts of kindness from strangers, some of whom became long standing friends. In following Sokolov I discovered the glories of European art, architecture and culture. I, who had once been too nervous to go to the cinema alone, visited a hundred and sixty five towns and cities in more than twenty countries as an independent traveller, exploring their galleries and museums, cathedrals, castles, national monuments and gardens, where I was able to indulge my love of photography. Many of my trips included scenic rail and bus journeys too: along the Rhine Valley with its fairytale castles, the shores of Lake Geneva, through the Swiss and Italian Alps, the forests and lakes of Finland, the sunflower fields of Spain, the acres of lavender in Provence. Even without the music this seemed like an embarrassment of riches.

I soon became so familiar with Sokolov's schedule that people I met at concerts sometimes asked me when he was going to be at a certain venue and invariably I could provide the information without consulting my diary. Once, as I left Sokolov's room, I turned and said, "See you on the 29th", which was barely a week away. "OK", he replied, then followed up with, "Where will I be?"

Back in the 1990s, the process of planning concert trips was laborious. For the first few years I was dependent on travel agents to find flights for me but eventually I discovered the internet. With no computer of my own I began using those provided by the local library or internet cafés. I rarely booked accommodation in advance, preferring to search for somewhere cheap on arrival. This led to several close shaves when flights were delayed and I arrived at concert venues by the skin of my teeth with my luggage in tow, but finding somewhere to stay after the performance could be an even bigger problem.

Doing it all on a shoestring enabled me to attend a far greater number of performances, and I spent much of my spare time not only looking for cheap flights but also combing the charity shops for suitable concert wear. For the first seven years on the Sokolov trail, I stayed in the most basic accommodation I could find: occasionally in a backpackers' hostel, but more often in a family run guest house or one star hotel. As soon as I began receiving a state pension in addition to what were by then part-time earnings, I was able to sleep in less spartan surroundings, but up until then I endured protruding bed springs, hostile pillows, horribly stained carpets, corridors reeking of cigarette smoke or other substances, mouldy bathrooms with geriatric plumbing, single glazing combined with all-night trams outside my window, nightmare neighbours who partied or played musical instruments into the night, and the occasional unwashed bed.

In the early days I carried emergency rations in the shape of home-made sandwiches – usually cheese - which I would supplement with a carton of fries or something sweet from a bakery, but shortly after the outbreak of foot and mouth disease in 2001 my supplies were confiscated at the airport and forbidden thereafter. But very occasionally I was invited to a plush reception, a festival dinner or a post-concert supper in a classy restaurant or private house, which was always a stupendous treat. I never knew when they were likely to happen, but from time to time Sokolov would be invited by promoters or organisers to such events, and as he generally preferred to return to his hotel after the evening's exertions, the invitations would sometimes be extended to me, and I got a decent meal as well as a glimpse of how the other half lived.

After several years of exhausting pre-dawn departures from Birmingham Coach Station to catch morning flights from Luton, Stansted, Heathrow and Gatwick, I chose instead to fly from Birmingham whenever possible, even if it meant catching connecting flights from the major European hubs in Amsterdam, Brussels,

Copenhagen, Paris, Frankfurt, Düsseldorf or Munich. As a result I took in excess of nine hundred flights following the scary hop across to Dublin, and apart from an unforgettable take-off involving a kangaroo jump, a couple of aborted landings, several episodes of seriously bone-shaking turbulence and one lightning strike, I never felt in any danger.

Sokolov played each half of his programme for twelve months at a stretch, and I often heard him play the same piece as many as thirty times. Most fellow enthusiasts understood why I did this, but others sometimes asked why I travelled such distances to listen to the same music over and over again. My answer was that no two performances could ever be the same, in terms of the atmosphere in the hall, the position of my seat, the character of the piano, the quality of the acoustics, the behaviour of the audience, the mood of Sokolov himself. I could also hear how each piece evolved throughout the season. Staying at home and listening to precisely the same performance on a CD had never been an option; there was simply no substitute for a live experience. Sokolov had always been a musician's musician. I saw many prominent artists and conductors in attendance at his recitals and as a guest I occasionally found myself sitting next to a well-known face.

A frugal lifestyle at home enabled me to lead a charmed existence on the concert circuit. Occasionally a photograph of me talking to Sokolov after a recital would appear on a Facebook website dedicated to him, so my face became familiar to many of his admirers. I also began commenting on the performances I attended, and before long, wherever I went, someone would recognise me. Although I loved receiving the attention, I could never quite believe I deserved it. When a German broadsheet newspaper published a full page article about me I was enormously proud, but some time later I was asked at a moment's notice to give a short interview for a Norwegian TV documentary about Sokolov, and I was so self-conscious that my few minutes of red-faced incoherent waffling was largely axed, leaving only a ten second clip.

Over the years I enjoyed the hospitality of numerous people I met at performances, when I was invited to share drinks or meals and sometimes offered overnight accommodation. On these occasions there was always talk of my travel experiences and my impressions of Sokolov as well as plenty of laughter, music and human warmth. Sometimes my hosts would arrange for piano music to greet me in the morning – by way of a recording or an impromptu performance on their own instrument. One weekend I stayed in the luxurious home of a Swiss couple I'd met at a recital in Zürich, who lived in a small town surrounded by verdant meadows and rolling hills. Their three storey open plan house, which they'd designed themselves, sported a glass fronted elevator. The room they used as an art studio was bigger than my entire flat and the mod cons included spacious walk-in wardrobes, a his-and-hers master bathroom, air conditioning and a dust extractor. Within the space of a week I was in the Netherlands spending the night in a derelict school building smothered in graffiti, where my host was legally squatting. I slept in the corner of a vast empty classroom but the main living area was the school's gymnasium, which contained redundant climbing frames and other apparatus, a few items of furniture and my host's grand piano.

So many diverse experiences, all of them precious, most of them falling somewhere between these two extremes, but every single one of them infused with the spirit of Sokolov.

1. SPAIN & PORTUGAL

A FEW WEEKS after the early Scandinavian concerts I visited Spain for the first time, and the only affordable direct flight was from Luton to Madrid with a budget airline called Debonair. Entrusting my life to an unknown low cost carrier felt like an act of recklessness, but Debonair proved to be a smart and efficient little outfit which I was sorry to see go out of business a year later. The bus into the centre of Madrid terminated in an underground car park, and in a dimly lit corner stood a small accommodation kiosk. A charmless woman with a cigarette wedged in the corner of her mouth fixed me up in a B&B on Gran Via, the so called 'Broadway of Madrid', and a battered taxi driven by someone I suspected might be a relative of hers, dumped me unceremoniously outside the premises and charged me a fortune. Hostal Hispano Argentino occupied the sixth floor of a very old building with an unexpectedly grand interior, and my room was simple but perfectly adequate.

On my city map, the Auditorio Nacional looked such a long way from where I was staying that I decided to spend the afternoon trying to locate it using public transport. This foolish exercise coincided with the rush hour and took so long that it left me with little time to prepare for the evening and set out again. As a result, the dummy run was pointless and I felt obliged to take one of the dozens of taxis cruising the district. With agonising slowness we nudged our way towards the Auditorio in impossibly heavy traffic, and my anxiety mounted as the minutes ticked by. At the last moment I arrived at the box office to find there was no ticket reserved for Barbara Truman and the performance was a complete sell-out. I was horrified, but a member of staff hastened away to investigate, and minutes later returned with a very good ticket for the dress circle. Sokolov had been consulted in his dressing room and had confirmed that I was a *bona fide* guest, but I was upset that he'd been disturbed on my account immediately before a concert, especially as this one was being filmed for Spanish TV, and afraid that the interruption may have interfered with his concentration and added to the pressure. In the future there would be a further handful of similar breakdowns in communication, flavouring each trip with an added dash of uncertainty.

The TV company did an excellent job with three strategically placed cameras, and Sokolov's splendid programme comprising Rameau's Suite in G, Beethoven's Sonata No.16 Op.31/1 and Brahms' Sonata No.1 Op.1 was captured for posterity. In the second half I was offered a seat downstairs, much closer to the piano, from where I could see Sokolov's hair almost standing on end with the fierce heat from the lighting trained in his direction, and a constant stream of perspiration coursing down his cheeks. These conditions were the absolute opposite to his usual preference for darkened halls, and he looked drained as he finally left the platform after the third encore.

Members of the London Symphony Orchestra were scattered around backstage, preparing their instruments for a late night concert, and Sokolov's room was crowded with visitors. When the last of the public had departed, leaving a small circle who appeared to know him personally, I was drawn into the room by his recording manager, Yolanta Skura. Sokolov wanted to discuss the mix-up over the ticket and I was eager to find out if I might be allowed to have a copy of the video recording. I also asked him when his programme was likely to change, but realising this might have seemed impolite, I quickly backtracked and assured him I didn't mind *what* he played, or for how long. This made everyone laugh, but when he revealed that at the end of the summer he would be introducing another Beethoven sonata and some rarely performed pieces by William Byrd, there was a great stir of excitement. In my innocence, I'd not realised that for him to divulge his plans for the following season so early in the year was virtually unheard of. Maybe I'd caught him off guard, but the cat was out of the bag, and everyone in the room was delighted. This willingness to share such information was very rarely repeated, and his future programmes usually remained undisclosed until shortly before he began performing them in public.

At that moment the door opened, a finger beckoned Sokolov to give an interview to accompany the recording, and he was gone. The next morning I took a brisk walk in Retiro Park, little realising that my journey home was destined to be a nightmare. After a five hour delay, my flight eventually left Madrid, but Luton was enveloped in thick fog, and after several aborted attempts to land, we were diverted to another airport much closer to Birmingham. The sensible thing would have been to make my way home from there, but I sat like a chump waiting to be transported all the way back to Luton in a dodgy looking double decker bus, on which a worrying amount of heavy luggage had been hauled onto the top deck. This was by far the most terrifying part of the journey and I arrived home at three a.m., twelve hours behind schedule. It was on occasions such as this that I was especially happy to be a free agent with no one at home waiting and wondering.

I'd seen precious little of Madrid itself, which was a pity, and although Sokolov continued to perform there every year, I never returned. However, I was to pass through Madrid-Barajas Airport many times in subsequent years on my way to recitals in other Spanish cities. Sokolov often began the year with a tour of Spain, and his 2020 tour took place immediately before the pandemic struck. In 2021 he was again able to perform in several Spanish cities at the beginning of the year, albeit under strict Covid-19 constraints.

In 2000 I was apprehensive about a planned trip to Bilbao on account of a sudden resurgence of bombing activity by the Basque Separatist Group ETA. It was already four in the afternoon when I landed at Bilbao Airport and the recital was due to start at seven-thirty. The seats were unallocated, so I was determined to be part of the free-for-all which would take place at seven o'clock or even earlier. I learned the service bus would take fifty minutes to reach the city so I went by taxi straight to the Filarmonica with the intention of finding a room close by, but the concert hall was nowhere near any hotels or other accommodation, so I walked towards the river, spotting a modest looking hotel on the other side. Suddenly there were several loud explosions and I almost ran for cover, but then I saw a large group of demonstrators processing slowly and silently along the river bank, carrying banners and discharging powerful fireworks at regular intervals. The hotel had only a double room available, so I inspected a number of others but found them to be cramped, gloomy and stifling hot. At six o'clock I returned to the first hotel and took the double.

It seemed astonishingly mild for a January evening, but on my walk towards the Filarmonica I noticed many women sporting ankle length fur coats, and outside the hall a sizeable crowd of cultivated and prosperous looking people had already gathered. The recital had been organised by a private music society and the walls of the foyer were adorned with signed photographs of some of the greatest singers and musicians of the twentieth century. At seven, the queue began filing in, showing their membership cards. By the time I'd explained who I was and waited for the all clear, very many people had overtaken me and I feared I would end up sitting far away from the piano. I glanced around the front seats but they were all occupied, except for one on the aisle, just a few rows back from the platform with a perfect view of the keyboard, on which was pinned a 'Reserved' notice bearing my name.

Sokolov's programme was devoted to Froberger, Beethoven and Schumann, and the audience displayed warmth and discernment. There were four spectacular encores: the first, Ravel's Toccata from Le Tombeau de Couperin, was a complete *tour de force*, and at the end of a Chopin mazurka there followed a few seconds of absolute silence, with the exception of an elderly gentleman sitting behind me, who murmured with feeling, "Si, senor!" Afterwards, as Sokolov asked me about the current 'flu epidemic in the UK (he was shortly to give recitals in London and Manchester), the concert organiser burst into the room, took Sokolov's face in his hands and planted a kiss on his forehead. The evening had been a triumph.

My hotel provided nothing in the way of nourishment the next morning, but I broke my fast with some bread and cheese I'd brought with me and a drop of warm mineral water. Stepping out into a pleasantly mild, misty atmosphere, I strolled through the narrow deserted streets of the old quarter and wandered round the Sunday morning flower market. Along the river bank stood the Guggenheim Museum of Modern Art, a surreal building clad in stainless steel, which had opened in 1997 and put Bilbao firmly on the tourist map. There was insufficient time to go inside, but as the sun broke through the mist, the municipal band began dashing off a selection of Spanish pieces to an audience of locals gathered on benches beneath the trees, and I joined a group of old men in black berets to drink in the spirited gallop of the music, the dappled sunlight and the jumbled images of ornate and crumbling buildings reflected in the water.

The downside of this charming scene was the stench of pollution coming from the river, which looked as if gallons of disinfectant had been poured into it. I realised I was sampling this unpleasant aroma at a mere eighteen degrees, and shuddered to think how it might smell in high summer. The city was also surrounded by an ugly sprawl of industrial chaos, but beyond all of that were rolling green hills and in the far distance, the mountains. On the long journey back to the airport, the bus wound its way through an unsightly landscape which was somehow fascinating in its hideousness and almost begging to be photographed. Despite its blemishes, I concluded that Bilbao had real heart and I resolved to return one day. On the flight home, the rugged coastline of northern Spain looked magnificent from the air, bathed in sunshine, with a high tide and huge rollers sweeping in. It reminded me that I'd not been close to the sea for two years and I realised how much I missed it.

My trip to Almeria in 2001 brought me closer to the sea, although I'd dithered beforehand, questioning whether it was worth travelling all the way to the south eastern corner of Spain, where a fusspot like me would be reluctant to eat the food, unable to drink the water, speak the lingo, survive the heat or tolerate the inevitable hordes of tourists. I'd read that Almeria was the hottest and poorest region of Spain, with a desert landscape in which *Lawrence of Arabia* and numerous spaghetti westerns had been filmed. The idea became increasingly unenticing, but I felt an overwhelming urge to be on the move.

I flew to Barcelona and waited for five hours for my connecting flight, during which time I'd hoped to take a quick look at the city, but I was advised against the idea in case of traffic jams. It was nine in the evening by the time I landed at Almeria's tiny airport, and I wanted to avoid using taxis, so I sat in a bus shelter watching everyone else on my flight disappear into hire cars, taxis or vehicles driven by welcoming loved ones. By ten o'clock no bus had materialised, so with reluctance I climbed into a cab and asked the driver to take me to a budget hotel.

I was tipped out in front of a tall, narrow building, inside which I was greeted warmly and offered what seemed like a real bargain: a basic room with a clean bed, an air cooler and a bath for twenty four pounds a night including breakfast. No English was spoken, but the family who ran the hotel were kind and welcoming. The only drawback was that the narrow streets surrounding the building served as a racing circuit for local youths, who whizzed round the block on scooters and mopeds until two in the morning. I remained calm and tried to concentrate on reading my book, reminding myself periodically that this was, after all, Spain.

Sleep eventually overtook me, and I breakfasted in the tiny hotel bar which was open to the street and occupied by elderly locals reading newspapers. The scooter brigade were already zipping past the open doorway, and from the bar a battered radio was dispensing strangulated flamenco singing. As I sat down, the barman attracted my attention, pointed at the coffee machine, held up an orange as if he was about to perform a magic trick and brandished a large bread roll for my inspection. I nodded hopefully and within minutes I was presented with a cup of excellent coffee, a glass of freshly squeezed orange juice and the bread roll, spread lavishly with margarine and jam.

My plan for the morning, before it became too hot, was to visit the city's main attraction, the Alcazaba, a ruined Moorish fortress. On my way there, I got lost and strayed into a widespread area of tumbledown hovels on unsurfaced roads, where ragged children played in the dust and toothless ancients sat outside doorways on rickety chairs. There was an overpowering smell of drains, every human I saw looked dirt poor, and undernourished dogs roamed around searching for scraps. I was regarded with curiosity, and as I tramped along with my camera slung round my neck and all my valuables in my rucksack, I wondered if I might be pushing my luck. Every flight of crumbling steps led to a dead end, and whenever I sought directions I was asked for money or cigarettes. Eventually a black youth led me through a maze of alleyways and finally pointed to the steps leading to the entrance of the Alcazaba. To my surprise, he asked for nothing in return, and later I felt guilty that I'd failed to reward him for his trouble.

At the top of the steps a stone archway led into a terraced garden full of heavily scented blossom trees in vibrant colours. The panoramic views from the top of the fortress were spectacular, both inland and out across the city and harbour towards the open sea. Until the heat became unbearable at around one-thirty I scrambled happily among the ruins, which I seemed to have pretty well to myself. The siesta period between two and five was spent back at the hotel, where I luxuriated in a tepid bath. There was little hope of finding anything to eat during the afternoon, so I resorted to some squishy banana sandwiches I'd brought from home. Later on, venturing out for a stroll in the shade, I bumped into the youth who'd led me out of the labyrinth earlier in the day, and this time I gave him some money.

Sokolov's recital venue, the Auditorio Municipale, was miles away further along the coast. Located in the exotic sounding Avenida del Mediterraneo, it was a stylish, air conditioned hall overlooking the seashore, and at the front of the building stood palm trees, fountains and an expanse of marble where concertgoers gathered with pre-performance drinks to gaze at the glittering Mediterranean. Despite my initial doubts, it was a splendid evening, the trip had turned into a most satisfying experience, and I came away from Almeria feeling I'd had a brief but authentic taste of Spain.

In 2002 I embarked upon a trip which took me to concerts in two different countries. The second performance was in Spain, but firstly I travelled to Sintra in Portugal, where Sokolov was to play at the Olga Cadaval Cultural Centre. Lisbon was baking in the afternoon heat as my aircraft flew low over the city's rooftops to make its approach. From the airport I took a bus to Rossi, one of four railway stations scattered across the city, where I scrambled onto a crowded train bound for Sintra. The forty-five minute journey cost less than a pound and we stopped at fourteen stations, firstly in the ramshackle outer suburbs of Lisbon and later in a succession of small, impoverished looking villages. A young beggar woman holding aloft a tiny infant progressed slowly along the carriage, outlining in a singsong chant the parlous state of her finances, ending with a long drawn out, almost operatic, "Por favor!" which was met with a mixture of complete disinterest and dismissive swatting gestures.

Towards the end of the journey I was one of only a handful of people remaining on the train, and the contrast between the shabby little places we'd passed through and Sintra itself could not have been more striking. At the neatly kept railway station, a blessed veil of cloud and a pleasant breeze greeted me. No wonder the Portuguese royals had chosen to build their summer palaces in a place such as this, far removed from the stifling heat of the city. Sintra was every bit as enchanting as the guide books had promised, with densely wooded hills all around and fanciful Romanticist architecture, each building possessing its own individual character. High above the town were the ruins of a Moorish castle, and the centre itself was dominated by the National Palace, a mixture of Moorish and Gothic styles with two extraordinary conical towers, which stood in the main square right opposite the unassuming Hotel Central, where I hoped a room might be available. As I dragged my luggage towards the square I bumped into Sokolov's manager, Franco Panozzo, who asked me how I planned to get to the recital in Granada two days later. When I told him I'd not given it much thought he stared at me in disbelief. The truth was that I'd failed to consider the logistics of this trip and was left with three equally unappealing options: a twenty-five hour train ride with six changes, any of which I might easily miss, an express bus which would take considerably more than a day, or a very expensive flight. I couldn't bear to think about any of them.

The Hotel Central was a solid, well worn nineteenth century building offering simple accommodation. There was a large bathroom and an inviting looking bath tub but the bed might well have been there since the hotel was originally built, designed for someone much shorter than me. Beyond my window I could see pine forests and hills in the far distance, and at closer range a profusion of pantiled roofs and lines of washing. After a preliminary inspection of the immediate area and a surprisingly drinkable cup of tea in a bar filled with infectious Latin American rhythms and young olive-skinned men in leather jackets, I toddled back to my room for an early night. My pillow felt more like a bag of King Edward's, but the smiling receptionist delivered a softer option within minutes. I'd expected to spend the night sweltering and swatting insects, but thanks to Sintra's cool mountain air I lay huddled beneath a blanket wishing I'd packed my winter pyjamas.

The next morning I seemed to be the only guest showing any sign of life, so it was a surprise to find several uniformed waiters standing to attention in the dining room. A pot of good strong coffee with orange juice and delicious lemony buns were more than I'd hoped for, and I was soon bounding outside to make the most of my day. The cobbled alleyways I'd strolled along the night before were already teeming with shoppers, and several coachloads of sightseers had been deposited outside the National Palace for the first guided tours of the day. According to the guidebook, Sintra's main attraction and national monument, Pena Palace, could be reached either by taxi or a ninety minute walk uphill. Luckily, a shuttle bus had been introduced recently, which picked up passengers outside the little tourismo every half hour, slogged up the winding forest road and delivered them to the Moorish castle ruin, or if they preferred, they could ride further up the hillside to the extensive grounds leading to the palace.

I joined a jostling crowd of good natured but determined Portuguese weekend trippers and elbowed my way onto a bus bound for the castle ruin. Climbing on foot up to the highest ramparts in what felt like a force nine gale was an exhilarating experience, and the views of the Sintra region and beyond were amazing. Even higher up could be seen the pastel coloured domes and towers of the palace, my next objective. A second bus ride up a steep cobbled road brought me to the gates of Pena Park and the palace. The interior was preserved exactly as the royal family had left it when they fled in 1910 to avoid the Revolution, but my impression of the building's exterior was that it looked rather neglected and was better viewed from a distance.

That afternoon I felt drawn to a park at a place called Monserrate, three miles away. There was no bus, so I set off along a rough road sheltered by woodland. There was very little traffic, and occasional gaps in the trees offered views of open countryside. After a while it occurred to me that this could be the perfect place to be attacked and robbed of my possessions, but I pressed on, arriving at the entrance to the park an hour or so later. It covered a vast area and all I could see were endless trees and shrubs. Somewhere among them was a palace with gardens, but I was destined never to find them. My feet were already in a sorry state and the prospect of the three mile walk back was dispiriting, but I gritted my teeth, thought of Prokofiev and limped back into Sintra just in time for tea.

At the concert hall things finally got going at nine forty-five. Returning to my seat after the interval I could see the piano tuner was on his knees, wrestling with one of the pedals which had emitted loud groaning noises during the Haydn sonatas. Sokolov continued with a set of dances by Komitas, Prokofiev's blistering 7th Sonata, and was still turning out encores at twelve-thirty. It was a gripping performance, but my thoughts kept straying to the question of how I was going to find my way to Granada the next day. Throughout the evening I'd switched from train to bus to plane and back again, finally persuading myself to concentrate on the music and forget about Granada until morning in the hope of a clear decision on waking.

Back at the hotel the night porter, a smartly dressed man in his seventies, seemed keen to converse. I had a raging thirst, so he fetched me a glass of orange juice and told me there was no charge since he'd accidentally broken the neck of the bottle when he opened it. I'd intended to drink it down in one almighty gulp, but felt obliged to sip it with caution through compressed lips in the hope of filtering out any stray particles of glass. Our conversation went deeper and deeper into the realms of politics, economics, history, philosophy and other nebulous regions I normally tried to avoid, and it took me so long to finish my drink that it was well after two when I finally crawled into bed, too tired to worry about Granada.

The next morning I rushed into the dining room, knocked back a cup of coffee, buttered some rolls to take with me and raced off to the station just in time to catch one of the rush hour trains. Increasing numbers piled on at each of the fourteen stops and it was already scorching hot. The way ahead suddenly became clear: the idea of sitting on either a train or a bus until evening was unthinkable, so I headed straight for Lisbon Airport, where I handed over a huge amount of cash for an afternoon flight to Granada via Madrid, lamenting that I could have gone by train or bus at a fraction of the cost. Sokolov was booked on a later flight, so I dressed for comfort, secure in the knowledge that I would see no one who mattered. It was therefore a shock to find myself on the same flight as Franco, who was no longer going to Granada but returning to Italy. While boarding and pre-flight checks were completed he knelt on the seat in front of mine in order to chat. Groomed to perfection as always, he looked down at me and I suddenly remembered that not only had I failed to apply any make-up that morning but I'd also neglected to comb my hair.

I landed in Granada at five-thirty in stupefying heat. The airport bus dropped me in the main shopping street, Gran Via, which also contained most of the city's budget hotels, but the atmosphere was so frenzied and the traffic so thunderous that I decided to look for something in a quieter area. The tourist office gave me a city map and a list of cheap accommodation, and I headed towards the hill on which the Alhambra Palace stood, choosing a cheerful looking B&B at the foot of the steps leading not only to the palace but also the Auditorio Manuel de Falla, where Sokolov would be performing the following evening. The house was quirkily decorated, the price ridiculously cheap, and my tiny room had air conditioning. The kindly proprietor made me a disgusting cup of tea, so I quickly found a nearby café where for a small outlay I purchased a large glass of fresh orange juice, a drinkable cup of tea and a jumbo-sized pizza.

The colour and clamour of Granada were just as attractive as the sedate greenery of Sintra, and I loved the part of the city in which I'd chosen to stay. Away from the crowded thoroughfares were narrow streets, tiny squares, ancient little churches and seductive alleyways hung with flower baskets. At eight in the evening the place came alive: people poured out onto the streets to promenade or fill the pavement bars and restaurants, children played ball games in the squares, groups of youngsters flirted and fooled around, dogs rushed to and fro barking excitedly and music poured forth from windows and doorways. It was completely chaotic and would have been intensely irritating at home, but here in Granada it was an entertainment which probably continued well into the night while I slept, blissfully unaware, tucked away at the rear of the B&B. At breakfast the next morning I decided to sample the coffee but it was only marginally less revolting than the tea. There was also a perfunctory repast described on the menu as 'toast', but it consisted of a small white roll which, rather than being browned, had merely been hardened and smeared with a thin coating of watery jam.

At the top of the long flight of steps behind the B&B a friendly local directed me towards the Alhambra Palace ticket office, at the same time offering to shine my shoes, which made no sense to someone about to spend a couple of hours tramping round a dusty ruin. By nine o'clock I was inside the Alhambra with the first group of visitors, and the royal palace alone justified the air fare. Had I travelled to Granada by any other means, I would have missed the opportunity to see this breathtaking example of Islamic art. The palace was wonderfully cool inside, but by the time I reached the Generalife gardens, the temperature was soaring. The fortress was less crowded, possibly because of its exposure to the sun, but the views of the city from the ramparts were stunning.

Almost every walking surface in Sintra and Granada consisted of either ancient cobbles or a more modern variant with stones of all shapes and sizes set in concrete. Despite wearing sensible loafers, I'd acquired an impressive collection of blisters, and having descended the steps from the Alhambra and walked the length of Gran Via and back again, I realised I couldn't manage another step. In the shade of the cathedral I rested until I felt capable of shuffling as far as my local eaterie, where I adventurously ordered a cheese and ham 'fillet' with fried egg and chips. The cheese and ham were wrapped in an unspecified meat which I took to be pork, and for many hours afterwards I anticipated the onset of gastric complications. Nothing unpleasant manifested itself and I took a long siesta before preparing for the recital, which was scheduled to begin at the preposterously late hour of ten-thirty.

At the Auditorio I sat in the front row next to a latterday Spanish grandee, complete with waxed moustache and silver-topped cane, who spoke English with a mesmerising accent. Sokolov had warned me about the extreme heat in Granada, so I'd chosen something suitably flimsy to wear and been glad of it on my way to the hall in the soupy atmosphere. Inside the building, however, the air conditioning was so efficient that I sat shivering through the first half, clutching my bare arms. An added distraction was the presence of one of the Alhambra's feral cats, perched on the roof directly above the platform, which meowed lustily throughout the first half. Returning to my seat after the break, I remarked to my neighbour that this was the first time I'd ever felt the need to go outside during the interval to get *warm*. Before you could shout, "Olé!", he was up on his feet, and like an ageing matador he removed his elegant jacket with a grand flourish and swept it around my shoulders. Unaccustomed as I was to such acts of gallantry, I felt obliged during the second half to check from time to time that he was warm enough.

The performance ended at one-thirty and it was much too late to visit the artist's room. Outside, the car park was emptying fast, and although there were several shuttle buses calling at the larger hotels, none of them seemed to be passing my humble hostelry, so I joined a group waiting for taxis. The Spanish, like some of their European neighbours, were not inclined to queue, and it was no surprise to find that I was the last person standing. It was almost two in the morning and deliciously warm, with moonlight flooding the Alhambra and the lights of Granada twinkling below; a more romantic setting could scarcely be imagined. The last taxi driver to depart had assured me another would be along shortly, and sure enough, one soon came snarling to a halt. I scrambled inside and became instantly aware of an unpleasant aroma which I couldn't quite identify. The back seat was draped with a bedspread, and by the time I'd realised it was also soaking wet we'd begun hurtling down the hill at breakneck speed. I was saturated to the skin and hopping mad. The driver conveniently spoke no English, so when I shouted at him to stop and let me out, he shrugged and drove even faster. There had obviously been some sort of unfortunate 'accident' in the back of the vehicle, and the driver had washed the seat but made no attempt to get it dry. Refusing to pay didn't seem like a sensible option at that time of night, so I threw the fare at him and stormed off, consoling myself that at least I'd not detected the smell of bleach or disinfectant.

It was such a late night that I overslept, and at nine-thirty I shot out of bed in a state of panic. My return flight was from Malaga and there were only three trains per day from Granada. I threw my still damp clothing into my bag and took a taxi to the railway station. As soon as I'd paid and got out, I realised the driver had dropped me at the bus station by mistake, but it turned out that he'd done me a favour; I was just in time to catch an express bus to Malaga Airport. On board I was cool and comfortable, and saw far more of the rural scenery than I would have done from the train. We were close enough to the Sierra Nevada to have marvellous views all the way, and as the road wound through sun-drenched countryside, endless olive groves stretched across the hillsides and we passed fields full of stately sunflowers. As I watched from the bus window, enthralled by the subtle colours of the landscape, the hills fading to a dusky orange in the distance, my practical side made a mental note that the next time I planned a double date with Sokolov in different countries, it might be an idea to take the distance between venues into consideration.

In December 2002 I escaped the winter chill and paid a flying visit to Seville, where I landed at three in the afternoon. A series of tiresome incidents and errors on my journey from the airport to the city resulted in a lot of wasted time, and when a taxi driver dropped me next to an unmanned tourist kiosk which looked as if it hadn't dispensed any useful information for half a century, it seemed like the last straw. Close to tears, I had no idea where I was or which direction to take, but a friendly German student happened along and offered to help me find a room. She took me to the Barrio Santa Cruz, a most attractive part of the city, right next to the Cathedral and the Royal Alcazar, where we found a traditional, colourfully decorated Sevillan house offering a tiny room with washbasin for next to nothing.

Once settled in, I walked as far as the river in warm sunshine beneath heavily laden orange trees. Tall palms lined the promenade, pleasure boats chugged past, and haughty Spanish orchestral melodies floated out across the water from a loudspeaker on the opposite bank. At the entrance to the Alcazar, a genteel looking Spaniard with a rolled umbrella offered to take me on a guided tour of the palace for thirty euros. The look on my face must have said, "No way, José!" so he reduced his fee to twenty. Had there been more time I might have succumbed, but a quick look inside the cathedral had to suffice. It could hardly be called sightseeing, but the concert was always the main event and sometimes it was necessary to settle for a mere flavour of a place and promise myself there would be a next time.

Tiny white fairy lights twinkled in the orange trees as I set out for Teatro de la Maestranza. The hall was impressive, but during the performance the entire repertoire of inappropriate audience behaviour was explored to the full. Scarcely a few seconds passed between bronchial outbursts, sweet paper rustlings and the dropping of miscellaneous items on the wooden floor. Initially I was irritated, but I gradually drew consolation from sitting next to a man who responded to every nuance of Sokolov's playing, with slight inclinations of the head, gentle sighs, small movements of the hand in anticipation of what was to come. It was clear he knew every piece intimately, so I was surprised when he asked if I could identify two of the five encores. I learned later he was José-Antonio Garcia, the person responsible for writing the programme notes. He spoke little English, but with the aid of the concert hall director he told me he'd enjoyed sitting next to me, sensing my connectedness to the music and the artist.

Back at the B&B a cold room and a damp bed lay in wait, but with the aid of extra layers of clothing I slept surprisingly well. Rather than face the complications of using public transport to get back to the airport the next morning, I took a taxi driven by a reckless young hothead who had no intention of allowing a thick blanket of fog to prevent him from belting along the motorway at his customary rate of knots. With visibility at the minimum, he periodically turned round to regard me on the back seat, laughing heartily at my terror-stricken features and telling me with more than a degree of relish, as if I might not have worked it out for myself already, that he couldn't see a thing. It was an awful experience, but by the time we reached the airport the fog had lifted. In the terminal building I spotted a fawn mackintosh containing Sokolov, who was pushing a trolley bearing what looked like the world's largest suitcase. Not for the first time, we were on the same flight, and as we stood waiting in the departure lounge we discussed the fear and reality of lost luggage.

In 2017 and 2019 I attended recitals in Valencia, but on neither occasion was I in good enough shape to do much walking, so I chose to find a room close to the concert hall. The Palau de la Música stood at the edge of the Turia Gardens, an imaginatively landscaped nine kilometre stretch of drained riverbed which wound through part of the city. The Turia River had been diverted following a catastrophic flood in 1957 and the park now provided an ideal place to walk, jog, cycle, or simply relax. In Valencia there was no rushing around; I arrived the day before the performance and spent my free time sitting in the Turia Gardens with a book, or simply watching and waiting.

My first visit to the Palau coincided with the beginning of an unforgettable period in which Sokolov revisited Beethoven's Sonata No.32 Op.111, and having heard him play it many times back in the 2003/04 season I was ecstatic that it was to be repeated. The last few bars of the first movement always propelled me towards a heavenly antechamber, in preparation for the celestial journey which followed in the second and final movement. In Valencia there was a lot of coughing, but as we were taken on Beethoven's voyage to the stars there was a long silence in the hall and Sokolov's mastery prevailed.

On my second visit, he began an exploration of Brahms' Piano Pieces Op.118/Op.119, some of which I thought I knew very well, but he succeeded in illuminating hidden corners to reveal a wealth of fresh detail I'd never noticed before. From the impassioned turmoil of the first Op.118 Intermezzo to the ardent tenderness of the second, and on through the remainder of this beautiful collection of pieces,

Sokolov seemed to convey something personal, as if we were not only hearing the outpouring of the composer's heart, but also that of the artist. With Sokolov there was always something more.

Barcelona's Palau de la Música Catalana: an almost indescribable explosion of colour and creativity, the greatest example of architectural exuberance I think I'd ever seen, and surely one of the most beautiful concert halls in the world. Often listed as the most interesting building to see in Barcelona, it inevitably attracted visitors who were unaccustomed to attending classical performances, but were tempted to buy tickets for whatever type of music was on offer at the time of their visit. As a consequence, at Sokolov's recital in May 2013, quite a few audience members were there primarily to admire the interior of the building, and the actual performance was a secondary consideration. At first I was anxious about the possibility of random flash photography, but an announcement was made beforehand and the audience contained themselves until the end of the evening in that regard. But there were untimely bursts of applause which broke out every so often among the tourist element, followed by exasperated shushing from the regulars. It was an unwelcome distraction, but Sokolov's cast iron concentration seemed undisturbed. In the second half, applause broke out at the end of the first movement of Beethoven's Hammerklavier sonata, but this time the opposition was so vociferous that the offenders were finally silenced.

This fabulous hall was said to be the only one in Europe illuminated purely by window light during the daytime, so the lighting conditions were not ideal for Sokolov, whose own preference was quite the opposite. Nevertheless, the performance was a roaring success. From my seat in a side box, I could appreciate the staggering amount of detail lavished on the interior of the auditorium, and this surfeit of visual splendour, combined with Sokolov's inspirational programme, was such a feast for the eyes and ears that it was almost too much for my senses to absorb. In a concert which began in full window light, gradually fading to twilight and the deep blue of late evening, the beauty and spectacle of the Palau provided stiff competition for the music, but the music was in safe hands and Sokolov was more than equal to the challenge.

After my visit to Sintra in 2002, each subsequent performance I attended in Portugal took place in the admirable Grand Auditorium of the Calouste Gulbenkian Foundation in Lisbon. The complex also housed two other concert halls, a museum and art gallery, an art library and a museum of modern art. The building itself was rather austere but I always found a hotel room close by so that I could spend time in the Foundation's attractive natural garden: a tranquil haven for wildlife and mankind which grew more verdant each time I visited. Sometimes I felt too travel weary to venture further afield and merely strolled contentedly along the garden's shaded pathways, but the first time I was in Lisbon in 2011 I was eager to see as much as possible, so I roamed around the Parque Eduardo VII with its panoramic view of the city and walked the length of Avenida Liberdade into downtown Lisbon's neoclassical Baixa District, stepping into the famous Santa Justa Elevator to reach the viewing platform at the top and finally passing through the massive triumphal arch into the immensity of Commerce Square, beyond which lay the gleaming waters of the Tagus Estuary.

The Gulbenkian Auditorium was managed with military precision and the staff did their utmost to ensure the audience had a memorable experience. The 1,200 plus seats were sold out and I was half way back, but the acoustic was excellent, the seating raked. Sokolov's Bach was superb; the Italian Concerto in particular was a positive joyride, but three extravagant and well spaced out sneezes were discharged by the same person during the Sarabande of the French Overture, and another idiot directly behind me chose the quietly mysterious opening of the Schumann Op.32 Fughette to embark upon a prolonged nose-blowing spree. I was ready to commit murder, and was reminded of a conversation I'd had with a man whose father was a former conductor of the Luxembourg Philharmonic Orchestra. As a child he'd been obliged to attend many of his father's concerts, but in later life decided to give them up altogether, concluding that the appreciation of music was such a deeply personal and emotional pastime that he no longer felt able to put on a suit and share it with a bunch of strangers. I could see his point, having had several hard-earned evenings ruined by the thoughtlessness of others, but how else was I to experience live performances?

In later years I became friendly with Isabel Serra and her husband Quim, who took me all over the city: to the hilltop Castle of St. George, along the coast to Queluz National Palace and the beach resort of Cascais; introduced me to the delights of Portuguese cakes and pastries and entertained me not only in their home, but in some atmospheric cafés and restaurants. All I could do in return was encourage Isabel to meet Sokolov in the artist's room, but she seemed to consider it a fair exchange.

In March 2016 I walked into the Gulbenkian Auditorium with a heavy heart, having discovered my seat was in Row 27, which in anyone's language meant the back of beyond. My mood switched to one of jubilation when I realised that Row 31 was in fact at the front, which meant that my seat was after all only five rows away from the platform. The piano, which had come from Granada, was well known to Sokolov and was to accompany him to Porto for his next recital. Although it began the evening with a beautiful creamy tone, in the second half the middle register developed a metallic resonance, but this took nothing away from the majesty of the performance. Unlike a music magazine critic who had recently written a scathing comment regarding Sokolov's Schumann Arabeske, I'd always admired his approach to the piece. Furthermore, this same critic, who had scarcely a good word to say about Sokolov's performance in Brussels three days earlier, had accused him of brutality in both the Schumann and the Chopin. There was no brutality in Lisbon; there was Herculean strength, there was power and pain, there was muscularity, but the music was never brutalised. We were all entitled to our opinion but I doubted very much that there had been any brutality in Brussels either.

The following year I had the exciting opportunity to attend recitals on three consecutive evenings in Portugal: firstly in Lisbon, then on to Coimbra further up the coast and finally Porto, both of which were unexplored territory. I felt unwell when I set out for Lisbon, and by the end of the recital there I knew I would have to abandon the other two performances. The Lisbon audience displayed exemplary behaviour on this occasion with no misplaced applause; quiet passages were respected, critical silences honoured. The Mozart produced some sumptuous playing and the Beethoven was immense. It was all there: an elegant venue, no distractions, just a beautiful stillness leaving the artist free to take us wherever he chose. As the mighty Beethoven Sonata Op.111 drew to a close I remember thinking it was one of the finest examples of Sokolov's art and one of the greatest expressions of Beethoven's genius. I probably made the right decision to cut my visit short, but I grieved for many weeks over those two lost performances.

In May 2019, Sokolov delivered the Beethoven Sonata No.3 Op.2/3 crisply and incisively, scampering through the exuberant finale, jaunty and carefree as a young buck. A spirited response from the Gulbenkian audience received the briefest acknowledgement before he continued to work his way through the Eleven Bagatelles Op. 119, leaving me with the impression that since I'd last heard them he'd examined each one afresh, made some subtle adjustments and polished them until they shone.

In the second half, fully in command of his forces, Sokolov was ready to subject his audience to a rigorous emotional workout. Travelling with him through the glorious Brahms Op.118/Op.119 programme always felt like another of life's great journeys. After the initial outpouring of the A minor intermezzo he presented the A major with lingering transparency and enough devotion to melt a block of granite. The infectious rhythms of the G minor ballade and the limpid beauty of the F minor intermezzo gave way to even greater wonders, and the finale of Op.119 was in itself a full-scale production worthy of separate billing.

Among the diverse selection of encores that night, Rachmaninoff's Prelude Op.32/12 brought with it a chill wind and a flurry of snowflakes as it took us into the mysterious heart of Russia, and who better to convey this superb evocation of his homeland than Sokolov?

2. ITALY

THE FIRST RECITAL I attended in Italy was at the Conservatorio Giuseppe Verdi in Milan. I remember collecting my ticket during the afternoon and being elated to discover that the seats were unreserved, so I figured if I arrived early enough in the evening I'd be able to choose a perfect place. Later, my hopes were dashed when I was told that the first eighteen rows were reserved for subscribers. I did return to the Conservatorio on one further occasion, and although I managed to sit marginally closer to the piano, the experience was far from enjoyable on account of undisciplined audience behaviour with corresponding tutting, shushing and loud sighs of exasperation which were equally distracting. Several people even stood up and wandered round looking for a better seat while Sokolov toiled on regardless, but after the disruptive element had left, three Rameau encores played at a fast clip proved to be easily the most enjoyable part of the evening.

Two trips to Rome followed, where I fared much better. The first visit was for two orchestral concerts at the Accademia Nazionale di Santa Cecilia, where generations of audiences had been entertained by a host of great opera singers of the Golden Age. The performances were of Tchaikovsky's 1ˢᵗ Piano Concerto with the resident orchestra, under the baton of the South Korean conductor, Myung-Whun Chung.

The following week I returned to Rome, this time for a solo recital. The train from Fiumicino Airport was crowded, unbearably hot and piled high with luggage. The underground journey from Termini Railway Station to San Pietro was even more suffocating, but I became transfixed by two young women sitting directly opposite, both in their early twenties. One was blessed with masses of dark pre-Raphaelite curls cascading about her shoulders, flawless olive skin and a voluptuous figure poured into a clinging burgundy velvet ankle length dress, the open side seam of which revealed matching knee length suede boots. The other was prim, pale and bespectacled, dressed in a nun's grey habit, feet planted firmly together in sensible lace-ups. Two such contrasting images of Roman womanhood sitting side by side on the metro would have made a wonderful photograph, but I lacked the courage to ask permission to take it.

I'd booked a cheap room at a two star hotel which appeared to be run by a rough band of Al Pacino lookalikes straight out of *The Godfather*. My room was more or less what I'd expected: threadbare carpet that hadn't seen a vacuum cleaner in months, peeling wallpaper, ramshackle furniture and an unfriendly looking bed. It was situated next to a communal bathroom containing a lavatory with prehistoric plumbing and a bath with no shower curtain or plug. A hand-held spray attachment delivered a choice of ice cold or scalding hot water and a bath towel cost an extra five thousand lire. It was a relief to know I'd be leaving there at crack of dawn the next morning to catch an early return flight, arranged to enable me to put in an afternoon shift at the office.

The recital was wonderful and the pieces by William Byrd were very well received. All that remained was to survive a night at the hotel. The WC next to my room was used regularly during the night and I heard the cistern refill at least eight times. Someone even took a bath, having brought their own plug or hired one from reception. I slept for a couple of hours before my wake- up call, and by four-thirty I was out on the street, the hotel door firmly locked behind me, waiting for a cab to take me to Fiumicino. I'd been warned it was a forty-five minute drive which would cost at least thirty pounds. The taxi arrived in spectacular fashion, screeching round the corner in reverse on what looked like two wheels. This didn't bode well for the journey, but I jumped in with gritted teeth and braced myself for a crash landing. The driver tore through the streets and out onto the autostrada as if he'd just robbed a bank, depositing me at the airport in half the specified time but charging me the full amount.

On a later trip to Rome in 2000, I'd pre-booked a room close to Termini Station which proved to be even more disappointing. Situated in a downtrodden side street, the B&B occupied the fifth floor of an old building and the room I was ushered into contained a grubby shower cubicle with no curtain and a washbasin bisected by a dark crack. A shabby tartan camping wardrobe with zip fastening provided one solitary wire hanger; there was no sign of a mirror in the room, and more importantly no toilet. A roughly hewn sheet of hardboard served as the only useful surface on which to place anything; patches of mould meandered across the walls and ceiling, and the bed was full of lumps and bits of spring straining to escape. It was rather late in the day to start searching for something better, but I marched back to reception and returned the key, determined to be on my way. The manager looked unsurprised, and persuaded me to view an alternative room right next to the reception area. It was infinitely more acceptable, and I wondered why he'd not offered it to me in the first place, but when I drew back the curtains to take a look outside and get a breath of air, I found myself staring into a communal kitchen-cum-dining room, where supper was being prepared by a crowd of backpackers. The clatter of pots and pans and youthful banter was strangely soothing, although I wondered how long it would continue, but at eleven sharp the kitchen closed, the place fell silent and I slept like a baby.

Three years later Sokolov gave two recitals at the Sapienza University of Rome, and close to the campus I found the delightful Hotel Adventure. Staffed by a pleasing selection of cheerful and attractive young men, it was an uplifting establishment decorated throughout in boudoir pink and gilt, with crystal light fittings, swags and flounces, fancy ornaments and extravagant plasterwork. My room overlooked neighbouring apartments and the view was mostly of people's smalls fluttering in the breeze, but I was in a quiet corner of the building, far removed from the sound of traffic, and it suited me perfectly.

In the University's Great Hall there were no crystal chandeliers; the auditorium was illuminated rather harshly by a series of fluorescent tubes, and behind the platform glowered an enormous and somewhat depressing mural. Painted crudely in an assortment of sludge colours, it depicted a gathering of historical figures engaged in a variety of activities which seemed to afford them little in the way of enjoyment. Frequent gusts of cold air swept through the building and the audience, evidently accustomed to unheated winter performances, sat in their overcoats for the duration. By way of compensation, the piano sounded marvellous, and Sokolov's programme of Beethoven Sonatas No.9 Op.14/1, No.10 Op.14/2 & No.15 Op.28, Bach's Sonata after Reincken "Hortus Musicus" and the Bach/Brahms Chaconne for the left hand went swimmingly. But as Sokolov left the platform at the interval, he slipped off the shallow plinth on which the piano stood, narrowly escaping a nose dive. I worried about it for the rest of the performance, but at the second recital the following evening, a wafer thin ramp had been fashioned and pushed into place.

It was always good to know that Sokolov was being well looked after, but this hall's ministrations did seem a little excessive. Each time Sokolov appeared, the director escorted him onto the stage, applauding strenuously as if to chivvy the audience along ("OK, come on ladies and gents, he's a little bit shy so let's give the boy some encouragement!") A mature lady in a voluminous fur coat took up position at the side of the platform each time Sokolov walked off, waiting for him like a doting grandmother, clapping excitedly and offering him an adoring smile which he chose to ignore, marching past her with his usual blank expression. I would imagine he disliked this kind of behaviour, but was much too polite to ask them to desist. When it came to the numerous encores, the director, the fur coated lady and half a dozen others crept forward to watch from the wings, scuttling back out of sight each time Sokolov rose from the piano stool.

Before he could even reach his dressing room at the end of the evening, he was besieged in a corridor by a surging mob, in the midst of which he turned round and round, happily scribbling autographs and answering questions. He must have been longing for a drink, but was the soul of patience and good humour. As the crowd began to disperse, the scowling director grabbed him firmly by the arm and attempted to yank him away from the last few stragglers, including myself, but Sokolov stood firm and exchanged pleasantries before being frogmarched back to his room, possibly for a compulsory hug from grandma.

The next morning I was served with a jolly decent breakfast by one of the lads, after which I decided to ride round on the metro all day and surface wherever there was something worth looking at, which in Rome was virtually everywhere. On my first short journey, a boy of no more than ten climbed aboard lugging a full-sized accordion, on which he dashed off a fleet-fingered Latin American dance tune, displaying musicianship and body language way beyond his years. With a breezy "Buon giorno, tutti!" he then collected his small rewards from anyone feeling generous, and I felt confident that such a boy would never go hungry.

My first stop was Piazza Spagna, where I treated myself to elevenses in the long-established and reputedly splendid Babington's Tea Rooms at the foot of the Spanish Steps. It was all dark oak and doilies, and if you ignored the view from the window of the Barcaccia Fountain and the sun baked facades across the square, you could imagine you were in the poshest teashop in Cheltenham Spa. It was a novel experience, but I paid three pounds fifty for a small cup of tea.

Next I visited Piazza Barberini and walked towards San Pietro. It felt rather like swimming against the tide with hundreds of people swarming in the opposite direction and I suspected I must have missed something significant. Sure enough, a few minutes earlier the Pope had delivered his midday blessing. I was disappointed to have missed it, but my timing improved as the day wore on. I arrived at the Quirinale Palace just as a military band entered the parade ground, flanked by soldiers and sailors in fetching uniforms who marched up and down a few times, presented arms and stood to attention while the modest public gathering sang the national anthem. It was better than nothing, but a glimpse of Pope John Paul would have been much more of an event. A bitter February wind followed me to Piazza Venezia, the Forum and Palatine Hill, where the sun was sinking behind the ruins, reminding me that I needed to prepare for another evening with Sokolov.

At the second recital the director had ruled out a repeat of the previous night's ambush in the corridor, and Sokolov's feet must have scarcely touched the floor between platform and dressing room as he was hustled away. By the time the mob caught up with him he was safely ensconced with a Russian journalist and photographer, and the director stood outside, arms folded, looking triumphant. It was normal practice for journalists to wait until the public had been received, but not on this occasion. Deprived of the opportunity to say goodbye, I mentally thumbed my nose at the director on my way out.

In more recent years, Sokolov's Rome recitals took place at the Auditorio Parco della Musica, a huge entertainment complex containing several music venues. Each year his performances attracted capacity audiences to the largest hall, the 2,800 seat Sala Santa

Cecilia. I was there in 2016 and took my place with some trepidation, having heard adverse comments about audience behaviour there. My feathers had already been ruffled on my way into the auditorium when the ticket checker refused to allow me in unless I left my camera in the cloakroom, which seemed ridiculous in view of the hundreds of people filing past him with smart phones in their pockets. Sure enough, mobile photography began the moment Sokolov set foot on stage and continued throughout the Schumann Arabeske. One of the phones soon began ringing, then a young boy sitting directly in front of me began displaying signs of boredom; applause broke out in all the wrong places and the piano had an unpleasant metallic edge to it, so the evening was shaping up to be far from ideal. In the Schumann Fantasy I felt confident there would be no opportunity for anyone to start clapping between the second and third movements as Sokolov always left barely a millisecond between the two. Sadly, the beautiful transition into the final movement was ruined by a further burst of applause, which was swiftly stifled by those familiar with the piece, in particular the man sitting next to me who bellowed out an exasperated, "NOOO!!"

After the interval, the President of the Accademia appeared on stage and spoke to the audience in avuncular fashion. I assumed he was asking them to switch off their mobiles and hoped he might also be attempting to educate some of them in the matter of untimely applause, but my neighbour told me it was purely about flash photography and the effect it could have on an artist's concentration. And so it was that this became a recital of two distinct halves. After the interval it was as if a completely new audience had been shipped in; there was absolute silence throughout a magnificent Chopin Sonata No.2 - one of Sokolov's finest and the true expression of a soul laid bare. The tuner had also worked wonders on the piano in the interval, and Sokolov presented six Chopin encores as a succession of individually packaged delights, each of which the audience devoured with rapt attention and wild applause.

The little boy in the seat in front had fidgeted to such an extent during the first half that I'd longed for his parents to take him home at the interval, but they dragged him back in for a second helping, presumably in the hope that he might be inspired to take up the piano himself. But unlike the very young Grisha Sokolov, who I imagine sat in wide-eyed concentration whenever his father took him to listen to his idol Emil Gilels in the Philharmonic Hall in Leningrad all those years ago, the little boy in the Parco della Musica sank into a coma and remained unconscious until the final encore had come and gone.

Back in the early days I sometimes came away from Rome with the impression that the inhabitants of that city were ever so slightly mad. In the safety of the airport terminal I often shuddered at the memory of death-defying attempts to cross the street, perilous white knuckle taxi rides and the abysmal nature of some of the budget accommodation, but Rome's shortcomings were manifestly outweighed by its wealth of historic and cultural splendour, and of course, Sokolov was always there.

In the Autumn of 1999 on a train journey from Milan to Turin, I shared a carriage with a young Jack-the-lad type who looked like the last person you'd expect to be exchanging pleasantries with a female well past her best. We sat in silence until a few minutes before pulling into Turin, and then, as sometimes happened on such journeys, we struck up a last minute conversation. He was amazed that I should be arriving in a strange city so late in the day with no pre-booked accommodation. I told him I always managed to find somewhere, often thanks to the kindness of people I met on my travels. He looked mystified, as if it had never occurred to him to be helpful to a stranger, but the idea obviously appealed to him because he began searching through his newspaper to see what time my concert started, carried my bag off the train, found an information kiosk, secured a city map for me and located the Conservatorio as well as pointing me in the direction of a good place to get a cup of tea.

I'd taken with me the address of a likely B&B and I asked for directions in a book shop, where I was told there was indeed a small hotel nearby, but it was 'full of prostitutes'. The Yellow Pages were consulted, which revealed that the B&B in question was a fifteen minute walk away. To save me a wasted journey, the kindly shopkeeper picked up his phone, established that there was a room available and booked it for me.

The lady who ran the hotel single-handedly with only a threadbare cat for company was a complete scatterbrain. On my way out that evening, she handed me a huge bunch of keys which scarcely fitted into my evening bag, and I dreaded getting into difficulties later when it was time to get back in. At the Conservatorio I heard Sokolov's manager telling someone that Maestro had to be up at five the next morning to fly to Paris, then to New York on Concorde, for the start of a three week tour of the US. In the artist's room he seemed unhappy at the prospect of a long haul flight; jet lag would be a problem, and continually flying from one city to the next would leave him with limited time to practise.

I gained access to the hotel with some difficulty and slept badly on account of the heat. My hostess breezed into my room at eight the next morning and presented me with breakfast on a tray, which consisted of a minuscule pot of luke warm tea, two slices of stale white bread, an individual pot of jam which had separated with age and a foil wrapped portion of grey-green butter. "Buon appetito!" she chirruped as she left the room. I was soon knocking on the kitchen door to show her the rancid butter, and as she rummaged around in a chaotic looking fridge for something a little less out of date she let out a piercing shriek of laughter, whereupon the startled cat flew outside for a bit of respite.

Reluctant to head straight for the railway station without seeing anything of the city, I spent half an hour detouring towards the River Po, which proved to be well worth doing. Shrouded in mist, the grandiose buildings, wide boulevards and tall colonnades looked mysterious and theatrical. The incoming trains from Milan to Turin had run every hour and I'd foolishly expected a similar service in the opposite direction, but I arrived at the station to find there was a two hour wait for the next one. Realising I could easily miss my flight I enlisted another crazy cab driver to fling me across the city to the bus station, where I leapt aboard a coach bound for Milan.

I needn't have panicked. My flight from Milan to Brussels was seriously delayed, I missed my connecting flight from Brussels to Heathrow and consequently failed to catch the coach I'd booked from Heathrow to Birmingham. When I eventually boarded a much later coach I was pleased to see just a handful of passengers, all of them looking ready for sleep. As we settled down for a peaceful journey, the coach called at another terminal and picked up a crowd of lively Norwegians bound for Crufts Dog Show at the NEC (which they referred to as 'the neck') who were in varying stages of drunkenness.

They were impossible to ignore and there was nothing for it but to join in the fun.

Many of my Italian concert trips included memorable rides on public transport. I recall lurching through the dusty old streets of Bologna as dozens of scooters and mopeds darted in and out of the traffic, many ridden by young girls with streaming hair, skimpy summer dresses and stiletto heels. I boarded a rickety old train to Ravenna which belted along between fields of crops at what seemed like suicidal speed (I swear it left the track as it flew over the points just outside Bologna). In Ravenna I had time to visit five separate sites displaying the city's famously beautiful mosaics, as well as Dante's tomb. More importantly, it was in Ravenna's Teatro Alighieri that I discovered the art of moving from a poorly positioned seat into a fantastically good one at the very last moment. For the past ten years I'd watched other people perform this trick and marvelled that, unlike at home in the UK where changing seats was frowned upon, in continental Europe it seemed to be perfectly acceptable.

In Ravenna I found that my seat was almost at the back of the hall on the right-hand side. I sat there for a few minutes feeling pretty hard done by, but in the final seconds between the closing of the doors and the auditorium being plunged into darkness, something in me rebelled, and before I knew it I'd shot out of my seat, pushed ungraciously past a number of people and found myself marching down the central aisle towards the platform, scanning the first few rows. An unoccupied seat on the end of the third row presented itself, into which I sank with a sense of wonder at my newly acquired audacity. From that day onwards I never looked back, and if I was unhappy with my seat I simply went in search of a better one. It didn't always work, and sometimes the rightful occupier turned up for the second half, but it was always worth a try. Occasionally I was received with hostility if I took an absent subscriber's seat, but once I'd explained how far I'd travelled and mentioned that I was well acquainted with the artist, I was welcomed like a guest of honour.

Unreserved seating was always an irresistible temptation, and in late November 2007 I hastened to Varese in northern Italy, where just such an arrangement was on offer. The journey was tedious, but the gorgeous view of Lake Como from the train lifted my flagging spirits. A local bus took me into the city and dropped me in an elegant, leafy district where my B&B was said to be situated, but with no street map to consult I asked a young man for directions to via Dante. He was Marco, a locum GP, who on learning this was my first time in Varese, not only offered to help me find the B&B but also volunteered to pick me up the following morning and drive me to a local beauty spot. During our search for via Dante I told him he must be one of the legion of guardian angels who always seemed to be around to lend a helping hand, which pleased him no end. As he strode away, he turned and shouted, "Wow, I'm an angel!"

The proprietor of the B&B welcomed me into his home and introduced me to a couple of friends who were eating lunch in the kitchen, right next door to my bedroom. I was disappointed to find no wardrobe, washbasin, television or reading lamp at my disposal, but my main consideration that afternoon was to buy a pair of support tights designed to assist with poor circulation, which I normally found in Boots or M & S but had forgotten to bring with me. I visited several department stores and shops selling hosiery, including one located in a side street with industrial strength girdles in the window. The mature lady behind the counter looked thrilled to have a potential customer so late on a Saturday afternoon and gamely mounted a step ladder, bringing down a pile of dusty boxes. Donning a pair of white gloves she began to unfurl pair after pair of staggeringly ugly flesh coloured monstrosities and drape them across the counter. She'd engaged the assistance of a man from the shop next door to translate, and I begged him to tell her to stop, conveying my thanks and explaining that they weren't quite what I had in mind.

As I settled into my room for the evening, the household was in a state of characteristic Italian excitability, with much crashing and banging of cupboard doors and the television going full blast. I filled the time from six o'clock onwards with spells of reading, eating various items I'd bought from a supermarket, and sorting my belongings into regimental order. Events next door alternated between short periods of calm and sudden explosions of shouting and crockery. I longed to be in a quiet hotel room, drifting off to sleep to the murmur of my own television.

My host was unusually tall for an Italian, with matinee idol looks, and his spacious bathroom was equipped with an exercise machine, an assortment of weight lifting equipment and a plethora of masculine toiletries. Framed photographs of himself engaged in various outdoor pursuits adorned the walls, and in my room there were scale maps of remote corners of Siberia marked with routes he had followed, which I found myself studying closely, simply to pass the time. At nine, despite the domestic hubbub, I sank back into crisp cotton sheets smelling comfortingly of washday, rammed home my ear plugs and knew no more until seven the next morning.

Marco arrived at nine, happy that he'd been called out only once during the night, and we drove the eight kilometres to Sacre Monte, leaving the car at the foot of the hill. It was a glorious morning, the trees ablaze with colour, the views of the lake magnificent. The winding footpath led upwards through a towering gateway and passed nine distinctively decorated chapels containing frescoes and scenes from the New Testament, in which the figures were so realistic it was as if huge biblical paintings had been brought to life. Perched at the top was a village with covered cobbled passageways leading to exhilarating viewpoints. We talked about religion, life and love on our walk, but I didn't let on that my friend Antonio Giancotti had also arranged to drive me to Sacre Monte that afternoon; neither did I admit to Antonio that I'd already been there that morning.

In the evening I arrived at Palazzo Estense, one of Italy's national monuments, an hour before the performance began, but already a dozen or so people stood waiting. We were separated from Sokolov by glass panels, through which we could hear him rehearsing quite clearly, and I could see that Salone Estense was a long and narrow, exquisitely decorated room dominated by massive chandeliers. As more and more people arrived, the volume of their voices increased to a roar, obliterating the sound of the music, which seemed a pity. I was joined by Antonio and we sat just a few feet from the keyboard, knowing exactly what to expect, but it was an even greater experience than we could have imagined. It was a whirlwind of a performance: Schubert's Sonata D958 and Chopin's Op.28 Preludes with six encores, each of them greeted with deafening choruses of "Grazie!" from the audience. Antonio lamented that he might never sit quite so close to Sokolov again, and we agreed it had been an event we would never forget.

In January 2008 I attended one of the early performances of Sokolov's new Mozart programme in Vicenza, and another Italian friend, Filippo Furlan, arranged for me to stay overnight in the home of a friend of his, but the keys to the apartment could not be made available to me until after the performance. I flew to Venice at daybreak via Munich, arriving at midday, and took the vaporetto along the Grand Canal to Piazza San Marco. The performance didn't start until nine o'clock so a long afternoon stretched ahead with no opportunity to rest or smarten myself up before the concert, but the city was bathed in mellow winter sunshine, the square uncluttered by tourists, and I enjoyed photographing the palazzos and the lagoon in the fading light. At five I caught the train to Vicenza, and was surprised to discover that Teatro Comunale was a brand new building, just recently opened.

The Mozart sonatas K280 and K332 were played wonderfully well, but I had the misfortune to be sitting next to a trio of ladies who took it in turns to unzip their handbags, forage for sweets and then, having rustled their wrappers, zip their bags smartly shut again. The encores were still coming thick and fast at eleven thirty and by then I was feeling desperately tired. I'd not slept the night before and had been awake for over forty hours. At last Filippo drove me to Franco Perretta's apartment on the outskirts of the city, and although Franco was due to return home later, he'd left word that I needn't wait up for him and had indicated which room I was to occupy.

Filippo opened an external gate with one key and the door to the entrance hall with another, but when it came to the front door of the apartment, the key refused to turn. Franco's mobile was switched off, and although Filippo was reluctant to leave me there, he needed to drive to Verona urgently. I assured him I would be fine; it was just a matter of waiting until Franco got back. I was on a small landing with nowhere to sit and it was necessary to press a time switch every so often to keep the lights on. Leaning against the front door with my eyes closed I prayed for Franco's swift return. Behind one of the other doors I could hear the comforting babble of a television, but from upstairs came the sound of bawdy singing and people crashing about. At a quarter to one I began to wonder if, imagining I was safely tucked up in bed, Franco might have decided to stay out until morning. The thought of another sleepless night was too awful to contemplate; I was also feeling cold and began fishing spare items of clothing out of my bag.

I went downstairs and into the street several times for no particular reason, and at two o'clock I decided I couldn't remain on the landing any longer and wandered outside again with no plan of action other than to escape from the building. A thick, penetrating mist had descended and I walked the silent streets, encountering nothing but unlit apartment blocks and dead ends. I could hear the murmur of traffic in the far distance, but I was a very long way from the city centre and afraid of getting lost so I turned back, intending to wait in the ground floor hallway all night if necessary. As I struggled with the wrought iron gate someone rode past on a bicycle and I thought to call out a feeble, "Scusi!". To my eternal relief a young woman wearing a hijab and a friendly smile dismounted and walked towards me. She spoke no English but understood French, so I attempted to explain my predicament, and without hesitation she beckoned me to follow her and wheeled her bicycle round the corner into a neighbouring street, telling me her name was Fatima and offering me shelter for as long as I needed it.

Her small apartment was sparsely furnished: a table and chair, a double mattress on the floor and little else. Fatima offered me food and drink, even a shower if I wished, but all I wanted was to lie down and sleep. As I sank back onto the mattress she tucked a blanket round me and placed a bottle of water and a glass by my side. We spoke very little, but she said that the next morning she would telephone a friend who understood English. As she lay beside me and turned out the light I felt a deep sense of gratitude mixed with amazement that in the dead of night fate had sent me a guardian angel on a bicycle.

I fell asleep instantly, but my mobile rang some time later and it was Franco, just returned home and anxious to know my whereabouts. Fatima wanted me to stay until morning but Franco felt duty bound to collect me straight away. Out in the street I hugged and thanked my rescuer and she looked genuinely sorry to see me go. Back at Franco's apartment my bed was much more comfortable but it felt cold, and I regretted leaving the warmth of Fatima's mattress.

The next morning as Franco prepared my breakfast he undertook to ensure Fatima received some flowers on my behalf. He also offered to drive me to Venice Airport that afternoon, which gave me sufficient time to visit Vicenza's Teatro Olimpico, a magnificent Renaissance auditorium built in the 1500s, still in use for dramatic productions and the first theatre in Italy to be built with a roof. An ingenious and meticulously painted *trompe l'oeil* stage set installed in 1585 (the oldest in existence) gave the illusion of elegant streets radiating from a central square and disappearing into the distance. A party of Americans was already inside, one of whom used his admirable baritone voice to test the acoustics with an operatic aria.

Back in Venice in May 2009 I chugged along the Grand Canal on my way from the station, full of anticipation at the prospect of hearing Sokolov perform in the city's renowned opera house, Teatro La Fenice, where Antonio Giancotti had arranged a seat for me in the front row. The theatre had been virtually destroyed by fire in 1996 and reopened with a newly built interior in 2004. The auditorium was sumptuous and colourful, but lacked the air of faded grandeur one associated with Italy's historic theatres. Sitting in such close proximity to the piano was a bad idea acoustically, but I witnessed one of Sokolov's finest performances of that season, and a demonstration of boundless physical energy one would only expect from someone half his age.

La Fenice Venice

Every year Sokolov performed at the most prestigious European music festivals as well as those devoted solely to the piano, and in

Italy one of the major annual events was the International Piano Festival in Brescia & Bergamo, founded in 1964 by the great Italian pianist Arturo Benedetti Michelangeli. I first attended the festival in 1998, and returned to those two ancient cities in the north of Italy many times for Sokolov's recitals in Teatro Grande in Brescia and Bergamo's Teatro Donizetti, both equally impressive inside, decorated predominantly in red and gold with many balconies divided into separate boxes, reaching up to exquisitely detailed ceilings. In these venues the mood of the audience was often demonstrative, with loud cheers breaking out before Sokolov had even lifted a finger, and occasionally premature cries of "Bravo!" before he'd barely struck the final chord, but the adulation he received in Italy came straight from the heart.

On these trips I spent many happy hours exploring, especially in Bergamo, where the old medieval city stood high on a hill overlooking its modern counterpart. On my first visit, the recital took place in Sala Greppi, and I wasted a lot of time wandering around in sweltering heat on the afternoon of my arrival, trying to locate the venue and secure my ticket. At last I happened upon an ancient gateway with a small brass nameplate beside it, leading to a cobbled courtyard and an office where I found the director of Sala Greppi, a bit of a charmer with a commanding voice. Neither he nor his male assistants appeared to speak English, but after a short period of uncertainty the director boomed, "Signora Truman?" and all was well.

Time was short, but I couldn't resist leaping aboard a bus bound for the old city as it wound its way slowly up the hillside. It was my only chance to see anything of the historic part of Bergamo and I spent twenty precious minutes darting through the narrow streets, passing ancient courtyards, archways and statues, glancing at wondrous medieval buildings. Everywhere was flooded with late afternoon sunlight, the trees were changing colour, and it was all rather spellbinding. I walked back down the hillside, stopping occasionally to gaze at the wonderful views of the surrounding countryside with a distant glimpse of the Alps, vowing to return to Bergamo with more time to do it justice.

Mindful of the unallocated seating that evening, I was soon hot-footing it back towards Sala Greppi in order to be one of the first in line. A large crowd soon gathered with not the slightest semblance of a queue, then the director appeared and began greeting some of the especially attractive females. Catching sight of me he shook hands briefly and then pounced on someone better looking. A free-for-all ensued when the doors opened, but I more or less held my ground at the head of the stampede and secured a seat in the centre of the third row. The interior was colourfully decorated, the platform draped with yards of green velvet, abundant foliage and a prominently displayed national flag.

The newly introduced pieces by William Byrd were priceless and the early Beethoven sonata which followed was even more technically demanding than the previous one had been. The encores continued until shortly before midnight, whereupon I was escorted to the artist's room, presented with a long-stemmed rose by a member of staff, and Sokolov broke away from a conversation to ask me about my journey. "How did you arrive?", he wanted to know. At that moment the director swept into the room, bearing a tray of glasses and a bottle. With an extravagant flourish and a thunderous, "Maestro Sokolov! Signora Truman!", he handed each of us a glass of champagne, and my happiness knew no bounds.

A reporter from a national newspaper came in to conduct an interview, mainly in Italian but occasionally lapsing into English. The final question he put to Sokolov was, "What does it take to become a great pianist?", to which came the reply, "You have to realise that music is not a job; it's your whole life". By this time, the director was consulting his watch, so I knew it was time to make myself scarce.

The next day, Milan Central railway station was hot and crowded with nowhere to sit, so with time to spare and no inclination to stray very far, I sat outside in the fresh air on a nearby bench, albeit in a seedy area frequented by drunks and dropouts. Fascinated by their antics I couldn't help noticing that in Italy even the most poverty-stricken individuals seemed to possess a sense of style.

It was several years before I returned to Bergamo, and this time I approached the historic part on foot, following directions provided by Antonio, who lived in the city and was able to secure some very attractive and hospitable B&B accommodation for me on my earlier visits. The route to the old city firstly took me along narrow cobbled streets and then climbed a steep road lined with villas until I reached one of the city gates, beyond which lay the maze of narrow thoroughfares and open cobbled piazzas, lined with bars and cafés, food stores and gift shops. The largest piazza was overlooked by medieval churches and palazzos of breathtaking beauty. My first evening there was free, so I returned to the old city after dark and walked among the floodlit buildings, gazing out across the sea of lights below, and at ten o'clock a great cathedral bell began tolling mightily, drowning out all other sounds for many minutes. The late spring air was still warm and the mood magical. The following evening I attended my first concert at Teatro Donizetti, where I was captivated by the warmth of its interior and the relaxed atmosphere backstage.

In Brescia two evenings after that I stood outside the crumbling and decrepit looking Teatro Grande imagining it would be a disappointment after the beauty of the theatre in Bergamo. On the contrary, the interior was sumptuous and even the anteroom in which everyone stood waiting for the auditorium doors to open was like a state room in one of Europe's great palaces. Quite apart from the visual splendour, the performance in Brescia was awe inspiring; Sokolov was so fired up I feared he might spontaneously combust. The raw energy of the man was astonishing, and at times during Schumann's Sonata in F sharp minor No.11 he bounced around on the piano stool, kicking and stamping as if he were driving out demons. Antonio, who was sitting beside me, had told me before the recital that he didn't much care for this sonata, but in little more than half an hour Sokolov persuaded him otherwise and at the end we leapt to our feet and hugged one another in celebration.

Two evenings later I was in Brescia, discovering that my seat was up in the fourth balcony with pillars partially obscuring the view. My only consolation was that I'd taken my binoculars and was able to study Sokolov's hands. I was also in a perfect position to examine the glorious painted ceiling and look down at the dozens of richly decorated boxes full of spellbound faces. It was an amazing performance, and the acoustics were such that even from so far away, the lightest pianissimi were clearly audible. Antonio moved downstairs at the interval, having earmarked an empty place in the front stalls, but by the time he got there it had been bagged by someone else, so he was forced to sit much further back. Realising what a cut and thrust business this seat-hopping was, I decided to stay put with my binoculars.

Teatro Grande Brescia

The following year Antonio managed to wangle a front row seat for me at Teatro Donizetti, and I took my place feeling deliriously happy. This was an evening of almost unparalleled satisfaction in which Sokolov produced the greatest Mozart sonatas of the season and an electrifying Chopin programme; a real 'blood and bone' performance in which he exposed the inner workings of the more dramatic Op.28 Preludes and delivered the lighter ones with grace and lyricism. As if this were not enough, he chose for his final encore the Bach Chorale Prelude BWV639 'Ich ruf zu dir, Herr Jesu Christ'. Whenever Sokolov ended the evening with Bach I always felt a deep sense that all was resolved and nothing more needed to be said; that I could go on my way having received some sort of blessing.

In 2017 Sokolov played a new Mozart programme combined with Beethoven's Sonatas No.27 Op.90 and the sublime No.32 Op.111. There was so much to relish as this great odyssey swept us up into the firmament and sent us spinning through a wilderness of stars. The overwhelming certainty of the closing bars and the air of solemnity they engendered called for a long silence before the intrusion of applause. This happened at some venues, and when it did it was wonderful. In Teatro Donizetti, after the initial burst of excitement following Op.111 the encores began, but many in the audience were so busy comparing notes that they seemed to forget to put their hands together and I feared we may not get the usual quota. Thankfully at the end of the third encore everyone suddenly began shouting for more and ultimately Sokolov delivered six of the best and received a hero's send-off.

At the 2018 recital in Brescia the first of Schubert's Impromptus Op.142 seemed to envelop the theatre in a cloak of velvet, and in the second piece I marvelled that between the two of them, Schubert and Sokolov had turned the humblest melody into something majestic. I was so glad that Sokolov was never tempted to play anything too fast and he always gave his audience the opportunity to stand back and admire. After the flesh-and-blood reality of the two opening pieces and the diverse imagery of the third impromptu, the finale abounded with riotous mischief and unearthly antics until the inhabitants of Schubert's elfin domain were sent scampering away into the night, generating a predictably explosive reaction from a delighted audience.

I noticed that in Brescia, although the applause between encores often seemed in danger of fizzling out because the audience were so busy discussing what they'd heard, they always remained firmly rooted to their seats knowing that Sokolov would return with six encores. On one particular occasion he produced out of the blue Debussy's strange and haunting Des Pas sur la Neige (Footprints in the Snow) which went on to draw many future evenings to an enigmatic conclusion.

Those who had never experienced the Sokolov phenomenon at first hand sometimes asked why I didn't stay at home and listen to his CDs, conserve my energy, reduce my carbon footprint and spend my money on more practical things. I always pointed out that a CD recording was forever set in stone, whereas what Sokolov produced at each recital was a constantly evolving, living organism. The countless hours spent travelling were a small price to pay to hear what he had to say. It might be the smallest assemblage of notes, a phrase here, a passage there, or a piece in its entirety. Whatever he offered was always worth the journey.

My most recent visit to Bergamo was in May 2019, when Sokolov played at Teatro Sociale in the historic part of the city while Teatro Donizetti was closed for refurbishment. In the first half I sat in a box to listen to the Beethoven Sonata No.3 Op.2/3 and the Eleven Bagatelles Op.119, but was disappointed with the remoteness of the sound, so I ventured downstairs at the interval and found a seat in the third row which provided a different experience altogether. I'd been desperate to hear the Brahms Op.118/Op.119 programme at full throttle, and this was my opportunity. With all the immediacy I could wish for, I settled back to enjoy the feast. For me, this music was all about nature; not just human nature but also the beauties of the natural world, the wonders of God's creation, so passionately described by Brahms and so eloquently expressed by Sokolov. The opening A minor intermezzo, played with devastating passion, full of anguish and uncertainty, the rapturous A major intermezzo sounding as if Sokolov worshipped every note, the freewheeling adventure of the G minor ballade, the fairy orchestra in the central section of the F major romanze. The six encores included Rachmaninoff's Prelude Op.32/12, and I recognised that night how rewarding it was to hear Sokolov performing works conceived by his own countrymen. His incisive account of this Russian gem was utterly beguiling: a mysterious blend of ice and fire, the opening and closing bars sparkling, crystalline; the final notes, amounting to no more than a scarcely audible 'plink', like the first drop of moisture falling from an icicle, heralding the distant approach of spring.

Two more of Italy's historic theatres were my first ports of call in 2016: Genoa's Teatro Carlo Felice and Parma's Teatro Regio. The Steinway looked lonely on the huge stage in Genoa, normally the home of grand opera, ballet and orchestral performances, and I discovered later that the piano was making its first public appearance. It was one hell of a christening, but the instrument gave a splendid account of itself, remaining in excellent shape throughout. Chopin's 2nd Sonata became one of the monumental achievements for which Sokolov would long be remembered, and in Genoa I sat next to a conductor from Birmingham who was hearing Sokolov perform live for the first time and who confessed to having a problem with Chopin's music. At the end of the sonata he declared himself deeply impressed by the humanity of Sokolov's playing. Indeed, there was so much more to this sonata than the passing of a life.

The following day Sokolov moved on, and naturally so did I, as did the infant piano, which by all accounts had found the vastness of the hall in Genoa something of a challenge, but I was assured it would feel more at home in the compact space of Teatro Regio in Parma. It was my first time there, and what a heart lifting experience it was to walk into that ornate little jewel of a theatre, blazing with light and colour, to find the piano sitting in front of the graceful classical backdrop I'd seen so many times in one of the well-known photographs of Sokolov at the keyboard. This was an exceptional evening where any reservations I might have had about the Schumann Fantasy were blown away. It was as if Sokolov took me into the innermost recesses of this piece and showed me just how amazing it was. The undeniably beautiful final movement was infused with enormous pathos and the declaration at its heart seemed to have travelled from the very core of Sokolov's being, right through to his fingertips.

I visited Bolzano, the capital of South Tyrol, several times, usually in August and occasionally for the final performance of the season. Not the easiest place to reach, it involved a five hour journey from Milan Malpensa, but the performances were often exceptional. The Auditorium Bolzano, a compact, friendly and comfortable venue, always seemed to bring out the best in Sokolov. In 2016 he'd only recently given his annual recital at the Salzburg Festival in the massive Grosses Festspielhaus where microphones and cameras had probably piled on the pressure, but in Bolzano one could sense he was thoroughly enjoying himself, communing with three of his favourite composers and spreading their message to every corner of the auditorium. He played with the utmost freedom, keeping nothing in reserve. With the music flowing like liquid gold, the entire programme was laid before the audience like a banquet for the senses.

I often wondered what kind of works he might have produced had he turned instead to writing, painting, composing or any other artistic endeavour, but it seemed more than enough that he could transform what someone else had written into a piece of art that he might have created himself on the spur of the moment. From the grandest sonata to the simplest encore, he painted, he sculpted, he narrated. His mind and body were so intent upon their work that there was no call for any kind of showmanship. He could hold an audience in his thrall without resorting to any such device.

Two years later in the same hall, Sokolov stepped out to begin the momentous task of laying his beloved Haydn sonatas to rest.

I'd heard him play them many times throughout the season, and for me this performance surpassed all others. It was like attending a well organised funeral and walking away feeling satisfied that the deceased had received the best possible tribute. Even at that late stage Sokolov revealed hitherto undiscovered nuances, and every small detail was given its moment. Each piece might have passed through an intellectual furnace somewhere inside his mind, where new ideas were constantly forged in an endless search for fresh revelations; a tireless journey towards the very essence of the music, a process culminating in the miraculous symmetry of heart and mind, feet and fingers. Sokolov worked his way through the three sonatas with lingering reverence and affection and the audience sat in rapt communion. This was his final opportunity to give voice to Haydn's creativity, and the audience produced the response that composer and artist deserved. He returned to the platform many times, as if drinking in sufficient applause to keep him nourished for the following eight weeks during which he would toil away on new repertoire to replace the Haydn sonatas. Whatever came under his scrutiny would receive his undivided attention for an intensive period of exploration, and when he finally presented it to the public two months later, it would remain, right up until the very last note of the final performance, an ongoing work in progress. There was no room for complacency in Sokolov's world. I saw him as the embodiment of artistic integrity: no grand flourishes, no gloss, no glamour. His final Haydn was pure genius.

Another evening I will never forget was spent in the lovely medieval hill town of Asolo in northern Italy, where Sokolov played in the 13th century Chiesa di San Gottardo, a small deconsecrated building used expressly for musical performances. At a previous recital I'd told Sokolov of my intention to be in Asolo, but he'd looked doubtful and said, "But it's only a church", so although I didn't expect too much from this particular experience, I was enchanted by the beauty of the setting. Approaching Asolo in Filippo Furlan's car, we could see the little town in the distance, clustered around the summit of a hill, bathed in the golden light of evening and looking like a scene from a fairytale. By the time we'd stopped for a pre-concert drink half way up the hill, the ancient church was illuminated by an almost full moon. A brightly lit awning outside the entrance threw the surrounding trees and the gathering throng into silhouette, and the buzz of anticipation was stilled as the doors opened to reveal a small interior with maybe two hundred canvas seats. The space was dominated by the piano, behind which an arresting altar painting depicted an angel in full flight. Wide corrugated panels had been applied to the ceiling in an attempt to capture and redistribute the sound, and this arrangement worked very well.

As the angelic sounds of Rameau's Suite in D began their decorous journey I went into silent raptures and remained in this blissful state throughout Mozart's Sonata KV310, Brahms' Variations & Fugue on a Theme by Handel and the Op.117 Intermezzi. Sokolov routinely turned out exceptional performances but this one was worthy of mention in the annals of pianistic history and I wanted everyone I knew to hear it. It was an object lesson; it was immense. This was pure magic without the trickery. I heard the Brahms for the last time two evenings later in Bolzano and walked out of the auditorium feeling bereft. In the artist's room I lamented the loss of the Handel Variations, which I told Sokolov I'd now heard twenty-nine times. He laughed, spread his arms wide and quipped, "What to do now?" What indeed.

3. MONACO

THE EXPRESSION ON my boss's face was priceless when I told him one Friday afternoon in November 1998 that I was off to Monte Carlo for the weekend. His attempt to look pleased for me failed to disguise the peevishness he undoubtedly felt that while he was playing a round of golf on Saturday morning and eating Sunday lunch with the family, an underling would be disporting herself in one of the major playgrounds of the rich and famous. He wouldn't have enjoyed every stage of my journey, but I kept the less palatable details to myself. Starting at three o'clock on Saturday morning I boarded a coach bound for Heathrow, having firstly sampled the dim violet glow of the bus station's malodorous night toilet. On the inside of the cubicle door was scrawled, "Bollocks to you, whoever you are!", a discouraging welcome if ever there was one, for any visitor arriving in the city of Birmingham for the first time.

My budget flight with easyJet left London on schedule, and it felt good to be flying south, away from the dreariness of late Autumn in the UK. The landing in Nice was so thrilling I resolved to sit by the window on the return journey. As we skimmed over the Maritime Alps and out across the sea, circling back to land on the edge of the outermost runway right on the shoreline, we flew perilously close to the water until the very last moment. The sun-drenched resort of Nice looked spectacular, and the bus to Monte Carlo cut through several long tunnels in the rock, passing steeply terraced properties growing an abundance of produce, and finally emerged high above the famous harbour. I gazed out of the bus window at a glittering blue sea dotted with tiny yachts and speedboats, masses of swaying palm trees, and a magnificent clutter of buildings surrounding the bay, stretching way up the hillside. The descent into Monte Carlo was breathtaking; in the harbour, big white luxury yachts gleamed in the sunlight, jostling with smaller craft. The bus dropped me outside the

Casino amid ornamental fountains and lush gardens; such a far cry from that ghastly WC in Birmingham Coach Station.

Budget accommodation was thin on the ground, but I found a room in a modest little hotel tucked away in a side street at the less salubrious end of the harbour, where a canary sang its heart out in the dining room window. The Congress Centre's Auditorium Rainier III was a fair step away at the opposite end of the harbour. I was bitterly disappointed with my seat on the far left of the front row with just a view of Sokolov's rear, and to make matters worse I was unexpectedly required to pay for it. Nevertheless Sokolov played a blistering Rachmaninoff Piano Concerto No.3 accompanied by the Monte Carlo Philharmonic Orchestra conducted by Walter Weller. After the audience had been treated to a Chopin encore I found my way backstage with the help of Mrs Sokolov, and the artist's room was soon filled with members of the orchestra wanting to pay their respects before they returned to the platform to play a symphony. Sokolov kept a small group of us entertained for the next forty-five minutes with experiences he'd had with various conductors and orchestras, but mentioning no names.

He related the well documented story of how, as a four year old, he'd stood on a tiny podium and conducted all his parents' classical recordings. Unlike many pianists who turned to conducting later in life, he'd done it the other way round. I said I was glad he'd got conducting out of the way so early, and everyone else agreed. He talked about his strong desire to play repeated passages because it gave him the opportunity to express the music in a different way and say everything he wanted to say. Some conductors preferred to dispense with repeats, which he seemed to find frustrating. We were so eager to hear what he had to say that we suddenly became aware that the second half of the concert had finished and the musicians were back in their dressing rooms. Sokolov had hoped to avoid the crowds, but he was spotted by a group of stragglers outside and he patiently answered their questions despite the evening chill. It was suggested I might like to walk back along the harbour with the Sokolovs so that I could see the floodlit fountains outside their hotel. Sokolov asked me what I thought of Monte Carlo and I said it was difficult to imagine ordinary people living there. He then told me that a most unsatisfactory seat had been allocated to his wife for the concert and I couldn't resist telling him about my own, including the fact that I'd been charged for it into the bargain. When we reached the hotel he invited me into the lobby, where he delved into his bag and produced the money for my ticket, which at first I refused to take, but he insisted on it as 'a matter of principle'.

The harbour by night was a fairyland spectacle of shimmering reflections, but back at my hotel I slept badly on account of the cold. The little canary sang to me the next morning as I sat alone in the dining room with a simple breakfast, and before nine I was on the bus back to Nice Airport. With an hour or so to spare I hopped on a local bus to the seashore and strolled along the famous Promenade des Anglais, passing the opulent Hotel Negresco. Sipping delicious coffee at a pavement café I also drank in the warmth of the sun and the smell of the sea, and as I walked along the streets of Birmingham later that evening, it was incredible to realise how and where my day had begun.

I returned to Monte Carlo twenty years later, but on this occasion there was no affordable accommodation in the city, so I was obliged to stay in a hotel over the border in France and ferry myself back and forth from the harbour by bus. Sokolov's performance was to be a solo recital this time, and I had a much better seat than on my previous visit. In preparation for his arrival on stage we were plunged into total darkness, with the exception of the piano and the surface of the platform, providing a classic image, as if nothing existed but Sokolov and his faithful companion, steering their course through an evening of sumptuous music-making.

The sound quality was ideal and Sokolov took command of Beethoven's early Sonata No.3 in C major, describing its mercurial progress with his trademark technical mastery, and a smooth transition from the sonata to the Op.119 Bagatelles was made possible by the audience maintaining a spellbound silence. The multi-faceted collection of eleven bagatelles began and ended with grace and decorum. In between, there were many unexpected gear changes and we were catapulted from the angelic to the demonic and back again at the turn of a hand. Anyone new to the bagatelles may have sat back expecting a succession of dainty miniatures but would have realised very quickly that some of these short pieces had teeth.

The magnificent Brahms Op.118/Op.119 programme was a feast for the imagination: starting in tumult, ending in triumph, overflowing with pictorial images, distant dreams, the tenderest love and longing; every detail of these narratives handled with consummate skill. I luxuriated in the familiar pieces as they passed through Sokolov's rigorous artistic process, whilst experiencing the thrill of discovery with those which were new to me. This was his first solo performance in Monte Carlo, so the audience were unfamiliar with his customary string of encores. Consequently there were gasps of astonishment and yelps of delight each time he swooped back onto the piano stool, ending the evening with Debussy's Des Pas sur la Neige, its delicate luminescence in sharp contrast with the waves crashing against the rocks just outside the hall.

Before leaving Monaco the next morning I sat in the manicured gardens of the Casino surrounded by unimaginable wealth, contemplating the endless promise of the Brahms programme, the sublime set of encores I'd heard the night before and the beautiful life I still had, thanks to Sokolov's music. I felt no envy for the inhabitants of Monte Carlo or indeed anywhere else; Sokolov's art was the one luxury I had, and I knew it was all I would ever want.

4. FRANCE

A PERIOD OF twenty years separated my two visits to the city of Bordeaux. The first was in the early days, when I sat up in the balcony of the Grand Theatre in the Lord Mayor's private loge, feeling like the cat that got the cream. More recently in 2017 I returned to Bordeaux for a performance in the relatively new Auditorium, an impressive modern building and a comfortable and spacious venue where I had a perfect view of the keyboard. Sokolov was in great shape and it was reasonable to expect that something mouthwatering was in store, but in the event it was a deeply disappointing experience thanks to a small number of people scattered across the auditorium who effectively spoiled the evening with a variety of avoidable disturbances. My neighbour was equally exasperated and we exchanged many looks of despair as the evening progressed. I was particularly incensed when, at the moment Beethoven's Op.111 reached its conclusion and Sokolov sat with head bowed in silent homage, someone who had no intention of waiting for the applause to begin stomped towards an exit, their heavy footsteps resounding on the wooden floor. It seemed nothing was sacred that night, but the audience's response was ecstatic and Sokolov assured me afterwards that he'd been largely unaffected. For my part it had been impossible to fully engage with the music, and for once I took scant pleasure from a long and costly journey.

My first concert experience in Paris was in 2003 at the iconic Théâtre des Champs-Elysées. On arrival in the city it seemed sensible to head straight for the famous boulevard itself, where I expected to find a tourist office and hoped to see the concert venue close at hand. The tourist office was at the far end, close to L'Arc de Triomphe, where I joined a long queue and stood for almost an hour before reaching the enquiry counter. There was no budget accommodation anywhere near the theatre so I was despatched to a far flung and unappetising corner of the city, where exactly five hours after my flight had landed in Paris, I took up residence at a humble address in rue des Petits Hôtels.

From the train that morning the domes of Sacré-Coeur, touched by early sunlight, had looked majestic, and there was time enough to ride to Montmartre and climb the steps to the basilica. I took a quick turn round the Tuileries gardens, overlooked by elegant buildings and still alive with the colours of mid-October. At the centre was a small pool with a fountain, where an old man with a long grizzly beard, a sailor's cap, smock and sandals, hired out toy sailing boats from a handcart. A long gravelled drive directed the eye to a hazy view of L'Arc de Triomphe in the far distance, and the Eiffel Tower could be glimpsed through the trees. With little time at my disposal I was glad I'd spent it there, and returned to the hotel content that my afternoon hadn't been wasted.

How my hotel came by its solitary one star rating was anyone's guess, but it certainly wasn't for the provision of hot water. Suitably refreshed after a bracing cold splash, I headed towards the sophistication of Avenue Montaigne and the famous theatre. From the outside it looked unexceptional but once inside there was elegance in abundance and the predominantly red décor was sumptuous. Two balconies were divided into open loges, each lined with figured dark red silk and containing half a dozen gilt chairs. One such loge was set aside for invited guests, into which I proudly stepped and took my place next to Franco Panozzo. Judging by appearances, the cream of Parisian society seemed to be in attendance and I felt a little out of my depth. Sokolov played Bach's Reincken Sonata BWV965 and the Bach/Brahms Chaconne for the left hand, followed by Beethoven's Sonata No.11 Op.22 and the great Sonata No.32 Op.111, which was nothing short of a miracle.

Sokolov's first commercial DVD, a recording of a live performance in Paris the previous year, masterminded by the highly respected French film maker Bruno Monsaingeon, was being released onto the market that very evening. At eleven o'clock the entire length of the corridor leading to Sokolov's room was jam packed with enthusiasts, many unwrapping DVDs to be signed. Some of them gave the impression that they knew him personally and I could sense this was going to be a long process, so I cheekily squeezed past, having seen enough queues for one day, and quickly paid my respects. Outside, I gasped at the closeness of the Eiffel Tower, covered in twinkling lights with a revolving beam at the top. The weekend had been one of frustration and elation in equal measure, and as I rode back to the hotel on the metro, my thoughts were already turning towards Germany, where in less than two weeks I would hear that glorious Beethoven sonata again.

The following year I was back in France, arriving in Toulouse mid-evening. Outside the railway station a gathering of vagrants stood comparing notes on another day spent dragging discontented dogs around on lengths of rope whilst tapping the local populace for cash. Behind them I saw a busy dual carriageway, on the opposite side of which were neon signs advertising a number of small hotels. I chose to stay at the two star des Ambassadeurs, which was cheap, scrupulously clean and managed by a kindly young couple.

After breakfast the next morning I sat in my room watching torrential rain bounce off the rooftops and it was early afternoon before it eased off. There were deep puddles to negotiate as I made my way into the centre and located Sokolov's concert venue, Halle aux Grains, and Place du Capitole, a vast open square dominated by the immense neoclassical pink brick facade of the city hall. The River Garonne looked depressingly brown after the rain and my feet were already soaked. Taking refuge in the cathedral I sat in a pew admiring the interior and was thrilled when the organ suddenly exploded into life and ploughed through an apocalyptic piece. I'd intended to spend time in the Musée des Augustins, currently exhibiting a collection of Cézannes, but the need to change into dry footwear was paramount, and by the time I'd squelched back to my room I'd lost the inclination to go out again before evening.

Halle aux Grains looked small from the outside, but the 2,500 seat auditorium occupied virtually the entire building, leaving no foyer to speak of and no corridors in which to move around. Once inside there was nowhere to go but through the appropriate door leading to one of the twelve separate seating areas: six on the ground floor, extending right around the building, and the same number in the steeply raked gallery, where I found my place at the end of a row. It seemed my seat had been designed to accommodate either a small child or an adult with no legs, with barely four inches of space available once it was lowered. An usher noticed my predicament and gave me permission to find another seat, which I succeeded in doing at the last moment, much to the annoyance of everyone I disturbed in the process. During the interval, ladies with vending trays slung round their necks patrolled each section, selling packets of potato chips. I couldn't have been more astonished if they'd been flogging buckets of popcorn or party poppers, and imagined all those empty crisp packets being trodden underfoot during the second half.

Sokolov's programme of Bach and Beethoven was of the highest order, and I walked into the artist's room to find the French promoters trying to persuade him to perform at a music festival in Toulouse the following year, in the Convent of the Jacobins, where the bones of St. Thomas Aquinas were said to lie beneath the altar. Sokolov had taken against the idea due to the complexities of the acoustics in that particular building, part of one end being exposed to the elements. It was an uphill struggle for the promoters and I sensed he would never agree, but they persisted until his hands started to flap - a useful adjunct to the Sokolov vocabulary which came into operation whenever polite refusal had failed, and in any language meant the matter was now closed.

My journey to Avignon, also in 2004, was far from straightforward, involving a flight to Munich, connecting there for Marseille. From the airport bus, the streets of Marseille looked uninviting as we drove past areas which at first glance looked like bomb sites awaiting clearance, but on closer inspection were evidently inhabited. By the time I'd queued for forty minutes for a rail ticket, I'd missed the high speed TGV service to Avignon and was obliged to take a slow train. It was packed and sweltering hot, and despite the windows being wide open it reeked of tobacco and diesel. The driver seemed intent upon death by derailment; the noise was unbelievable, and on the rare occasions the brakes were applied, they gave off a deafening hiss. As we flew over points and lurched round bends I concluded that if this was the slow train I was jolly glad I'd missed the fast one. The scenery wasn't hugely diverting either, apart from a stunning view of Marseille harbour as we left the city behind.

By four o'clock I longed for a quiet room and a cool pillow, but as yet I had nowhere to stay. Facing Avignon's station entrance were the medieval walls encircling the old part of the city. A massive gateway led to the long rue de la république, towards the end of which lay Place de l'Horloge and the Opéra Grand d'Avignon, the venue for the following evening. Beyond that lay the colossal Palais des Papes overlooking the Rhône, and the famous bridge of Avignon, Pont Saint-Bénézet. I decided it would all have to wait until the next day, and turning down the first side street showing a hotel sign, I checked myself into Hotel d'Angleterre, a traditional and peaceful place where a friendly receptionist fetched me a tray of tea.

My back muscles had become increasingly uncomfortable during the long day of travelling and were close to seizing up altogether, so I took to the floor of my room and attempted some exercises. Concerned that a night in a strange bed might make matters even worse, I wondered if I would be in a fit state to see the best of Avignon the following day, sit through the recital in the evening and then withstand the journey home. After a good night's sleep I walked gingerly to Place de l'Horloge and regarded the vast cobbled courtyard in front of the world's largest Gothic palace and fortress; an awesome building dating back to the 14th century, where nine popes had resided in splendour, apart from the most recent official resident, Pope Benedict XIII, whose occupancy was said to have been austere.

I felt fragile and had to admit to myself that the planned tour of the building was out of the question. I'd looked forward to walking the battlements and roof terraces, peering into the vaults and seeing the ceremonial rooms and private papal apartments, but settled instead for a brief walk round the outside of the building, after which I needed to sit down urgently. I made for a café beside a large duck pond with a fountain, manned by a surly twosome who slouched on a wooden balcony and glared at anyone bold enough to approach the seating. Despite the graceless fashion in which plates of lacklustre food and beverages were being slapped and slopped onto the tables I took my chance, but even the wildfowl seemed disgruntled, squawking and squabbling incessantly, so it was nothing like the tranquil interlude I'd hoped for.

It was barely midday, but I headed back to the hotel in the hope that my increasingly crablike gait wouldn't attract too much attention. An afternoon of alternate periods of relaxation and repeated exercises brought about a marked improvement, and I arrived at the hall feeling optimistic. The opera house's glossy brochure had promised a sumptuous red and gold interior, but at close quarters it looked in need of a lick of paint. The red plush seats were alarmingly close to the floor, and when I sat in mine it was like sinking into a velvet-lined bucket, my knees rising almost to shoulder height. The prospect of enduring more than two hours in a semi-squatting position, even with Sokolov to look at and listen to, was unthinkable. By the time the lights were lowered I'd negotiated a move into a loge, where I perched happily on an upright chair in an elevated position.

In Avignon Sokolov had been able to dictate his own terms with regard to illumination. He sat in his own solitary pool of light and the rest of us were in complete darkness. To enable him to negotiate the steps down to the exit, each time he left the platform a spotlight came on at the side which was then extinguished until he reappeared. This arrangement worked well until the third time he gave his characteristic swooping bow and launched himself in the general direction of the steps, when the spotlight failed to come on and left him floundering in the dark for several seconds. Terrified he might go cartwheeling into the front row, I looked away and imagined Mrs S reaching for the smelling salts. At last the light came on and Sokolov strode away, presumably to put a flea in someone's ear.

The second half of the programme was new to me. Still mourning the loss of Op.111, I couldn't imagine a fitting replacement, but I should have had faith. The first Chopin piece, the Fantasie-Impromptu, was so utterly thrilling that it took me until the end of the evening to recover. As I prepared to leave the artist's room, having congratulated Sokolov on the new Chopin programme, he announced, "I'm coming to Birmingham tomorrow!" as if this might have come as a surprise to me. Naturally I'd been looking forward to his visit to my city, but his confirmation carried me home on a wave of renewed anticipation and my back pain all but disappeared. On the flight to Munich the next day I felt ridiculously happy, knowing that he might at that very moment be on his way to Gatwick or Heathrow. Ahead of me were three concerts in the UK, a further three in Germany and possibly three more in France. After a twelve week summer drought, suddenly it was raining Sokolov!

A six day trip to France in December with three concerts in different cities seemed like a challenge, and the long walk through Paris CDG airport terminal to the railway station was always a tedious trudge, followed by the tiresome wait in the queue for tickets. Just getting to Gare du Nord took long enough, but on this occasion I had to change to a different line for Gare de Lyon in order to catch the train to Dijon, and the metro concourse was a sea of jostling travellers and commuters, fractious children, yapping dogs, packed escalators, impenetrable barriers and endless queues. I was accosted by countless beggars of an especially resolute variety, had my baggage sat on without apology and was treated with utter disdain by more than one railway employee. Welcome to Paris, I thought, and then remembered I'd often suffered similar tribulations in London.

Gare de Lyon was equally nightmarish, and as I struggled to get my teeth into a super-crusty baguette on a cold, windswept platform with nowhere to sit, I was assailed by a flock of marauding pigeons and had a sudden longing to be back at home. At least my seat on the TGV was in the quiet zone, and as we left the environs of Paris behind, eventually slipping into rural Burgundy, the landscape changed to one of simple rustic beauty. Ancient villages slumbered in the winter sunshine, some of them amounting to no more than a dozen houses clustered round a tiny church. At last I began to sit up, take notice and look forward.

The closest budget hotel to the Auditorium in Dijon was on the edge of town, and as soon as I walked through the door I fell in love with it. Originally an old coaching inn, it was a glorious assemblage of sunken floors, ill-fitting doors, creaking stairways and tiny casement windows. My large double room with its corner fireplace and ancient furniture looked like a hastily knocked up amateur theatrical stage set for a pantomime, inexpertly decorated in livid shades of tangerine, turquoise and fuchsia. The reception and dining area was in the former stable building overlooking a cobbled courtyard and tall archway. The hooks driven into the walls for tethering horses were still in place, and it was easy to imagine coaches clattering along the street outside and trundling into the courtyard. The whole building was so lopsided and uneven that each doorway had a compensating shallow step. I lost count of the number of times I tripped over these, and every time I went to reception I quite literally fell into it.

The Auditorium was by contrast an astonishing piece of modern architecture combining a massive convention centre with a concert hall. The interior was one of ingenious design and innovative ideas applied to the smallest detail, all of which worked perfectly. Sokolov's insistence on dim lighting was honoured to the point where he was guided onto the platform by a torch-bearer. The performance was almost unbearably beautiful, and naturally I told him so.

I spent two nights in Dijon, so there was a whole day and an evening to fill. At the Grand Theatre, a Moscow opera company was performing Rimsky-Korsakov's *The Tsar's Bride,* so I went in search of the cheapest ticket I could find and enquired about leg room in the balcony. The girl selling tickets took me straight up into the top tier to try the seats for myself before buying. The interior was fabulous: an ocean of blue velvet with an ornate domed ceiling, colossal chandeliers and three precipitously raked balconies. I was elated that I had another taste of Russia to look forward to that evening and spent my day admiring the city's medieval and Renaissance architecture, the beautiful burghers' houses with multi-coloured patterned roofs and the central network of narrow streets lined with antique shops and little bistros, formerly occupied by metal workers, basket weavers and glass makers, from whose crafts the streets took their names.

On my way to the opera I passed the Dukes' Palace, where coloured moving images were being projected onto the front of the building, depicting the seasons of the year. I was just in time for autumn, and the massive pillars on either side were transformed into tree trunks entwined with creeper. On the stone facade a forest scene showed leaves fluttering down and a procession of elves marching through the woodland carrying axes over their shoulders. As the image changed to wintertime the branches were stripped bare, the falling leaves turned into snowflakes and a herd of deer moved among the trees. The final image was of a flame travelling along a fuse wire which zigzagged across the front of the palace and finally exploded into a silent firework display.

My visit to the theatre was exhilarating. I'd always considered the Russian voice to be a unique and extraordinary instrument, and I knew that at least one of the voices I would hear that evening would make my hair stand on end. The reality far exceeded the expectation and there were three memorable voices among the soloists: a ravishing soprano, a rich, fruity mezzo and a tenor of the kind I especially admired, possessing a quick vibrato, whose singing moved me to tears, but sadly he managed only one aria before being executed. I wondered how the huge orchestra and chorus of more than a hundred managed to scrape a living from their chosen professions. On my way to the theatre I'd seen musicians approaching from all directions carrying instruments, so presumably they'd been scattered across the city in low cost accommodation. They received a roaring reception, the soloists looked genuinely delighted and I came away from the performance in high spirits.

On arrival in Paris the next day I decided to stay near Gare de Lyon, which was on a direct metro route to Théâtre des Champs-Elysées. My chosen hotel's geranium-filled window boxes seemed out of place in the maelstrom of traffic and the preponderance of strip joints. Invited to inspect the only vacant room, I was told it was a non-smoking hotel, but if I promised to lean out of the window they would turn a blind eye.

On my customary dummy run to the venue I crept into the foyer and heard Sokolov powering through the Chopin Polonaise-Fantasie. Later that evening there was tension in the air as the performance was to be recorded for radio transmission with the added possibility of a CD recording. An announcement had been made with regard to switching off mobiles and keeping any noise to a minimum, but this was December and someone coughed roughly every twenty seconds. At the conclusion of each piece there was an almighty clearing of throats, along with unbridled sneezing and vigorous nose blowing. Sokolov's concentration was tested to the extreme, and whoever was in charge of the sound equipment must have been foaming at the mouth. It seemed like a foregone conclusion that the performance would never be broadcast.

In Dijon I'd exchanged a few words in the artist's room with a French couple, Mohamed and Marie Kouider, who'd been awestruck by what they'd heard, and I was surprised to see them again at the Paris recital, where I met their daughter, Paloma, a young concert pianist who was currently under the tutelage of a former colleague of Sokolov's in Paris. The family said that meeting me would always be linked with their discovery of Sokolov, and we became lasting friends.

The next day I moved on to Nancy and found a perfect little hotel, Les Portes d'Or, close to the centre. It was late afternoon and a Christmas parade with marching bands was processing through the streets, followed by carnival floats, each depicting a different fairy tale. The banging of drums and the blare of trumpets continued until well after dark, when I dived into a nearby pizza restaurant to enjoy my first hot food in four days. The next morning I spent some time in the Musée des Beaux Arts, where I felt especially drawn to the works of the 19th century French artist, Emile Friant, and later I stood open-mouthed in Place Stanislas, Nancy's vast and spectacular central square, each of its entrances guarded by a massive gilded wrought iron gate. The square was flanked by elegant buildings, including the city's top hotel and the town hall, the edge of whose roof was decorated with ornate stone urns and huge lanterns suspended from the beaks of golden cockerels.

After the recital that evening a large Russian contingent flooded into Sokolov's room, and by the time they'd all left it was late and Sokolov had to be up early the next day, so I quickly handed him a small Christmas gift for his wife and turned to leave. It was after midnight and he had precious little sleep to look forward to but he began telling me that I'd now heard the current Bach programme for the last time, then mused upon his forthcoming trip to Scotland. He stood rubbing both eyes as I walked away, and I was touched that he'd been prepared to spare me a few minutes of his time.

In April 2006 the Kouider family organised tickets to hear Sokolov in Bourges, central France, and invited me to join them. Taking an evening train from Gare de Lyon to Sens in Burgundy I was met by Mohamed and Marie and taken to see the magnificent floodlit bulk of the medieval Cathedral of St. Étienne, where Thomas à Becket sought refuge in 1163, having fled from Canterbury. I stayed overnight at their home in Villeneuve l'Archevêque and the next morning we set off, taking a scenic route which passed through ancient towns and sleepy villages with endless vineyards ranged along the valleys, the muted colours of early spring enlivened by occasional splashes of yellow forsythia. Crossing the River Yonne, we stopped for a picnic lunch in a field dotted with cowslips and violets overlooking the valley of the Loire.

At four o'clock we drove into Bourges and made straight for the concert hall. While Marie, Paloma and I took photographs of one another beside a giant poster in the foyer, the irrepressible Mohamed wheedled his way into the management office and told them he'd brought with him a very important friend of Sokolov's. I was horrified to think this wildly inaccurate announcement might filter through to the artist's room. With time to spare we wandered the historic streets and had dinner in the concert hall's restaurant. On leaving, we learned that while we'd been eating, Sokolov had come into the restaurant to look for his mystery friend, but luckily our table had been positioned behind a screen and he'd seen no one he recognised.

The hall, which occasionally doubled as a cinema, seemed unpromising, with a poky little platform free of any adornment, walls of a uniform black, and the squeaky old plush seats looking and feeling as if they'd been sat upon since before the Revolution. Worse still, the audience looked inescapably provincial with a generous scattering of young children and very old folk. I anticipated much fidgeting during the performance and a mass shuffling out before the first encore, but I was so wrong: there was scarcely a murmur throughout, and everyone sat tight through the encores. The piano was superior to the one I'd heard recently in Bonn, although the acoustic didn't convey the beautiful plucked harpsichord sound I'd so enjoyed there in the Bach pieces. In Bourges the Beethoven was emphatic and authoritative and the Schumann more impassioned than ever. In a comparatively remote venue such as this, with just 600 seats, it was as if Sokolov felt free to give rein to his emotions, without the pressure of a recording to consider. He took the ultimate number of risks and they paid off handsomely. The piano was left in no doubt that Sokolov was in charge, and at times it appeared to be on its last legs. In the artist's room Mohamed took photographs as Sokolov signed a poster for Paloma, and we all came away feeling elated. By eleven the next morning we were back in Sens, where I took my leave and began the long trek home, thankful for the opportunity to have seen a particularly beautiful part of rural France and to have established a firm friendship with the Kouiders, whose extraordinary home was filled to the brim with energy and interest, life, love, art and music.

In the spring of 2007 a trip to Lyon was left in the balance when my flight was cancelled two weeks before the event. The options available were to abandon the trip altogether or fly to Geneva and take the train from there, and I chose the latter. Although the journey from Geneva to Lyon was on a dilapidated two carriage train, we rumbled past vineyard-clad hillsides with carpets of primroses along the embankment, and I remember feeling an overwhelming sense of freedom and excitement. The final stretch of the three hour journey ran alongside the Rhône, passing clear, tumbling streams, picturesque small towns with avenues of manicured trees and gardens full of blossom. Whatever else the day had in store, I knew I'd made the right decision.

As we approached Lyon my high spirits began to ebb away as I contemplated the reality of getting back to Geneva Airport by nine the next morning. I had to choose between a train at five-thirty with one change or a direct bus at six o'clock. The Auditorium Maurice Ravel was situated in the business quarter of the city and all the budget accommodation, along with anything worth seeing, was on the other side of the river. I wandered round the immediate vicinity for almost an hour before settling for a room in a neighbouring district costing an arm and a leg and necessitating a tram ride to the concert. I needed to be back at the hall by seven-thirty so it was all a terrific rush, with no time to eat or rest.

It was a massive auditorium, shaped like a Roman theatre, and when I'd ordered my ticket over the phone I'd been assured there would be an excellent view of the keyboard, but I discovered that my seat was on the extreme left-hand side, where I could see absolutely nothing. I was bitterly disappointed, but with very little persuasion on my part, a young male usher with wings and a halo made it his personal mission to find me a better place to sit, and as the lights went down he whisked me into a prime position in the centre block. There had been many disappointments that day since I'd gazed out of the train window at the primroses, but thanks to another angel my evening was one of complete satisfaction. Schubert's Sonata D958 was played sublimely and the piano was well modulated with luscious tone, producing the softest pianissimi. The Scriabin programme was finely articulated, the audience behaved exactly as they should; anyone with the effrontery to venture a cough between movements was severely rounded upon. Even after six encores including a new one by Scriabin, Sokolov took the long walk across the platform to receive countless further ovations.

I rose at four-thirty the next morning with only a swig of mineral water to start what turned out to be a day of relentless tedium. The station was almost deserted and no shop was open to buy anything to eat. I eschewed the bus, fearing hold-ups on the motorway, and instead put my faith in the train, changing at a small station in the village of Culoz where I sat in solitude for half an hour waiting for my connection, wondering what would happen if it didn't materialise but also reflecting that despite the anxieties, the lack of sleep, the absence of breakfast and the huge expense, the quality of the performance in Lyon had more than compensated.

On a subsequent visit to Lyon, Sokolov was playing a Mozart programme including Sonata K545, which often prompted people to exchange knowing looks, as if remembering their own attempts at playing this sonata, or perhaps thinking of their children or grandchildren labouring away at the piano with varying degrees of success. It was a piece well known to everyone, but no one had ever heard it played quite like this.

Such a vast stage necessitated a long walk to and from the piano and on this occasion I noticed that the edge of the platform sloped downwards into the wings. Sokolov approached it with visible caution each time he left the stage and I spent the second half in a state of anxiety that he might slip. In the past I'd sat, heart in mouth, at a number of venues where he'd calmly negotiated what could have been potential onstage hazards.

After the interval I heard my penultimate Schumann Fantasy, which was staggeringly robust. The beautiful final movement brought forth an enormous wave of appreciation and the audience became increasingly animated as the encores rolled out. The sight of Sokolov swooping back onto the piano stool again and again elicited choruses of shouting mingled with ecstatic screams. I left the hall feeling as if I'd witnessed a life lived out in its entirety in the space of a single evening.

One of my departures for Paris in 2009 coincided with a French general strike, and Air France had warned of delays and cancellations. I was hoping to be at concerts in Dijon and Metz and I worried that I might miss the Dijon concert and be forced to stay overnight in Paris. CDG's terminal building and the railway station were eerily quiet and it seemed this might be where my day would come unstuck, but a member of staff directed me to a waiting train bound for Gare du Nord, and with the ticket office closed and the vending machines out of commission, there was no charge. Better still, at Gare de Lyon I was lucky enough to find a connecting train to Dijon, and I arrived at three in the afternoon feeling immensely relieved.

That evening I was reunited with the Kouider family in Dijon's Auditorium, where the Beethoven sonatas were technical and musical wonders. Sokolov's chosen tempi were ideal; sometimes he slowed things down just enough to enable him to shape each phrase more carefully, allowing the listener to appreciate every detail to the full. This was never better demonstrated than in the new Schubert Sonata D580, in which Sokolov's approach lent the piece an even greater nobility, and it made much more sense to me than any other version I'd heard. The audience was attentive throughout but somewhat chaotic during the encores, hauling on coats and hats, standing but not leaving, then noisily re-seating themselves each time Sokolov reappeared. I walked with the Kouiders to their car and they handed me a large carrier bag full of surplus food they'd brought with them.

With a whole day to reach my next destination I ate a leisurely breakfast the following morning and sauntered to the railway station with the intention of catching the next available train. It was a shock to be told there were only two trains to Metz each day and I'd already missed the first one. The second one at four o'clock was fully booked so my only hope was to buy an unreserved ticket and try to persuade the train manager to allow me to travel. With five hours to kill I wandered round the town, dragging my luggage and the carrier bag full of bread, cheese, apples and oranges. The four o'clock train was delayed for a further two hours, but eventually I was allowed on board and reached Metz at nine in the evening.

My perambulations around the city the next day were hampered by a cutting wind, so I spent much of my time drinking tea and consuming the contents of the Kouiders' carrier bag. Later I discovered the city's cavernous auditorium, L'Arsenal, and although I was nowhere near the platform, I could see perfectly well on account of the steeply raked seating. In both Dijon and Metz Sokolov produced flawless performances, but I particularly enjoyed this one because of the amazing acoustics. In Metz the Beethoven took flight and the Schubert sonata was full of musical colour and deliciously accentuated rhythms. The naïve sense of wonderment I felt that night reinforced my belief that a limited knowledge of music theory might be considered a blessing. The sheer joy of simply listening was more than enough for me. There were only three encores in Metz, which was unusual for a Saturday evening, but with the temperature at six below zero outside, maybe the audience were hankering after their warm beds.

One of my summer journeys in 2008 took me to the annual music festival in Colmar, a picturesque French town in the Alsace region. I arrived in the evening and took a long walk the next day, filled with energy and enthusiasm, happy to be in such an attractive place. A narrow river flowed between pastel painted fishermen's cottages, gabled houses, window boxes overflowing with colourful blooms and a multitude of enticing little waterside eateries. Inside the Dominican Church I saw a much prized and exquisitely detailed altarpiece depicting the Madonna in a Bower of Roses. At the Musée d'Unterlinden I found another jewel in Colmar's treasury, the Isenheim altarpiece: a composite of paintings and sculptures originally intended to be in one piece but so huge it was presented in exploded format, showing the Virgin and Child, a particularly gruesome Crucifixion scene, the Annunciation and the Resurrection.

A festival atmosphere pervaded the streets surrounding the huge 13th century Église St. Matthieu that evening as the audience gathered for Sokolov's recital. Outside the church stood a faux grand piano fashioned out of wire and wood and decorated with flowers. Formerly a Franciscan church with a reputedly fine acoustic, St. Matthieu's interior was serenely beautiful, with more than sixty illuminated biblical paintings forming an unbroken frieze around the walls. During the afternoon I'd attempted to gain admission but had been rebuffed by two beefy bouncers guarding the door who told me that no one but Sokolov was allowed inside until the evening. Shortly before nine o'clock I took my seat and soon Sokolov appeared from behind a curtain at the rear of the piano to receive a noticeably warm welcome on this, his third successive appearance at the Colmar Festival. Against an atmospheric backdrop of ancient stone arches he steered an exhilarating course through Mozart Sonatas K280 and K332 followed by Chopin's Op.28 Preludes, reminding us what a unique experience it was to hear a great artist performing in a building with such a long history.

My only visit to Grenoble came the following year when I travelled there from Geneva on a comfortable air-conditioned coach which passed through wondrous misty mountain scenery, lulling me into such a relaxed frame of mind that I was quite unprepared for the reality of Grenoble's bustling city and the discovery that the tourist office was a half hour walk from where the bus dropped me. My hotel room was a little depressing, so I resolved to go out for the evening, and the best option seemed to be a free concert in the Maison de la Culture, or MC2 as it was snappily named, presumably to appeal to younger audiences. It was a huge modern complex containing performance areas catering for all tastes, but with events beginning and ending at different times I wondered if a crowded entrance hall might disturb performances still in progress. A large youth ensemble from Lyon, the Orchestra of the Alpine Rainbow (each member dressed in a different colour) performed an ideal programme for my taste, starting with Wagner's Prelude to Lohengrin, followed by Richard Strauss's Four Last Songs with a guest soprano, and ending with Prokofiev's Romeo & Juliet Suite.

The next day I climbed a steep track to the Fort de la Bastille in warm sunshine and descended by cable car. At the top, the viewing platform afforded a breathtaking mountain panorama, showcasing Mont Blanc in the far distance. Later that evening the foyer of MC2 resounded with a heavy bass beat escaping from one of the halls, and hordes of teenagers darted back and forth. It was hardly the ideal atmosphere in which to prepare for a profound musical experience, but once inside the auditorium there was no extraneous noise, the acoustic was excellent and the audience deathly quiet. At the interval, the piano technician attempted to eradicate an ear-tingling edginess somewhere in the middle register, but it soon re-established itself. No matter; Beethoven and Schubert were well served and Sokolov received a rollicking reception.

A memorable experience came my way in Reims in the summer of 2018, although my travel arrangements were perilously close to collapse on account of a protracted French rail strike. I arrived with only a couple of hours to explore the city, but the magnificent cathedral was more than enough to satisfy me, with its indescribably beautiful stained glass and the famous statue of the smiling angel, carved in the 13th century, whose head was destroyed during the First World War and restored in 1926.

The city's opera house was a stately, traditional venue possessing a compact and attractive auditorium with a relatively small parterre and three balconies. Directly behind the piano was a well concealed door through which Sokolov advanced and retreated many times during the evening to the sound of increasingly tumultuous cheering. The piano possessed a robust and full-bodied tone and Sokolov's relationship with the instrument was not so much one of master and servant but rather like old and trusted friends who understood one another perfectly. The supreme sound quality lent a fresh and dazzling luminosity to Sokolov's elegant progress through the three Haydn sonatas, and it quickly became evident that he was on a roll.

As the Haydn programme came to an end, a lady sitting next to me remarked: "I think all of that came straight from his heart". On the other side of me sat an enraptured Pierre-Emmanuel Taittinger, president of the Taittinger champagne house, who on hearing me speak English, began enthusing about Sokolov's playing. I told him I'd heard Sokolov on a number of occasions and he asked, "How many?" At that time I'd clocked up 469 performances, and when I told him, he almost fell off his seat. I hastened to explain that it had taken twenty-one years to reach that number but he said, "Oh, don't apologise! I think it's wonderful!" Mistaking me for a woman of means with a sophisticated palate, he whipped out a business card and invited me to call him next time I was in town so that he could arrange a conducted tour of his winery.

During the Schubert programme I had to smile when I heard the third Op.142 impromptu, remembering a discussion I'd had with a German friend and keen amateur pianist regarding my inability to find any feeling for this piece. "But Barbara", she'd exclaimed, "you should hear it played by a housewife!" The absolute clarity of sound lent a distinctly demonic flavour to the final impromptu, Schubert's vivid portrayal of creatures from another dimension who were deftly driven away as Sokolov chased them down the keyboard. The customary audience explosion occurred at this point and Sokolov then proceeded to emerge from his on-stage portal to deliver encore after encore. Waves of ecstasy swept through the theatre each time he approached the piano stool and sat waiting for everyone to regain their seats and simmer down. I'd not witnessed an audience in such a state of excitement for quite some time.

Sighs of contentment and whoops of delight could be heard from the audience as Sokolov approached each of his six encores as if it was the sum of his life's work. In the final Debussy prelude, the half dozen perfectly weighted descending notes at the conclusion demonstrated not only Sokolov's mastery but the constancy of the piano. So great was its contribution to this splendid evening, it might have received equal billing.

For many years Sokolov had performed at La Roque-d'Anthéron Piano Festival in Provence, one of Europe's most celebrated pianistic events which embraced all kinds of piano music, including jazz, performed in a variety of venues. Up until 2007 his recitals took place in the Protestant Temple de Lourmarin, which he'd warned me was always unbearably hot. By the time I got round to visiting the festival in 2009, his performances had been switched to the estimable Grand Theatre in Aix-en-Provence, a then recently inaugurated fortress-like building inside which spacious public areas could be found and a 1,350 seat curved auditorium, into which the public were summoned by stately fanfares. The raked seating offered a perfect view of the platform from any angle and the acoustic was exceptional. This air-conditioned haven had plenty of panache but all the dignity of a traditional concert hall and was manned by a team of young, stylishly coiffed and chicly attired staff; super-efficient and very much in tune with the public. On just one occasion in 2013 the recital was given in Marseille, at Théâtre de la Criée, but I believe the venue's air conditioning proved to be problematic.

Despite the long journey, which often involved a flight from Gatwick to Marseille, I travelled to Aix-en-Provence on a number of occasions in midsummer and was always stunned by the intense heat. Provence had a beguilingly exotic quality and it best expressed itself to me in the gardens of the Pavillon Vendôme which I happened upon quite by chance one afternoon as I sought refuge from the sun in a maze of narrow streets close to my hotel. I might easily have missed the unassuming gateway which led into a peaceful garden containing topiary, flowering shrubs and a bed of roses surrounded by benches on which people sat reading. Through another gateway lay a much larger formal French garden with a pond, and at the far end stood the Pavillon, a historic monument with an elaborately carved frontage, built in the 17th century. After serving many purposes (originally commissioned by Louis de Bourbon as a retreat in which to entertain his lover) it was now a museum exhibiting temporary art installations. On either side of the French garden were two rows of venerable plane trees, beneath which I loved to sit and listen to the tidal rustle of leaves in the warm wind and the incessant chorus of cicadas.

Apart from Aix's cool cathedral cloisters which I also visited on occasions, the only other sanctuary was the Grand Theatre, where, in the company of a piano-loving audience, a satisfying evening was always guaranteed when Sokolov was in residence and the reception he received was never less than rapturous. On one occasion the final note was struck well after midnight, but despite the lateness of the hour, Sokolov received quite a few visitors. One lady who'd studied with him in St.Petersburg told me, "At the age of eleven he was already a genius", but I didn't like the idea that this label might give the impression that everything came to him easily. In reality the possession of a superior intellect, deep musical insight and the utmost manual dexterity could never rule out the phenomenal amount of daily study and practice necessary to maintain such an exalted level of performance. To professional musicians this must have been obvious, but for me it was a matter of wonder.

Occasionally, as the lights came up at the interval, no one seemed particularly interested in moving, as if they'd all been glued to their seats. I remember this being the case following a performance of the Schumann Fantasy, when Sokolov had given us a heroic first movement, a swashbuckling second and a dreamlike third, building to a heartbreaking climax. At this particular performance Chopin's 2nd Sonata occupied the second half and the audience, having held its breath throughout the final presto, immediately broke into a torrent of applause and cheering. The encores provided a whole show of their own, generating lusty cries of "Merci!", and after teasing and tantalising with the seductive Chopin Mazurka Op.30/2 Sokolov turned to Schubert to bid us farewell. In his customary patch of light he paid every bit as much attention to the final encore as he did to the whole programme. These precious additions were as far removed from party pieces as it was possible to imagine, each one a singular labour of love.

My most recent trip to Aix was in the late summer of 2019, by which time I'd grown immensely fond of the two collections Op.118/ Op.119 by Brahms, in which Sokolov lovingly described image after image of earthly and ethereal beauty whilst engaging with Brahms' quirky rhythms. I loved the urgency and eloquence of the Op.118 A minor intermezzo, the angelic plucked strings in the middle section of the F major romanze, the powerful and eternally uplifting G minor ballade, which propelled me through a gap in the clouds into a realm where I could travel without limits, free as air. The scintillating variety of encores generated a barrage of cheering, concluding with Schubert's C minor Allegretto D915 which reminded me of being read to by a favourite teacher. It's a wonder Sokolov didn't ask if we were all sitting comfortably before he began to relate this gentle piece with its charming hesitations and simple, satisfying harmonies. Again, these encores were so much more than mere extras.

Following my first concert in Paris there were many subsequent visits. The annual recitals in November or December always attracted capacity audiences to Théâtre des Champs-Elysées, where a dazzling catalogue of celebrated artists had graced its platform for over a century. I was there soon after the terrorist attacks in 2015, and although it felt like entering a war zone, I decided that if Sokolov was willing to play there, I was more than happy to go and listen. As I sat watching the audience filling the seats and listening to the solid wall of sound created by their animated pre-concert greetings and exchanges, it was impossible to imagine such a commotion ever being quelled, but as soon as the lights were dimmed, all attention was focused on the familiar, unassuming individual emerging from the shadows onto the darkened stage, looking like some mythical figure, ready to join forces with his instrument. Sokolov always began his work swiftly; within a split second of reaching his seat he was on his way, with no prolonged acknowledgement of applause, no gathering of concentration. Everything was already under control, he knew exactly where he was going and it was up to the audience to climb aboard without delay for fear of missing one millisecond of the oncoming adventure.

The theatre seemed to have a special place in its heart for Sokolov, whose recitals generally sold out within days of their announcement. Much revered by Paris audiences, he studiously set about giving them a night to remember and created such an atmosphere that in the immediate aftermath of these evenings I sometimes felt I was returning to earth from a very high altitude. In 2015, as the Paris audience struggled to make sense of the recent carnage in their beloved city, a big spoonful of Sokolov's healing medicine was exactly what the doctor ordered.

On one occasion my flight to Paris was delayed because of snow, and by the time I landed it was too late to find my way to Paloma Kouider's apartment, where I was to spend the night, so I attended the recital complete with luggage and gifts, which included two boxes of chocolates and a large Christmas pudding. The cost of entrusting my outer clothing and luggage with the wardrobe attendant was so excessive that I took my handbag, a rucksack, the chocolates and the Christmas pudding into the auditorium with me. The seats were packed so tightly together I feared that if I put anything on the floor I might never see it again, so it all remained on my lap for the duration. A visit to the artist's room was out of the question that night; I was dressed much too casually, besides which the Kouiders were waiting for me somewhere in the outer suburbs. (In more recent times Béatrice Reuflet, whom I first met at a Sokolov recital in 2016, welcomed me into her home in Vincennes on the outskirts of the city and we attended several of the Paris recitals together.)

In November 2006 I travelled to Paris twice in the space of a week, the first time to hear Paloma's recital at UNESCO in front of a large audience, after which a lavish champagne buffet was held at the organiser's apartment in the centre of Paris. It lasted until two in the morning, and the highlights for me were the quality of the wine, a staggeringly impressive cheese board and an enormous platter of chocolate and coffee éclairs. Currently Paloma has a flourishing career as a solo artist and also as a chamber musician in collaboration with other artists and her own prize-winning ensemble, Trio Karenine, whose diverse recordings have received wide acclaim.

Three days later I was back in the city for Sokolov. In Théâtre des Champs-Elysées it was sickeningly hot and there was pandemonium up in the balconies before the recital began on account of numerous people sitting in the wrong seats. The first half of the programme received a rapturous response, and I thought the audience behaved rather well, but shortly before the second half began, a young man bellowed from the balcony such a deafening "Mesdames et Messieurs!" that the chattering throng was silenced. He went on to ask the audience to have respect for Maestro Sokolov and kindly refrain from coughing, which seemed to antagonise a few, who immediately took up the challenge, resulting in major episodes of bronchial activity between each of the Scriabin pieces.

Partly because of the heat, but mainly in an attempt to protect the knees of my new trousers which were jammed up against the seat in front, I carefully folded them up above the knee after the lights went down. As we filed out of the auditorium at the end of the performance and I strolled towards the cloakrooms surrounded by Parisians in elegant attire, I caught sight of my reflection in a full length mirror and noticed I'd forgotten to roll them down again. I offered up a prayer of thanks that I'd been spared the indignity of entering the artist's room with one trouser leg well above the knee and the other at half mast.

Ten years later, in November 2016, feeling pretty damned pleased with myself, I sat on a fancy chair in the first balcony with a perfect view of the keyboard as the opening bars of Mozart's Sonata K545 floated towards me, straight from the pages of an enchanting picture book. The audience clearly adored Sokolov's Mozart and the tempestuous conclusion of Sonata K457 was greeted with unanimous approval. In the second half I sat through the Schumann Fantasy with a foolish grin plastered across my face. At the beginning of the year this piece had been an object of difficulty and doubt, but it had gradually entered my bloodstream.

Paris 2019

On my most recent visit to Paris Sokolov played a relatively new Mozart programme. The Prelude (Fantasy) & Fugue KV394 provided a surprising departure from what I would normally have expected from Mozart, with its strangely mercurial prelude and densely constructed fugue, which at times sounded like a sonorous peal of bells. I'd grown fond of Sonata No.11 KV331 too, in particular the variations, and I believed no one but Sokolov could have persuaded me to appreciate their subtlety and charm. And then there was the beautiful Rondo KV511 which revolved like a long, slow, perfectly balanced pirouette.

The first half of the evening was blessed with silent concentration on the part of the audience, and I could have wept at the interval when so many cheers rang out for Mozart, because I knew that based on such a reaction, Sokolov's Brahms would surely generate even greater excitement. Indeed after the break, during the first three Op.118 pieces in particular, it was as if Sokolov held the mesmerised multitude in the palm of his hand. Under his craftsmanlike touch these richly detailed narratives seemed to be illuminated from within. At the dramatic conclusion of Op.119 the theatre erupted and a seismic release of energy emanated from the public, renewing itself after each of the six encores. How could Sokolov not be energised by this kind of response? It would explain how, having invested every fibre of his being in the main programme, he could still find the inner reserve to produce a further handful of miniature masterpieces.

Sokolov seemed to sit comfortably in whatever musical period he chose to visit, as if he was completely at home and of that age, and he always knew exactly how to gain the maximum impact with his choice of tempi. At his 2017 recital in Paris, the audience heartily approved of his Haydn sonatas, which received the kind of rousing reception one might expect at the very end of a great recital. After the break Beethoven took over and from the first commanding notes of Op.111's opening movement, through the divine deceleration and on towards the aching poignancy of the arietta, the music pulsed and shimmered in Sokolov's hands. Everything was so perfectly described: the vulnerability of the human heart, the grief and the glory.

A climate of infectious bonhomie prevailed in the artist's room; many people with long standing connections to Sokolov were gathered there and it was a privilege to be a bystander. Outside the theatre, the trees along Avenue Montaigne were a glittering fairy world of golden Christmas lights and the Eiffel Tower was dressed in its seasonal best, but inside the theatre the richness of Sokolov's yuletide gift to his public outshone any amount of festive finery.

Avenue Montaigne Paris

5. SWITZERLAND

THE FIRST RECITAL I attended in Switzerland was in February 1999, and on arrival in snowy Zürich my main concern was to find somewhere cheap to stay. I booked a room without bath or breakfast for a modest sum, but on my way out of the tourist office I picked up a leaflet for my chosen hotel and read that it was favoured by young people in search of a relaxed, informal atmosphere, close to all the hottest night spots with each bedroom dedicated to a famous rock star. I hastened back into the queue to change my booking and within the hour I was sitting with a tray of tea in the lounge of a sedate but considerably more expensive establishment within walking distance of the lake. I struck up a conversation with a Jewish American lawyer, and we soon got around to the subjects of divorce (he'd had three), marital infidelity (Bill Clinton's impeachment trial was in progress on a TV in the corner), and my relentless pursuit of Sokolov's live performances. He asked me what I proposed to do when my money ran out, and I told him I might consider selling my home. "Well yes, it's an idea", he said, "but if I were you I'd see a psychiatrist first."

I salvaged what was left of the afternoon by tramping to the lake in my rambling boots and every item of clothing I could muster. The trees were heavily laden with snow, small boats bobbed on the icy water of the lake, and the late afternoon sun illuminated the opposite shore. In the time it took to crunch my way back to the hotel, the temperature had dropped even further, but a log fire was burning in the lounge. Two enormous standard poodles sprang to attention as I entered, but I was more afraid of the formidable proprietress, whose penetrating voice, stately bearing and ambitious hairdo involving a complicated arrangement of plaits, cried out for a horned helmet and a regiment of Rhinemaidens.

An hour later I retraced my steps to the lake and found the Tonhalle close by. Its unexceptional exterior belied the spacious reception halls and resplendent auditorium, where the edge of the unusually high platform was planted out with brightly coloured flowers, lending a festive air to the proceedings. The grand interior had already set my pulse racing, and when I discovered my seat was very close to the piano, I could hardly contain myself. William Byrd, Beethoven and Ravel provided a deliciously diverse programme. After waiting at the end of a long queue I eventually put my head round the door of Sokolov's room, and he threw up his hands in surprise, saying he had no idea I was going to be there. The concert organiser was waiting to drive him back to his hotel and Sokolov asked where I was staying, possibly with a view to dropping me off en route, but the promoter claimed to have no idea how to get there so I plodded back on foot for a solitary drink by the fire.

The next morning's breakfast comprised a hot beverage, a dry brown roll, a slice of rye bread and a spoonful of jam. On subsequent visits to Zürich I stayed in a different hotel each time but returned to this one some years later, by which time the breakfast had improved to the extent that guests were permitted, under the watchful gaze of Brunhilde, to hack off their very own chunk of cheese and choose from a selection of three kinds of sausage, all of which looked similar and tasted the same.

Before leaving the hotel, a further chat with my lawyer acquaintance, whose name was Daniel, revealed that his home town was Seattle, and by an amazing coincidence he was friendly with another Daniel whom I'd met and spent time with in Stockholm twelve months earlier. He explained to me how close Jewish communities were; apparently everyone knew everyone. As we parted company he leaned towards me and whispered: "Remember to see that psychiatrist".

Most of my visits to Zürich were in wintertime, several of them shortly before Christmas, when the city's lavish decorations looked wonderful reflected in the river as I walked to and from the Tonhalle. In June 2000 I was there in sweltering heat, and rather than trudge round the city I chose to sightsee by tram, jumping aboard the first one that came along in any direction and seeing where it took me. Close to the lake I found some gardens full of lavender and wisteria with a lively beer garden attached where, in a world dominated increasingly by the young, it was heartening to see middle-aged and elderly couples ballroom dancing beneath the trees to a live band.

In the artist's room that evening, Mrs Sokolov and a friend of theirs compared notes with regard to tinnitus, demonstrating the variety of sounds they could hear, including continuous or intermittent buzzing, low pitched humming, high pitched whistling and rhythmic swishing noises. This gradually developed into a kind of duet, at which point Sokolov picked up an invisible baton and began conducting.

In March 2013 I approached the Tonhalle to find people studying notices posted on the outer doors and for one horrible moment I thought there might be a last minute cancellation, but they were merely announcing that Sokolov would be signing CDs after the recital. As a result, box sets flew off the sales table and the queue for the artist's room was a mile long. The auditorium was packed out with more than a hundred extra seats installed behind the piano. The performance surpassed the one I'd heard two weeks previously in Schaffhausen and I began to fully understand the enormity of Sokolov's task. This was a big programme, requiring unimaginable physical and emotional strength, beginning with Schubert's Four Impromptus D899 and Drei Klavierstücke D946, all of them beautiful, but I found the latter pieces the most fascinating, especially the second one, in which he struck the perfect balance between the opposing forces of the music. How often Sokolov prompted me to think long and hard about the composer; not only to admire the genius behind the composition but to wonder what was in his mind when he wrote it. The Schubert necessitated many returns to the platform, and after the break came Beethoven's Hammerklavier Sonata. It was a stupendous experience and frequently I found myself holding my breath for long periods. By the end of the main programme the piano, having been tested to the absolute limit, gamely handled four Rameau encores, but Chopin's Prelude Op.28/4 highlighted its declining state of health, and Sokolov's concluding choice, Op.28/20 was the final nail in the coffin.

In 2017, in addition to the packed Tonhalle auditorium, the platform was crowded with many extra seats, some of which looked worryingly close to the piano, but the entire gathering of add-ons remained silent and motionless and the audience as a whole allowed the music to exhale before expressing considerable enthusiasm. The trademark on the side of the Steinway read 'Musik Hug', and that's exactly what we got: a great Russian bear hug of a performance, ably supported by a steadfast piano and a lively acoustic (at close quarters some might say too lively, but I sat a little further back than usual and it was just about perfect). Sokolov presented his Mozart programme to the music lovers of Zürich and beyond with inimitable skill and eloquence, receiving immense applause at the interval. Thus it was easy to predict that Beethoven would have an even more devastating effect. The Op.90 Sonata alone was a small miracle, its compact length qualifying it for inclusion in this programme, but so full of ideas I couldn't help wishing it had been twice as long. Whenever I heard Sokolov play something new to me it felt as if he was explaining every detail for my express benefit so that I could derive the maximum pleasure from that piece in the future. He seemed to bring something indefinable to everything he touched; every phrase unique to his own distinctive soundworld.

The execution of Beethoven's final piano sonata No.32 Op.111 was simply incredible. The contrast between the first and second movements could hardly have been more stark. There was such a torrent of emotion in the first; there was desperation, but a certain amount of strut and swagger too, and there were impulsive plunges into sections of music of staggering modernity; music destined to evolve long after Beethoven's death. Had a group of youngsters been asked to listen to sections of this sonata I'm convinced they would have found the music pretty cool. The sublime second movement was for me the music of the spheres; a journey to the vault of heaven. In Zürich Sokolov played as if it was his mission in life to ensure our safe passage there.

Another Swiss city I visited many times was Basel, and in 1999 I was especially looking forward to hearing Sokolov play in the Stadtcasino, having learned it was one of his favourite venues. I awoke on the morning of departure with a worryingly familiar discomfort in my lower back, and the prospect of a bus ride into Birmingham city centre, a long coach trip to Luton Airport, a flight to Zürich and then a train journey to Basel filled me with dread. Somewhere between Coventry and Northampton the National Express coach left the dual carriageway and began chugging through winding country lanes, passing pretty cottage gardens and rustic inns, finally grinding to a halt at an impossibly narrow hump-back bridge, at which point the driver told us he'd travelled to Luton Airport only once before and confessed that he had no idea where he was. It took fifteen minutes to reverse into a narrow opening and an eternity to find our way to

Luton, the journey having been extended by well over an hour. By the time I stood up I could scarcely move, but somehow I survived the rest of the journey.

The train ride from Zürich to Basel was scenic, following the Rhine for much of the way. We sped through picture book villages, passing lush flower-filled meadows, dense woodland and, closer to the city, ranks of lovingly tended allotments, each with their own little summer houses. I took a tram into the centre of Basel, from which I glimpsed ornate medieval and Gothic buildings, craftsmen's houses, old taverns and finally the Stadtcasino. I got off in the market square outside the rust coloured gilded Rathaus, and asked a group of girls for directions to my hotel. Not only did they offer to escort me there, but insisted each of them carry a piece of my luggage. The long flight of steps up to the street on which my hotel was located would have been impossible without assistance, but in a matter of minutes I was staggering into the lobby with my retinue of helpers.

The hotel far exceeded my expectations and I was allocated a splendid double room, but a strong desire to take a closer look at the Rhine momentarily overtook the pain and I went straight out again to admire a six arched bridge spanning the river. The water was alarmingly high, and as it roared along it carried with it tons of mud, huge branches and anything else that got in its way. The surge of water was exhilarating, and I longed to take the riverside path and walk through the town, but reluctantly returned to my bed. Much of the following day was spent struggling from one bench to another. I was insufficiently mobile to cover much ground, although I did take a tram ride to a promontory jutting out into the Rhine river port of Dreilandereck, from which three different countries could be seen.

At the Stadtcasino that evening I forgot about my back for the duration of the concert, but the stiffness soon set in again as I approached the artist's room. Sokolov was sympathetic but said it had been unwise of me to undertake such a long journey. He was right of course, but I assured him everything would be back to normal in a couple of weeks: a prediction which proved to be woefully inaccurate. He talked about the excellent acoustic at the Stadtcasino and the impossibility of making a recording there due to the close proximity of a busy intersection where tramlines converged, resulting in constant noise and vibration. A hugely expensive project to insulate the building was undertaken some years later, and I heard the successful result for myself in 2008.

It took me half an hour to dress myself the next morning and I was tempted to ask the receptionist to tie my shoelaces. Unable to face breakfast, I sipped tea until a kindly taxi driver took me to the railway station. When I stood up to change trains at Zürich Hauptbahnhof I was in considerable pain, and an elderly lady took the largest of my bags and set it down on the platform for me. I stood beside it and burst into tears, whereupon another lady came to the rescue, carried my bags to the platform which served the airport train and spoke to the guard, who ushered me into a first class compartment and telephoned the airport.

On arrival at Zürich Airport I found two strapping hunks in uniform waiting on the platform to help me up the escalator, check me in and take me to the special assistance area, where I was offered a pain killing injection, which I declined for fear of doing more damage while under the influence. The special assistance supervisor asked me about my trip, and when I told her about the concert and expressed anxiety that I'd be unfit for work the next day, she said that the most important thing was that I'd done something good for my soul, and work would have to wait.

A young man appeared with a wheelchair, into which I gratefully subsided, and I was whisked through security and straight onto the plane. EasyJet had reserved a whole row of seats near the front to enable me to lie down if I wished, and I spent most of the flight with my head resting against the window, gazing down at the ground and pondering on the many kindnesses I'd received. Another wheelchair waited at Luton and a nurse in the medical centre helped me onto a bed, covered me with blankets and made me a cup of tea. I lay there for four hours until the next coach left for Birmingham, little realising I had several weeks of agony ahead.

Later the same year I was back in Basel just in time for the Christmas festivities, this time to hear Sokolov play Brahms' 1st Piano Concerto with the Basel Symphony Orchestra conducted by Walter Weller on two consecutive evenings. As daylight faded, the old town centre was transformed into a wonderland of twinkling lights and shop windows glowed with colourful seasonal displays. A Christmas market came to life in front of the church with dozens of stalls selling unusual and beautifully made toys and gifts. Inside the Rathaus courtyard stood a fifty foot Christmas tree decorated with baubles as big as footballs and stately baroque music floated out across the market square, adding to the yuletide magic.

In April 2001 I arrived in Basel on a much warmer evening, having pre-booked a room at a cheap and cheerful hotel I'd visited on a previous trip. It was a disappointment to discover that the jolly Wild West themed bar and restaurant attached to the hotel had closed down and the business had changed hands. The friendly manager I'd looked forward to meeting again had been replaced by quite the most hostile individual I'd ever encountered at a reception desk, and the Rottweiler at her side regarded me with equal disdain. With nothing to occupy the evening I decided on an early night, but soon found the duvet ended midway between my knees and ankles, and further up the bed a sandbag was masquerading as a pillow. I'd been obliged to use the spare blanket to wrap round an antique radiator belting out unwanted heat, and every so often a device on the ceiling expelled a puff of air freshener, emitting a sharp click followed by a gasping sound, not unlike an artificial respirator. Within an hour my head was banging, but the idea of lodging the smallest complaint seemed out of the question. Resigned to a hellish night I plumped up my sandbag, screwed myself into a ball and waited for the next blast of pot pourri.

Feeling deadly the next morning, I prepared to face a dining room full of bright-eyed breakfasters, but there appeared to be only four other souls in residence: three Italian students and a dishevelled looking man in his fifties who spent most of his time making excruciatingly slow progress round the hotel on crutches. A cheery young girl serving breakfast promised to organise a better pillow for me, but it turned out to be exactly the same as the one I already had, only bigger. It rained all morning so I visited a gallery housing some splendid Holbeins and early Picassos and also took in a museum devoted to the work of the Swiss artist, Jean Tinguely, whose ingenious moving sculptures were fashioned from scrap metal. By the time I emerged, the sun had broken through, and I walked along the river through Solitude Park, drinking in the scent of spring flowers after the rain and savouring the prospect of Sokolov. Later in the

Stadtcasino he gave an immaculate account of works by Couperin, Mozart and Franck.

In the dining room the next morning there was just myself and the man on crutches, who told me he was from Zürich, and although we sat at separate tables, his English was so good that it was impossible to avoid a conversation. We covered variously the state of the euro, the recent outbreak of foot and mouth disease, English football teams and several other topics he chose to raise. He asked for my address so that he could send me a post card, which I found rather strange, but I handed him an address card which he sat and gazed at, repeating my name several times, calling me his little ray of sunshine. Embarrassed, I concentrated on buttering a crusty roll, and at that point the Italians drifted in. Undaunted, my admirer handed me a scrap of paper torn from his diary bearing his name and address and a splodge of jam, observing that it would take him less than two days to reach Birmingham by rail and sea. I shuddered at the thought.

In November 2008 Basel was under a covering of snow, and many beautiful scenes presented themselves along the rail route from Zürich Airport. One of the highlights of this particular visit was the Fondation Beyeler Museum, where I saw a collection of John Singer Sargent's Venetian interiors. At the Stadtcasino, Sokolov was in phenomenal form, sailing through the Mozart sonatas with wings on his heels, the outer movements of both pieces fizzing with energy. His Beethoven was musically insightful and technically astounding, and among the six Chopin encores, Op.28 Prelude No.16 generated a gale of laughter any self-respecting stand-up comedian would have been happy to receive. As he concluded with a profound and beautifully executed Prelude No.15, the applause was intense, and the lady sitting beside me remarked, "Next week we have Pollini. It will be difficult for him to follow this". Moshe Atzmon, one of Sokolov's favourite conductors, was in the artist's room and we left the building at the same time. He told me that whenever they worked together Sokolov never gave less than one hundred per cent. I already knew this to be true, having witnessed their warm and fruitful collaborations on more than one occasion.

On my two most recent trips to Basel, in December 2017 and 2018, the Stadtcasino was undergoing extensive refurbishment, so the recitals took place in the Musical Theatre, a much less atmospheric venue but one which I thought served the purpose rather well. The occasional rumble of passing trams was the only reminder that outside the building, another world far removed from ours was going about its business.

In 2018 my attempt to reach Warsaw two days earlier had been thwarted by heavy snow in the UK and my airport experience, which involved queueing for five and a half hours to secure an alternative flight to Switzerland, had been appalling. I arrived in Basel at one o'clock in the morning feeling as if I'd been to hell and back. Failing to get to the Warsaw recital had caused indescribable anguish, as if a piece of my life was missing, never to be recovered, but as soon as I took my seat in the Musical Theatre and the first Haydn sonata began winging its way across the auditorium, it wrapped itself around me like a healing balm, and in no time at all I felt cushioned, comforted, compensated for what I'd lost. With the special combination of technical precision and poetic expression for which Sokolov was so admired, he skilfully demonstrated Haydn's imaginative devices, often with an impish sense of fun, the three sonatas overflowing with invention. In the new year Sokolov would continue to play the Haydn sonatas, at the same time introducing a new, as yet unspecified, half programme, and it occurred to me that Haydn was going to make a most congenial travelling companion for whichever composer Sokolov chose.

My final encounter with Beethoven's Op.90/Op.111 programme took place in Basel that evening. Op.90 was deliciously measured, beautifully poised, and from the tumultuous opening of Op.111 to the muscular reining in towards the end of the first movement, I was transfixed. The great transition from earthly suffering to heavenly release was for me the most reassuring moment in this sonata. The arietta took its ethereal course, with its agonisingly tender opening sequence and the eventual elevation into a cosmic province flooded with starlight. The conclusion was intense, the trills simply amazing, the accompanying orchestra of angels beyond beautiful, and Beethoven's ultimate resolution was finally reached. I came away with the firm belief that Op.111 would be considered one of the greatest triumphs of Sokolov's career.

In August 2005 I took the scenic and spectacular train journey from Geneva to Montreux. It was a perfect summer's day, the mountain views were stunning, and for the last half hour the track ran along the edge of the lake. From Montreux railway station, a lift took me down to promenade level where the tourist office fixed me up with a room in a cheerful little hotel, the Bon Port, where I felt instantly at home. In the afternoon I took a walk along the lakeside towards Château de Chillon. The water lapped gently against the rocks, stately willows and maples stood among a mixture of familiar and exotic flowering shrubs, clusters of sparrows twittered happily in the bushes, the sky was an uninterrupted blue and I felt indescribably happy to be there.

At the opposite end of the town stood Auditorium Stravinsky, where it was possible to sit with a pre-concert drink in a glass sided bar and watch the sun sink behind the mountains. During Schubert's sonata D959 a mysterious intermittent metallic tapping sound began to intrude. At first I thought it might be Sokolov's finger nails, which I sometimes imagined I could hear, but this was so loud it became a serious distraction. It turned out to be caused by an old man sitting close to the platform who was tapping his walking stick in time to the music with a ringed finger. Eventually someone asked him to stop, but I wondered if the recording for Swiss Radio might have picked it up. The lady sitting beside me had never heard of Sokolov until that evening, but someone had told her he was a monument so she'd come along to see if it was true. From the look on her face at the end of the evening I gathered she'd joined the club.

My first trip to Bern was in the spring of 2004, when I found a characterful room in the historic quarter of the city and rushed straight out into the sunshine with details of a short walking tour. The oldest and most interesting part of the city was enclosed within a horseshoe bend in the tree-fringed River Aare, a wide blue serpentine sweep of water, clean and fast flowing, with six bridges connecting the old city to the green outer suburbs. The three main streets in the old quarter ran parallel with one another and their pavements were sheltered by cool stone arcades packed with restaurants and obscure little shops. Outside the confines of these streets, picturesque postcard images presented themselves wherever you looked: richly decorated houses, colourful gardens and endless views of the river and surrounding hills. Clusters of scented wisteria cascaded from balconies, rambled across house fronts and clung to street lamps.

The walking tour took me across the river and along a shady woodland track leading to a narrow field path overhung with pink blossom. At my feet a profusion of clover, buttercups and orchids spread out like a carpet as I climbed up to a viewpoint sheltered by trees, behind which lay a peaceful rose garden offering a place to sit and enjoy the scent of the flowers and bask in the warmth of the afternoon. The roses were still in their infancy but the garden was crammed with luminous rhododendrons, azaleas and irises. Continuing along the route, I came to the only blot on Bern's landscape. I was already vaguely aware of the bear pits, but for some reason I'd not expected them to actually contain bears. A large enclosure housed several reasonably contented looking animals but the smaller pit was home to a huge, elderly bear who was a picture of misery, shambling disconsolately round in circles, occasionally looking up at his fascinated audience. I noticed that the entrance to his sleeping quarters was blocked off and there was scarcely any shade in which to shelter. His mournful and uncomprehending expression touched my heart, and the likelihood that he may have known no other life, having spent his entire existence in captivity, was no consolation.

Another climb to a high terrace in front of the Houses of Parliament provided a marvellous view across the city and surrounding countryside to distant mountains, with the Eiger and Jungfrau clearly visible. Apart from the sad interlude at the bear pits, my day had been hugely satisfying, and at seven o'clock I was in Bern's resplendent Kultur Casino waiting for Sokolov to begin his homage to Bach and Beethoven. During the performance I began to experience a worrying shortness of breath and a sudden wave of nausea. At the interval an elderly lady wearing an oxygen mask was carried down from the balcony to a waiting ambulance and I felt tempted to ask if there was room for one more, but thanks to an almighty dose of Op.111 my sickness subsided, my breathing returned to normal, and Mrs Sokolov collected me on her way to the artist's room.

In the summer of 2016 Sokolov performed for the first time in the Great Hall of the University of Fribourg. In almost all respects this was an impressive venue, with a moderate sized auditorium, steeply raked seating, an attractive stage setting, excellent acoustics and a fine sounding piano. Throughout the recital there was minimal coughing, no untimely applause or mobile intrusions and the audience maintained a respectful silence at the end of each piece, so conditions were just about ideal, apart from the hard wooden seats which creaked and groaned whenever anyone made the slightest movement; even the gentle repositioning of a foot was enough to produce a loud crack. I imagined Sokolov practising contentedly all afternoon in the empty hall and hoped someone had given him prior warning of the venue's one significant shortcoming.

A cast iron will was required to remain motionless, even for those of us who'd been lucky enough to notice that cushions were up for grabs in the foyer. Anxious to play my part in keeping noise to the minimum I was determined not to move a muscle, and at the risk of generating an attack of cramp or a deep vein thrombosis, I sat completely rigid throughout the first half, but conceded defeat half way through the second. Thunder rumbled overhead during the Schumann Arabeske, and part of the Schumann Fantasy was overlaid with the sound of torrential rain on the roof, but I doubt if such natural events spoiled anyone's enjoyment. Sokolov maintained perfect concentration and ultimately the music prevailed, transcending all earthly impediments. The squeaky seating was a big talking point in the artist's room, but Sokolov pointed out that if the wooden seats were replaced with upholstered ones, the acoustic would be quite different. The problem was an intractable one, but on the other hand there were far too many positives to consider that night.

A Swiss venue renowned for its fine acoustics was the one in La-Chaux-de-Fonds, a city tucked away in the Jura mountains, very close to the French border, famous for clock-making and the birthplace of the architect Le Corbusier. The first time I went there in 2001 I arrived by train from Lucerne, and the final leg of the journey passed through classic Christmas card scenery: steep fir-clad hillsides, rocky peaks, deep ravines, waterfalls, stretches of tumbling river, villages and valleys nestling beneath a blanket of white. A blizzard was in progress as I peered out of the small railway station, and with no information office or town map to consult it took me a while to establish that – miracle of miracles – the Salle de Musique was just a five minute walk away, and almost next door to it was the inexpensive Hotel Fleur-de-Lys. The last person I expected to see in the dining room the next morning was Sokolov, but there he was, helping himself to the modest breakfast buffet. I chose to sit in a corner, as far away from him as I possibly could, wishing to respect his privacy, but he came across to my table and asked about my journey home. When he'd finished his meal and walked towards the door, he turned and waved, and I felt inexplicably blessed.

I returned to La-Chaux-de-Fonds in April 2007 and this time the two hour train ride from Zürich took me through a dazzling spring landscape, gradually climbing to over a thousand metres and cutting through forest, farmland and countless pretty villages. On this occasion Sokolov was playing his Scriabin programme, and as he walked off stage at the end of the volcanic Vers la Flamme it seemed that everyone in the hall turned to a neighbour and made some comment. Many were laughing nervously as if attempting to make light of a narrow escape from some sort of catastrophe or recovering from a particularly terrifying funfair ride, but in the time it took for him to return to the platform the audience had decided Sokolov had delivered something extraordinary and greeted him with uproarious acclaim. At the hotel the next morning there was no sign of him, and I gathered he was staying in more salubrious accommodation out of town.

In November 2009 La-Chaux-de-Fonds Music Society had recently purchased a brand new Steinway with the aid of Lottery money, and Sokolov was to be the first artist to play it in public. The performance confirmed that his Schumann Sonata No.3 Op.14 had ascended to a dizzying level of technical and interpretative brilliance, and when I remarked afterwards that the new piano had received a baptism of fire and asked how he felt about its potential, Sokolov declared that as with all new babies, there might be a few teething troubles.

It was ten years before I sat in that wonderful hall again. The unpromising facade gave way to elegance within, and the glowing walnut wood panelling which lined the auditorium played a major role in producing the venue's much prized sound quality. For decades the hall had been favoured by prestigious record labels to create high calibre recordings, and some of the most celebrated world class soloists had performed there. In March 2019 Sokolov was also equipped with a fine piano and a discerning audience. From my seat in the balcony the clarity of sound was astonishing and in the context of such ideal conditions Sokolov produced a performance of immense magnitude. The early Beethoven sonata was full of freshness and vigour, the eleven bagatelles brimmed with unexpected departures, intriguing twists and inexplicable changes of mood; so many ideas condensed into little more than fifteen beguiling minutes. After the break Sokolov's expert navigation through Brahms' densely drawn emotional landscapes and pictorial vistas, right through to the triumphant pageantry of the Op.119 finale, were accomplished with magisterial ease. In his hands the music came alive, and a bedazzled audience savoured every moment of this rhapsodic journey. As I walked past the hall the next morning on my way home, I marvelled that its unprepossessing exterior could have contained such wonders.

On my first trip to Geneva in April 2009 I began with a walk from my hotel towards the lake through a maze of shabby back streets, where I encountered a prostitute on every corner. I found their blatant intention and unseemly appearance sad and unsettling. The subsequent stroll along the lakeside was much more appetising, with gorgeous views, a stiff breeze ruffling the water and drifts of daisies and forget-me-nots scattered across the grass. A group of infants from a local kindergarten came along, each clutching a knot in a long piece of rope. Supervised by three carers they joined hands in a circle under the shade of a tree, trotted forward into the centre and all collapsed onto the grass, lay motionless for a few seconds, then repeated the exercise several times more before reassembling to continue their walk.

At seven in the evening I was inside the imposing Victoria Hall, built in the late 19th century and dedicated to Queen Victoria. My seat was on the platform behind the piano, and looking towards the back of the hall I found the darkly ornate neo-baroque and rococo interior rather oppressive, but I was rewarded with an excellent opportunity to observe Sokolov at close range. From my vantage point I could see among the audience the celebrated Romanian pianist, Radu Lupu, looking completely absorbed. Later I watched him enter the artist's room to speak to Sokolov, and although few words were exchanged, the warmth of the handshake said it all.

Nine years later I was back at the Victoria Hall sitting in the parterre, and my impression of the auditorium on this occasion was completely different. As I looked up from the third row at the piano and the illuminated organ above it, I could almost imagine myself to be sitting in a church or cathedral. The piano produced a sweet, pure and perfectly balanced sound and Sokolov executed the irrepressible Beethoven Sonata No.3 Op.2/3 with poise and agility, in one section his expressive hands suggesting he might be nonchalantly flicking a duster down the keyboard. Each of the Op.119 Bagatelles had a life and a landscape of its own and likewise the Schubert Op.142 Impromptus presented an exquisitely detailed tracery of sound as he laid bare the many facets of human experience and covered limitless distances.

In the early spring of 2000 I was excited to be returning to Lucerne for the first time in twenty years. The train journey from Zürich was silky smooth and Lucerne's picturesque chocolate box image with its profusion of medieval buildings and the famous covered bridge looked exactly the same, apart from the recently built Culture and Congress Centre standing beside the lake. My accommodation was across the river bridge in the old town, and as I reached the little cobbled courtyard in front of the hotel, a clangorous peal of bells rang out from the baroque Church of the Jesuits on the opposite bank. At first I wondered if the promise of a room overlooking the river would prove to be such a good idea after all, but despite the endearingly old-fashioned fairytale furnishings - an enormous dresser, wall tapestries depicting medieval life, a creaky wooden bed and groaning floorboards - my room was blessed not only with double glazing, but also, to my extreme delight, tea-making facilities. Roaming the streets alone at night searching for a decent cup of tea had never been my idea of fun, so this latest discovery was like stumbling upon a holy relic.

I drank several cups at the open window, watching the lights reflected in the water and listening to the wildfowl settling down for the night with their occasional honks, quacks and splashes. The next morning I leaned out and gazed up and down the river and across the shining lake, feeling elated. After breakfast I sat on the hotel terrace watching the mist clear from the mountain tops. The sun was already warm, dozens of swans drifted past and bells rang out across the town. Feeling pretty pleased with everything, I ordered another pot of tea and dashed off a number of unashamedly smug postcards. I had many hours to wander at will before the pleasures of the evening, and I already knew that a very good seat awaited me at the Congress

Centre. Intoxicated by the beauty of my surroundings I burst out of the hotel doorway ready to turn cartwheels, but mindful that things had a tendency to go wrong whenever I became over-excited, I settled for a measured stroll along the lakeside, eventually climbing a steep wooded path to reach the gleaming Château Gütsch, an exclusive hilltop hotel with a panoramic view of the lake.

The swanky Congress Centre's vast auditorium was full that evening and Sokolov's Froberger and Schubert programme was received with a rapturous standing ovation. Sokolov was presented with a huge bunch of flowers and duly rattled off several encores. Backstage I encountered only a handful of people, and I was thrilled when Franco Panozzo suggested I take Sokolov's flowers away with me. It was great having them in my hotel room overnight, and the next day I left them with the proprietor, who gave them pride of place in the dining room. This was to be my only visit to the town in springtime, the other three falling in the autumn or winter, although in November 2001 the town still looked stunning, the trees along the lakeside promenade a vibrant copper colour, the water a brilliant blue and the massive bulk of Mount Pilatus capped with snow.

The Lucerne Piano Festival was one of those highly prestigious events where on arrival I always felt like a poor relation fresh from the provinces, surrounded by so much wealth and sophistication, but by the time I'd taken my seat I was no longer a fish out of water but back in my comfort zone, on a direct line to the music. On a Saturday evening in November 2016 huge tubs of cough sweets scattered around the foyer were being plundered by the handful, the provision of which was destined to be only partially successful. The piano gave out a pure and mellifluous tone and the delicious runs and trills in Mozart's Sonata K545 flowed effortlessly through Sokolov's fingers. I'd recently heard of a critic who'd been at his Geneva recital and was uncomplimentary about his Mozart programme. I almost felt sorry for this person and others like her who knew so much about music that they weren't open to other possibilities and developed such entrenched ideas about how certain composers should be played that they were unable to endorse anyone whom they considered to have broken a boundary or failed to conform. My uneducated view was simple: this was Sokolov's Mozart and I embraced it wholeheartedly, along with the public in Lucerne who also approved of it. The second movement of the Schumann Fantasy was more imperious than ever, the assertive bass notes in that wonderful march designed to intimidate anyone who chose to get in the way. The final movement was played with what I could only describe as desolate grandeur.

Two years later, as I walked into the Congress Centre someone was playing jazz on an eye-catching red grand piano in the foyer, surrounded by festival goers sipping pre-concert drinks. Although I normally appreciated all kinds of piano music this was for me a jarring prelude to the evening ahead. Part of the concert platform had been removed, leaving a more than adequate space between the piano and the first row of seats, into which I installed myself with enormous satisfaction. The piano possessed a gloriously full-bodied tone and a vibrant clarity; it was the perfect instrument to illustrate the uncontainable lust for life in Beethoven's youthful sonata. The adagio bore all the mighty Sokolov hallmarks, and as the sonata crept stealthily towards the dark and dramatic passages I anticipated how thrilling those massive chords were going to be. When they arrived, they were of such earth-shattering power that several unsuspecting people in the front row of the podium almost shot out of their seats. The final movement overflowed with delicate trills, cascading runs, cheeky little twists and turns, with a triple trill heralding the conclusion. Outside the hall, seasonal mist had descended for much of the day and dulled the remaining autumn tints, but in the confines of the Konzertsaal we were invited to enjoy a spell of high summer.

Whenever I mentioned to Sokolov that a piece sounded very different or especially lovely on a particular evening, he never took any of the credit for himself, always insisting modestly that it must have been something to do with the hall, the acoustic, the piano. The intricate inner workings of his beloved Steinways were a mystery to me, but I recognised they were works of art in themselves and objects of immense beauty. In Sokolov's hands they seemed almost human.

I visited Schaffhausen, a Swiss town close to the German border, in summer and in winter, and on both occasions I spent time at the atmospheric Rhine Falls, the largest and most powerful waterfalls in Europe. A viewing platform enabled visitors to get thrillingly close to the relentless torrent and whatever the weather, the roar of the water was exhilarating.

In the town's spacious High Gothic Church of St. Johann I attended Sokolov's final performance of his 2014/15 Bach/Beethoven programme. This particular church's acoustic lent itself especially well to Bach's Partita No.1, each note rising as if into a limitless space, yet with the absence of echo. Whenever Sokolov was performing a programme for the last time, there always seemed to be an audible sense of finality, the closing notes emitting a special kind of resonance, the squeezing out, even at such a late stage, of some small fresh detail; a 'remember this' moment. Sokolov had given almost seventy performances of this programme since it began in the autumn of 2014 and the ones I heard had always sounded newly inspired and pulsing with life.

The evening was not without its difficulties, and Sokolov had much to endure. Permission had been given for a photographer to take some shots during the performance, but this individual took his mission to the extreme, positioning himself in the organ gallery immediately behind the piano and creeping back and forth in full view of Sokolov and the audience, occasionally ducking down and then popping up again like a glove puppet. From time to time he descended the stairs in order to point his camera from various angles, and although he did his best to remain silent, he managed to locate some excruciatingly squeaky floorboards on his wanderings. It was a relief when he disappeared at the interval.

As if this were not enough, it happened that Schaffhausen was staging a gourmet meat marketing promotion which involved the installation of livestock in hay-filled pens scattered around the town centre. Directly next to the rear wall of the church were two such enclosures containing different breeds of cow, each with a cute little crowd-pleasing calf (beef and veal were the prime commodities being showcased). Confinement in such an alien environment was inevitably stressful, and in an attempt to protect their young from the unwanted attentions of curious passers-by, the cows were vocalising at regular intervals, often in deafening unison. As a consequence, the entire Bach sarabande, the quieter passages of the Beethoven adagio and the Moments Musicaux were accompanied by the lowing of cattle. At one point between movements Sokolov was obliged to sit and wait for a prolonged outburst of mooing to subside before continuing.

Over the years, many performances I'd attended had been affected by a wide range of intrusions: birdsong in Bisdorf, cats in Granada, trams in Krakow, firework displays, outdoor rock concerts, low flying aircraft, thunder storms and a whole variety of 'in house' disturbances, mainly medical emergencies, but also snoring, screeching hearing aids, whistling nostrils, restless children, the rattle of a guide dog's harness in Reading Town Hall and the vigorous unstrapping of velcro shoe fastenings in Zürich Tonhalle, the wearer having waited until the quietest possible moment in which to perform this vital adjustment. But cows? This was definitely a first.

One of the most exciting concert destinations in Switzerland for me was St.Moritz, partly on account of the scenic rail journeys from Zürich on the Gotthard Panorama and Glacier Express routes, or from Milan on the Bernina Express. As part of the long-established Engadin Festival, Sokolov's recitals took place in Église au Bois, a small church on a wooded hillside whose delicate cream spire stood like a sentinel among the trees. My first experience of this venue was in August 2017, and despite the rural setting I expected people to be parading around in fancy outfits and being 'seen', but the folk who trudged up the rough path to the church door looked like nothing more than a gathering of earnest music lovers, and they proved to be exactly that: silent, attentive, respectful. It was more like a devout congregation flocking to hear a spirit-lifting sermon from a loved and trusted minister.

On its small platform, the piano was dwarfed by a towering wooden pulpit and the ceiling above was bathed in violet light. In such a limited performance space Sokolov seemed larger than life, and the church acoustic had very little reverberation from where I sat near the front. The sense of immediacy was astounding, and rarely had I heard such a clear and direct transmission of sound in any type of concert venue. As a result of this refined sound quality the Mozart K545 second movement ornamentation was indescribably lovely and the whole performance was massive, reinforcing Sokolov's reputation as a true giant. What he achieved in the second half was superhuman, unearthly. The transition from the pastoral harmony of the second movement of Beethoven's Sonata Op.90 to the brutal landscape of Op.111's opening passage was made in one giant leap. As the first movement slipped seamlessly into the second, we were already prepared to cross the divide and begin our journey into the starlit kingdom. Sokolov's expression of Beethoven's grand design seemed more intense than ever before. There was always a spiritual dimension to his performances, but sometimes there was a kind of holiness, and I felt this very strongly in Église au Bois. I saw heads bowed, faces clasped between hands; doubtless there were a few tears as well. Had I been sitting at the back of the church I might have left before the encores began and stepped out into the night to hold on to the moment, to dwell upon what I'd heard and watch the flicker of lightning behind the mountains, but I sat tight while Sokolov produced six further jewels by Schubert, Chopin, Schumann and Rameau, and it wasn't until I walked down the path from the church that I acknowledged what a humbling experience it had been.

St.Moritz 2018

The following year I returned, and it felt good to be repeating the experience, to be among the fortunate few sharing an intimate venue in an idyllic location, with an estimable piano and a marvellous acoustic, combining to create the ideal environment in which to receive the full force of Sokolov's physical and intellectual energy. The Haydn sonatas sparkled; each phrase was meticulously enunciated, every note expressed as if freshly conceived. So much of human life was present in these pieces: the light-heartedness of youth, the reflective nature of maturity, the longings and regrets, the missed opportunities, the indignities of old age. I loved the rakish strut of the B minor first movement, and the way the presto took off like a rocket at kamikaze speed, setting us down gently just in time for the vanity and affectation of the C sharp minor first movement, the sonata finally fading into nothing, as if a candle had been snuffed out. In the second half, Schubert's four beautifully created impromptus received a clamorous reception. Sokolov produced such a diversity of sound that I sometimes closed my eyes, convinced that when I opened them again I would find him applying his skills to a different kind of instrument altogether.

That day I'd arrived in St.Moritz barely an hour before the recital began and found a torrential rainstorm in progress. As I watched a rainbow spanning the lake, it appeared to anchor itself somewhere on the hillside among the trees surrounding the church, where I imagined Sokolov, presiding over the crock of gold he would be sharing with us later that evening.

On my last visit I sat up in the tiny organ gallery at the rear of the building, and as soon as Sokolov appeared and began his gallant farewell to the Beethoven sonata and bagatelles I was thrilled by the volume and clarity of sound. The sonata was executed with immense energy, the bagatelles unfolded in all their fleeting artfulness, but all too soon Sokolov was disappearing behind the pulpit with an avalanche of appreciation following in his wake, his devoted service to Beethoven fulfilled. The recital began in daylight, and as night fell the coloured backdrop intensified, just as Brahms' music enveloped us. The middle section interlude in Op.118/5 was one of pure enchantment, and the church was shaken to its foundations in the bombastic finale. Each time Sokolov offered another encore the applause was mighty. After an electrifying Rachmaninoff Prelude

Op.32/12 came the Schubert Allegretto in C minor, delivered in the manner of a bedtime story designed to send us out into the night feeling calm and replete, but it was no surprise that at the end of this gentle lullaby the audience remained in a state of high excitement until they were quite certain Sokolov was not coming back.

This was possibly the most magical concert trip of the year, taking into account the beauty of the landscape and the special nature of the venue. In view of the cost of the flight and the train journey, my accommodation in St.Moritz was of necessity a basic room in a nearby hostel with a clean bed and a simple breakfast. As I left there on Sunday morning and began my scenic walk back to the railway station, I glanced across at the belt of trees encircling the spire of Église au Bois and at that very moment the solitary bell in the church tower rang out, as if to say, "Goodbye, see you next year!", and I continued on my way home, lingering along the lakeside, filled with immeasurable gratitude for what I'd experienced in that blessed little building on the hillside.

Eglise au Bois, St.Moritz

The last concert I attended before the onset of Covid-19 took place in December 2019 in the picturesque lakeside resort of Lugano, which was cloaked in thick mist for the entire duration of my short visit. It was my first time in the modern Lugano Arte e Cultura (LAC) concert hall, and I believe Sokolov's too, and it was the last performance of the Brahms Op.118/Op.119 programme. He described this magnificent profusion of narratives as if he had experienced every one of them at first hand. He depicted the agonies of the heart, the harsh realities of suffering, loss and longing, but there was also exhilaration and joy, lyrical glimpses of the natural world, and the Op.119 finale was pure theatre. Sokolov may have been approaching his three score years and ten, but he could still display formidable strength and the most exquisite delicacy imaginable.

6. AUSTRIA

MOST OF THE Austrian concerts I attended took place in the sumptuous Konzerthaus in Vienna. The first occasion, in December 1998, I remember quite vividly. On a wing and a prayer KLM deposited me in Vienna just two hours before the recital began and I had yet to find somewhere to sleep. The information kiosk at the airport sent me to a classy little pension in the city centre, but with no time to sit and admire my Regency style furnishings I was on my way to the Konzerthaus within half an hour. The icy pavements were too terrifying to negotiate so I resorted to a taxi, and as we drove through the city I sat open-mouthed as thousands of tiny white Christmas lights cascaded like frozen waterfalls from the rooftops.

I was equally stunned by the interior of the Konzerthaus, with its red and gold auditorium flanked by massive white columns. The audience was silent throughout the performance, but rapturously enthusiastic at the end of Sokolov's diverse Byrd/Beethoven/Brahms programme. In the artist's room I produced a small Christmas gift, and on the label I'd written a seasonal greeting in Cyrillic script, which Sokolov examined closely before pronouncing in teacherly fashion that it was "absolutely correct", except that I'd included accents which were not strictly necessary. He was complimentary about the Steinway at the Konzerthaus, which had a new keyboard. "In three years it will be a good piano" he declared. The concierge at the artists' entrance called a taxi for me, but the driver was unfamiliar with the street in which my B&B was located. As we studied a city map, Sokolov appeared in his outdoor clothes and joined in the search. "How come you found somewhere to stay that nobody's heard of?", he wanted to know, and not until the whereabouts of Pension Aviano had been established did he finally amble off round the corner to his hotel.

Breakfast at the Aviano was a dainty and delicious Viennese affair, served in an elegant little candlelit dining room. Overnight the pavements had been gritted but were still treacherous, so I checked out and slithered a few hundred yards to the opulent looking Café

Mozart and made a hideously expensive cup of coffee last for as long as possible. Numerous ankle length fur coats swept through the café's portals before I slipped out, skated past the Staatsoper where camping stools had been left outside overnight with notices attached ("One person – Aida"), and somehow made it back to the airport coach.

Three years later I stayed at the Pension Neuer Markt, another welcoming place in the heart of the city, next to St. Stephen's Cathedral. This time I had a free day in Vienna with time to enjoy the Christmas lights and watch some of the street entertainment. I especially admired a trio of Russians playing Bach on balalaikas and an accordion, and a young man who was the living image of the famous golden statue of Johann Strauss in the city's Stadtpark. He stood motionless until someone dropped a coin into his golden pot, whereupon he went through the motions of playing his violin whilst slowly rotating like a mechanical figure. When a group of young boys gathered round to taunt him, he yawned theatrically, lay on the ground and pretended to fall asleep.

The evening became so bitterly cold that before venturing outside again I donned almost every article of clothing I had with me, including my pyjamas. The city looked sensational by night: church bells boomed, horse drawn carriages clopped through the streets, and I was perfectly content to wander. The next morning I visited Schönbrunn Palace and walked in the vast formal gardens, climbing up to the Gloriette, a triple-arched triumphal gate built on a hill overlooking the palace. In front of the Rathaus a colossal Christmas market was set up, and in the subway beneath the opera house I visited a WC which resembled a miniature auditorium with tiered balconies on either side, the door of each cubicle decorated to look like the entrance to an opera box. A Viennese ballroom scene adorned the back wall and a constant medley of Strauss waltzes further enhanced the experience.

At the Konzerthaus Sokolov's performance of Haydn, Mozart and Franck was inspired and his encores included the showstopping Ravel Toccata. It was my last opportunity to hear the Franck Prelude, Chorale and Fugue, and when I told Sokolov I'd heard it twenty-six times, he laughed and gestured towards the practice piano in the corner of his room. "So now you can play it for me!" he quipped.

The following year the recital was in October, and a sea of umbrellas filled the Cathedral Square as groups of tourists drifted about in their waterproofs, making the best of a filthy day. As a token gesture I took a quick turn round the block but was back in bed before midday; a luxury I would never have allowed myself at home unless life had been hanging by a thread. The rain intensified and so I remained there all afternoon until it was time to prepare for the Konzerthaus.

My seat was next to a mischievous impresario I'd first met in Monte Carlo, who stood in the auditorium grinning at me. "What the hell are *you* doing here?" he bellowed, then quickly announced that Sokolov would be playing in the hall he managed the following January. "On my lovely new Steinway", he beamed. "You are of course invited to come. You can sit in the hall all day and listen to the rehearsal if you wish. You can do what the hell you like, it's entirely up to you!" That settled, we took our seats and I glanced up to see a striking female figure settling herself into the front row of the circle, a large bunch of flowers beside her which were no doubt intended for Sokolov. At the interval that same figure came careering towards me, arms outstretched, and I recognised an American girl I'd met before at a couple of recitals in the UK. She seemed disproportionately pleased to see me but was soon asking if she could tag along with me to Sokolov's room after the performance.

With a close fitting outfit accentuating her hourglass figure, a coquettish little pill box hat with a tassel, waist-length dark hair and luxuriant eyelashes, she was undeniably appealing, and I felt like the two ugly sisters rolled into one as I stood beside her in the queue. She was now a writer living in Vienna, and the piece she was currently working on had been inspired by the feelings she'd experienced on hearing Sokolov for the first time. She went into his room with her flowers and I waited outside, wishing I'd warned her that Mrs S would almost certainly be in there. Sure enough, a few minutes later she emerged looking utterly crestfallen. "Ohhhh", she wailed. "I didn't realise he was *married*!" "Oh yes", I said, unintentionally rubbing salt into the wound. "It's just another of life's disappointments, I'm afraid. They're completely devoted to one another and his wife takes extremely good care of him."

At four the next morning I quietly let myself out of the hotel, expecting a taxi to be waiting to drive me to the airport coach terminal. Twenty minutes later I was still there, unable to get back inside and with insufficient funds to take a taxi all the way to the airport. Finally it arrived in reverse, and I told the driver he had ten minutes to get me to the coach. He drove like a crazed gangster, breaking every rule in the book, trying various short cuts which failed due to road closures, frequently mounting the pavement and finally screeching to a halt some way off where the coach was parked. With barely a minute to spare, he grabbed my bag and ran with me to the coach, which was just about to pull away. It was an unceremonious departure and it took several hours for me to calm down, but for the remainder of the journey home I thought about the American girl and wondered how long it would take for her heart to mend.

In 2006 I was joined by an English friend and the visit to Vienna involved much more in the way of sightseeing. Numerous Christmas markets were explored and a lot of cake was consumed, mostly by me. We visited the Gustav Klimt museum shop, the Belvedere, whose landscaped gardens offered a wonderful view of the city, and a carol concert in the Rathaus performed by several choirs from Germany. We toured the interior of Schönbrunn Palace, then took tea in the Gloriette's stylish café. A string quartet provided background music, my friend ate something sensible and I devoured a large slice of heavenly confection involving almonds and icing. We went in search of a group of council flats in a quiet residential area which had been transformed by the Austrian artist Friedensreich Hundertwasser to illustrate his philosophy that 'the straight line is godless'. The resultant brightly coloured assemblage of misshapen apartments with slanting floors and ceilings, madly shaped windows and unexpected features became one of Vienna's top tourist attractions. When the residents first took up occupancy of these unusual dwellings they were pestered by tourists wanting to see inside, but now there was a small multi-storey shopping arcade across the street built in the same style, to satisfy their curiosity and also cash in on the sale of related merchandise.

At the Konzerthaus we sat in the organ gallery looking down on the piano. Bach's French Suite No.3 and Beethoven's Sonata No.17 went according to Sokolov's plan, but half way through the Scriabin programme he left his seat at the conclusion of Sonata No.3 and quickly walked off without acknowledging the applause and with several more pieces yet to play. This was so unusual that I feared he might be unwell. After five minutes no announcement had been made and a few people decided to go home, but he reappeared eventually and reached inside the piano before resuming. We learned later that a string had broken but the tuner had gone home, so a conflab had ensued as to whether he should continue. Luckily for us, he finished his programme and gave us a clutch of encores into the bargain.

Konzerthaus Vienna 2008

There were many further December recitals in Vienna, and sometimes it might be the last engagement of the year when Sokolov said farewell to half of his programme. One such occasion came in 2009, when I heard the final performance of Schubert's glorious Gasteiner sonata, which I'd grown to love very dearly. The Viennese audience, never over-demonstrative and rarely in the habit of standing, showed their appreciation with profound and prolonged applause. There was always a palpable warmth in the audience, and many seconds often elapsed following the end of a segment or encore before the flood of affection filled the hall.

That same evening there was also Schumann's Sonata No.3 Op.14, often referred to as the 'Concerto without Orchestra', which was swiftly working its way into my system, its complexities gaining clearer definition with each performance. It was executed with supreme technical prowess and musical vision, and as I sat up in the balcony savouring every note of the unforgettable alliance between Schubert, Schumann and Sokolov, my heart turned somersaults, soared heavenwards, then plunged back to earth at the end of the Schubert, the sheer exhilaration of the moment reinforcing my determination to devote whatever remained of my life to this man and his music-making. Whenever I set out on a journey to hear him I likened myself to a pilgrim travelling to Mecca, and in the same way that my journeyings could be considered acts of worship, I felt that every performance he gave was for him the very same thing. Earlier in the day I'd seen him near the Konzerthaus on his way to rehearsal and been reminded of something I'd read a long time ago in the memoirs of an English playwright. I don't remember the exact words he used, but in his youth he'd spotted a celebrated musician sitting in a pub and been struck by the realisation that an ordinary looking man in a raincoat could be an instrument of the divine.

In subsequent years it became necessary to install at least a hundred extra places on the platform for Sokolov's recitals, the first row almost within touching distance of the piano. I always hoped the few who were sitting in line with the keyboard realised how fortunate they were. The volume and quality of sound from behind the piano would be compromised, but to be able to watch those hands so closely, if only once in a lifetime, was surely worth the sacrifice. I'd only managed to sit on the platform once in eighteen years, and I would have given anything to change places with a lady sitting in that privileged position on a Friday evening in November 2015, who scarcely looked at Sokolov or his hands and chose instead to read her programme very slowly from cover to cover.

As the Schubert sonata progressed, the combination of the richly gilded interior and the jewel-like quality of sound that came from the piano was overwhelming, and I rejoiced that I would hear it all again two evenings later in Warsaw. With a splendid instrument and marvellous acoustic at his disposal Sokolov transformed the Konzerthaus into a cathedral of sound, and while Chopin's 2nd Sonata filled the space with power and intensity, the quieter interludes floated out across the auditorium like scraps of gossamer. The sonata and each of the six encores received mighty applause, and Chopin's Op.28 Prelude No.15 stood out for me that night. I'd heard Sokolov play it countless times, but never better than this: every single note finely judged, perfectly weighted. I lost count of the number of times he was called back to the platform, and the audience left him in no doubt that they were reluctant to let him go. As he made his final bow to those seated behind him, an elderly gentleman summed it all up by standing with arms stretched wide in a gesture of thanksgiving.

There were many great Sokolov performances in 2018, but what I heard in Vienna at the end of the year was something else entirely: a never to be forgotten, all-encompassing spiritual communion. The music completely outshone the delicate golden filigree above the platform as Sokolov's hands produced the smoothest silken runs, shimmering trills, featherlight pianissimi to die for. These performances of his were living organisms which by their very nature could never reach true perfection, but this one came as close as I'd ever known. For the first time since the start of the season the audience contained itself at the end of the Beethoven sonata and Sokolov was permitted to continue without interruption. The bagatelles tumbled out, each with its own distinctive personality, and finally the Schubert impromptus were relayed to us in all their glory and received with thunderous acclaim.

And so, without being captured for future generations, another moment in musical history escaped into the ether and another multitude of concertgoers left the building at best transformed, at the very least enriched by the experience. More than ever in Vienna I realised that the essence of that moment could never be truly captured; one simply had to be there to soak up the magic and hold on to the memory. On my way into the hall that evening it had been impossible to ignore the larger than life seated figure of Beethoven in the foyer, who seemed to be regarding the comings and goings of twenty-first century humanity with deep disapproval. At the end of the recital I could almost imagine that discontented statue coming to life and heading for the artist's room to offer his congratulations, a broad smile spreading across his troubled features.

On three occasions my trips to Vienna were paired with recitals at the 600 seat Stadttheater in Wels, a city in Upper Austria, close to the city of Linz. I was there in 2001 for the first time, and although the piano had its limitations, Sokolov seemed to coax the best possible performance from it. Before the recital began I spoke to a regular subscriber whose seat happened to be in my favourite spot. When we discovered that the seat I'd been allocated was in a poor position she insisted we change places. Her kindness was rewarded when the subscriber who usually sat next to her failed to turn up and we were able to sit together and share the experience.

In 2009 a Steinway still in its infancy and producing a beautiful tone had been shipped to Wels from Vienna. I was in the middle of the front row, virtually at Sokolov's feet, more than happy to sacrifice the sound quality for the spectacle of viewing the fingerwork from beneath; his hands illuminated as if disembodied with a life of their own, his face reflected in the light from the keyboard. I always felt that in the smaller and less significant venues, instead of coasting along in a lower gear, which he could so easily have done, Sokolov appeared to play with more intensity than ever, using the opportunity to push the boundaries. Maybe he was right: maybe it was all to do with the acoustic and the instrument, but the Schumann sonata seemed to be played with even greater subtlety than just ten days before in Stockholm. There was more light and shade, a strong sense of urgency but with less haste. Whatever the reasons the results were incredible, and excited audience members were quick to congratulate the team of organisers at Wels Round Table whose efforts had been so magnificently rewarded. The quality of the performance, the intimacy of the venue and the sense of fellowship Sokolov's concerts always generated among his audiences left me feeling quite emotional.

In 2012 I was lucky enough to sit in the front row of the Stadttheater again with a perfect view of the underside of Sokolov's hands. Rameau's Suite in D had already reached the pinnacle by the end of the summer and it was impossible to imagine he could raise the bar even further, but somehow he did. For some months I'd also found myself completely attuned to his Mozart, and with the exception of one skilfully disguised emergency gear change in Beethoven's Hammerklavier Sonata, the evening in Wels was gold standard.

On my first concert trip to Salzburg in June 2006 it was eleven at night when I reached my hotel after a gruelling ten hour journey via Stansted. My tiny room was like something out of a children's story, with an unpolished wooden floor, a rag rug and roughly finished furniture with heart-shaped cut-outs, decorated with brightly coloured painted flowers. Despite a virtually sleepless night on account of the heat, I was amazingly alert the next morning and spent a lot of time tracking down the Mozarteum box office to collect my ticket. I was tempted to sample a lunchtime buffet concert in one of the many churches, promising an hour of Mozart followed by drinks, sandwiches and savouries. This would have given my feet a rest, my senses a lift and my stomach sufficient fuel to last until teatime, but I decided to drift round the old town instead, climbing up to the fortress overlooking the city, with views of countless domes and bell towers, the swiftly flowing river Salzach and the surrounding mountains, whose white caps bore witness to the severe winter Salzburg had suffered that year.

Seats at the Mozarteum were unallocated and I arrived sufficiently early to bag one in the third row. The programme was Bach/Beethoven/Schumann, the performance immaculate but the aftermath was a disappointment on account of an intrusive female being evicted from the artist's room. The door was firmly closed and locked behind her lest she make any further attempt to gain access, thus preventing those of us still waiting in the corridor from being admitted. I didn't know it at the time, but I was destined to clash swords with this lady on a number of occasions in the future.

In 2009 Sokolov's recital was switched to Salzburg's huge Grosses Festspielhaus and he couldn't have produced anything finer for the occasion. As he walked to the piano for the first time I shuddered at the responsibility resting on his shoulders, performing in front of a particularly demanding audience of almost 2,200, many of whom had paid astronomical amounts for their seats. The excellent acoustic allowed the lightest pianissimo to float across to where I was sitting, way back in the affordable seating, and Sokolov gave soaring accounts of Beethoven and Schubert sonatas. The performance received tremendous acclaim from the audience and outstanding reviews in the press; I was elated to be present at such a momentous event.

After the first encore a young woman approached the platform and held up a bunch of flowers. Sokolov came out, failed to notice her, took his bow and disappeared again. She stayed put and held her flowers higher, but the next time he came out, he went straight across to the piano and began to play. The same thing happened between the next two encores, and in a final act of desperation the girl lobbed the flowers after him as he strode towards the wings, sparking a burst of laughter from the audience. The flowers landed face down directly in his path to and from the piano but he carefully skirted round them several times. Naturally the public expected him to pick them up and it would have been an easy matter to do so, but I sensed this could never happen because it would have broken down the impenetrable barrier between himself and the public which seemed so vital for him to maintain on stage. After he'd disappeared for the final time, Sokolov's intrepid admirer scrambled onto the platform, retrieved her offering and took it to the artist's room, where the barrier would without question have been lifted.

In 2011 I caught the last performance of Schumann's Humoreske and Four Piano Pieces Op.32 in Salzburg, where the usual collection of rich and famous gathered in the Grosses Festspielhaus, and as always it was a grand occasion. Firstly we had Bach's infectious Italian Concerto and his wonderful Overture in the French Style. In the sarabande I marvelled at Sokolov's use of the tiniest ornament possible on the last note of the repeated opening statement, and the central section of the gavotte was played so delicately it might have come floating in on the breeze from a neighbouring village. As for the Schumann, even in the final performance Sokolov searched out new forms of expression, and the Op.32 fughette provided a superbly understated climax to the programme. I told Sokolov I was now entering the end-of-season desert where I would wait patiently for the new programme in the autumn and he said he wished he had more time to prepare. I asked if he missed the orchestral repertoire and he said it had been five years since he'd played a concerto and he was happy with that, but never say never again. Did he have a favourite concerto? "No", he said. "It's all music; it's all beautiful".

On my first visit to Bregenz in 2010 I strolled along the shore of the Bodensee with the promise of springtime all around me, passing the famous outdoor festival arena and island platform. Surprised to find myself in yet another place I'd no idea I would ever see, I felt the usual sense of gratitude for Sokolov's gift of unwittingly re-writing the closing chapters of my life. A few hours before the performance began I sat a thousand metres up, surrounded by snowy mountains, listening to one of his recorded Schubert sonatas, and it felt as if I were surveying his kingdom.

That evening in the Festspielhaus's Grosser Saal the performance was overshadowed by far too many audience distractions. By the end of the Bach courante in Partita No.2 I'd given up any attempt to concentrate, and during the sarabande alone I counted twenty-eight disturbances. It was an insult to the artist, and I personally felt cheated, having travelled so far. As the Brahms took over I was determined to try and filter out the interference, otherwise the evening was going to be a complete write-off. I was rewarded with a blissful experience when each individual part of Op.116 spoke to me as a whole for the first time. The Schumann sonata was awesome, and in the final movement even the coughers were momentarily silenced. Someone I spoke to at the interval had remarked on Sokolov's stage persona. "Why does he behave in that way?" she'd asked indignantly. "Why does he not show some personality? Why is there never even a smile?". I tried to explain Sokolov's strict avoidance of self-promotion; that he merely delivered the composer's intention, albeit in his own distinctive manner. A week later in Helsinki another lady summed it up perfectly when she said, "Sokolov has no need to flirt with his audience; he has so much more to offer them."

Sandwiched between recitals in Warsaw and Vienna I visited Graz for the first time in December 2019, a charming and elegant city on the River Mur, possessing a wealth of Renaissance and baroque architecture. I spent a free day exploring the medieval old town, visiting the beautiful Roman Catholic Parish Church of the Holy Blood and finally taking the funicular up to the densely wooded Schlossberg to admire the views and see its ancient clock tower. In the magnificent Musikverein that evening, a classic statue of Beethoven sat surveying his palatial surroundings from the top of the staircase leading to the auditorium. This was another enormously thrilling night when Sokolov paid homage to Mozart and Brahms in spectacular fashion.

Back in 2009 my journey from Birmingham to Wattens in the Austrian Tyrol for a recital in Swarovski Kristallwelten took twelve hours and was fraught with anxiety. My first flight was to Zürich, where I had only fifteen frantic minutes to transfer onto another flight to Munich, and from there it took three trains to get me to Schwaz, during which time the gently undulating Bavarian countryside gave way to dazzling alpine scenery with snow capped mountains, rushing rivers and scatterings of wild flowers. At Schwaz I discovered the bus to Wattens didn't run on Saturdays but had I remained on the train it would have taken me to Wattens, so I waited an hour for the next one. In Wattens I was hoping my B&B would be in a homely, traditional little pension, but I found myself in a characterless establishment run by a David Hasselhoff lookalike with fake tan and blonde mullet, who hosted weekend table dancing and musical events. I prayed that whatever was to take place that night would be tucked away in a basement, but shortly before two on Sunday morning I awoke to the thump of techno bass which continued until six.

After a sub-standard breakfast there was nothing to do in Wattens other than visit Swarovski Crystal World, where products from the nearby factory were displayed in a dark underground warren which accentuated the brilliance of the exhibits. It was a right royal rip-off if ever there was one, especially as my interest in jewellery and crystal was non-existent. In the afternoon my room was suffocatingly hot on account of the balcony door refusing to open. No response had been forthcoming to my request for assistance so I wrestled and tugged until it finally became unjammed and allowed in a gust of muggy air, along with an army of ants who came marching across the threshold uninvited. I dealt with them as swiftly as I could, shut the door and thought I might take a walk to relieve the monotony, but a crop of thundery showers passed over and by the time I was ready to leave for the concert, a violent hailstorm with torrential rain and lightning had taken hold. Determined to be first in the queue for the unreserved seats, I practically paddled all the way to the concert hall, taking to a grass verge along the way in order to avoid being splashed by passing traffic. Leaving my saturated coat in the cloakroom I stood in the foyer, proudly sporting my second-hand Jacques Vert jacket and feeling as if I'd scrubbed up reasonably well all things considered, but on looking down at my lower half I saw that my trousers were soaked up to the knee, liberally splashed with mud and smothered in grass cuttings.

The hall was also underground with just 240 seats, and to my extreme disappointment the first four rows were reserved for regulars. The mad scramble for the remaining places left me in the seventh row with no view whatsoever so I decided to kick up a fuss, which landed me a third row seat among the subscribers. As I might have expected, Sokolov turned everything around for me and the moment he began his inimitable handiwork I forgot about the day's events and entered his world without a backward glance.

The audience behaved impeccably, with the exception of four restive children in the front row. I was all in favour of exposing youngsters to great music, but where piano recitals were concerned I believed no one under the age of twelve, unless they were studying music seriously, should be allowed to sit within the artist's line of vision. Although Sokolov admitted afterwards that he'd been well aware of their dangling legs swinging back and forth throughout the evening, this performance was flawless and I could only imagine that if Beethoven and Schubert had been listening, they would not have wished for a single note to be expressed in any other way.

7. POLAND

MY FIRST TRIP to Poland in December 1999 was fraught with warnings of fogbound runways, winds from Siberia carrying heavy snowfall, grumpy purveyors of tourist information, untrustworthy taxi drivers, pickpockets, numerous 'no go' zones and undrinkable tap water. Even worse was the thought of travelling all the way there to find that for some reason Sokolov hadn't turned up, which filled me with the deepest dread. I'd been unable to check on his whereabouts before leaving home at three in the morning to catch an early flight from Heathrow, but by eight o'clock I was tucking into a hearty in-flight Polish cooked breakfast which lifted my spirits enormously. As we began our descent towards the outskirts of Warsaw I could see a light covering of snow, and a forest of grim looking tower blocks rose up out of the gloom.

The arrivals hall was a sea of eager faces waiting for loved ones returning home or visiting for Christmas, together with a gaggle of pushy taxi drivers and random characters asking for money. I dived into an efficient looking Orbis Group office, seduced by the promise of a shuttle bus service to each of their establishments, which I foolishly imagined might be free. At the same time I feared the accommodation would be way beyond my budget, but I settled for the cheapest available room in the Hotel Polonia, and half an hour later I was climbing the steps of a building, once grand but now past its best, whose reception area, palatial dining room and wide sweeping staircases were bedecked with baubles and festive greenery.

I was soon outside again, contemplating the chaotic jumble of traffic and clanking trams in front of the hotel. Somehow negotiating the maze of underground passages beneath a huge intersection, I discovered that the Philharmonic Concert Hall was only a ten minute walk away. Eager to leave behind the area in which I was staying, with its shabby street trade and pitiful beggars, I strolled towards the old town along a wide boulevard lined with Christmas trees where numerous Father Christmases patrolled the pavements and young girls dressed as angels with golden wings handed out sweets and chocolates to passers-by.

The reconstruction of the old town was remarkable with everything lovingly restored to picture book perfection, especially the multi-coloured three storey merchants' houses surrounding the town square, where horse-drawn carriages stood at the kerbside in the hope of attracting custom. On my way back to the hotel I was drawn into an elegant coffee house complete with cloakroom attendant and immaculate waiters serving a relaxed clientele who were there to meet and talk with friends or browse the newspapers. By the time I emerged it was fiercely cold and almost dark, and as I hurried back towards my home territory I tripped on a cobble stone and went sprawling face down in the slush. The necessary clean-up job followed by a hot bath to ease my rapidly stiffening joints occupied what was left of the afternoon.

By six I was back at the concert hall, where I struck up a conversation with a distinguished looking man surveying the foyer from the top of a staircase. I suspected he might be the manager but he was actually there to represent the bank sponsoring the performance and was waiting for a party of guests to arrive. He suggested we meet Sokolov together at the end of the recital, and although I had misgivings, as soon as the third encore had been delivered I duly made my way to the appointed meeting place, where I was introduced to a smiling group of VIPs, including two Polish government ministers and the winner of the most recent International Frederic Chopin Piano Competition. I was swept along with the group and we were soon entering what I expected to be the artist's room, but was in fact an opulent reception lounge full of antique furnishings where waiters advanced bearing trays of wine and others held aloft silver platters full of artistically arranged canapés. On a long sideboard stood glass stands piled high with miniature cakes and pastries.

This was all very well, but where was the artist's room? I asked the question several times, but was assured that the Sokolovs would be arriving at any moment. Knowing this to be highly unlikely in view of their usual avoidance of such gatherings immediately following a performance, I felt trapped and far removed from where I wanted to be. I got into conversation with one of the ministers, but all I could think about was plotting my escape. I made several attempts but was told, "No, no! You must stay here. You are our *guest*. Sokolov will come soon". I then had the bright idea of suggesting I collect my coat from the cloakroom, but was met with, "Relax! We *all* have coats in the cloakroom!". The manager bustled off to ensure Sokolov was on his way, but came back with the news that there was still a long queue outside the artist's room. I should have been in that queue, and it felt as if I were being held hostage. In a way I was, because my name had been mentioned to Sokolov with the express purpose of persuading him to show his face at the reception. Eventually a ripple of applause filled the room as the Sokolovs appeared in the doorway, and he was immediately surrounded and pinned against a wall to answer a barrage of questions. Sokolov was all smiles as if nothing was amiss but his wife looked very unhappy. As soon as they left I excused myself and walked back to the Polonia feeling desolated. This had been the last recital of the year and the concert season would not resume for many weeks. I was mortified that Sokolov had been pressured into attending because of me and I would have been so much happier if he'd refused.

After a miserable night I crept into the dining room with a pounding head, and despite what looked to be a sensational breakfast buffet on offer, I couldn't face any food. Instead, I dragged myself outside for a walk in the fresh air, and along the street an earnest looking young man approached me, asking if I'd smiled three times yet that day. I told him I most certainly had not, and that it was unlikely I'd be smiling for many days to come, whereupon he tried to interest me in buying a set of saucepans. I politely declined and continued on my way but was stopped in my tracks when I spotted in the distance the Sokolovs strolling towards me arm in arm. My first instinct was to dive behind a street vendor's kiosk, but as they drew closer I realised that this chance encounter was a gift from God, and if I didn't set things straight with them and allow myself the opportunity to apologise, I would have the most unhappy Christmas imaginable. And so it was that I got to explain to Sokolov exactly what had happened at the Philharmonic Hall, and although he admitted he'd been very tired and would have preferred not to attend the reception, he fully understood my predicament and told me not to worry about it.

Subsequent trips to Warsaw were much more harmonious, and in November 2015 I discovered one of my favourite hotels in the whole of Europe: the Polonia Palace. It was a short walk from the railway station, grand enough to make you proud to be staying there but with surprisingly affordable room rates, the friendliest staff, and situated directly opposite the monumental Palace of Culture, the city's most useful landmark. A gift from the Soviet Union to the people of Poland and built in the 1950s, the palace contained four theatres, a 3,000 seat auditorium, a large swimming pool, a multiplex cinema with eight screens, two museums and an accredited university. I took the lift up to the 30th floor viewing terrace and stayed there until the sun set and the Christmas lights came on.

Later I heard Sokolov's final performance of the Schubert Sonata D784 and Moments Musicaux D780. Two nights previously I'd been at the Konzerthaus in Vienna and I'd arrived in Warsaw wondering if it might have been a mistake to attend a second concert. The Philharmonic Hall didn't possess any of the sumptuous grandeur of the Konzerthaus; the auditorium was neither colourful nor particularly ornate, but it had a kind of austere elegance. The chandelier closest to the piano gave out a dull yellowish gleam and the overall effect was rather sombre. I sat in the first row of the balcony watching the hall fill up, deciding that the subdued setting for this recital suited my mood and my seat in the balcony would be a good place from which to witness my final Schubert. The dim lighting left me free from distractions and I savoured every moment. Sokolov gave another heart-stopping account and the audience displayed a degree of deep concentration I'd rarely seen before.

I was curious to discover what a Polish audience would make of the 2nd Sonata by Chopin and a little apprehensive that Sokolov's comparatively unsentimental approach might not be to everyone's taste. Chopin was, after all, one of Poland's great national treasures. In the event, the effect upon this audience was profound. Sokolov's physicality, musicality, emotional insight and technical brilliance broke all boundaries, and the final flourish brought the entire hall to its feet in a clamour of thunderous applause and shouting. I'd so wanted them to like what Sokolov did, and to see such a reaction gave me an indescribable lift. Before an already ecstatic gathering, he then worked his way through five Chopin encores, seemingly paying even more attention to the tiniest details; teasing and flirting with the music and ending the evening with a shimmering Debussy prelude. No flamboyant gestures were required; it was simply a matter of supreme concentration and masterly finger and pedal work.

The Philharmonic Hall gave one the feeling that it had stood on Jasna Street since time immemorial, and crossing its portals the following year I sensed once more the solemn dignity of the auditorium: no frills, no frivolity. The audience radiated a sense of earnest application as they listened and their appreciation was fervent and unstinting. As the first sweet notes of Mozart's Sonata K545 took flight, the piano gave out a wonderfully full-bodied sound; a valiant instrument whose beautiful tone never faltered. The Mozart programme continued to gain stature with each performance and I was steadily coming to realise the full extent of what I was hearing and the challenge this opening sonata presented. In its very simplicity it exposed the performer to an unforgiving landscape where there was nowhere to hide. Sokolov, with apparent ease, executed and elevated this highly deceptive piece to a level which demanded phenomenal technique combining razor-sharp precision with balletic poise.

Schumann's masterwork followed, flooding the hall with every conceivable combination of sound and colour. If someone had told me before the season began that I would come to love the Schumann Fantasy so passionately I would have laughed. Such were Sokolov's powers of persuasion. The six encores ended with Schubert's Moments Musicaux No.6, a sublime parting gift to a devoted audience; a piece which spoke to me of separation and longing, the middle section suggesting a fond reflection on happier times. Each recital became a life lesson for me. In human form I sat in the audience and listened; in spirit I sat at Sokolov's feet and learned.

After the performance many people gathered in the corridor approaching his room and from outside it looked like the kind of ceremonial space in which one might expect to meet royalty, with its lavish golden drapes. For a moment I wondered if I might find a throne in there somewhere, but there was just a piano, behind which a smiling Sokolov waited to greet the thankful citizens of Warsaw and others from further afield.

Warsaw 2018

The only seat available for the Warsaw recital in December 2018 was in the front row. It was a little too close, but no matter; I was there. The first notes of Beethoven's Sonata No.3 Op.2/3 sang out as sweet and soft as honey, and as soon as the opening bars had set the scene Sokolov tore into the first movement like a greyhound in pursuit of a rabbit. The articulation was incisive, the dark solemnity of the second movement was expressed with profound sensitivity, giving way to a lilting and nimbly executed third, and before we knew it the exuberant finale was upon us. The unpredictability of the eleven bagatelles was always a delight, but the most uproarious response came at the end of the mesmerising Schubert Impromptus Op.142, when the audience stood to greet every one of Sokolov's subsequent appearances on stage. As he came out for the final bow, a thunder of rhythmic clapping still persisted and I wondered what was in his mind at that moment. Was he reflecting on the performance he'd just given, or already thinking of his next assignment; maybe craving a long cool drink, or merely wondering just how many encores he would need to produce before the audience were prepared to relinquish their seats and go home?

On a dreary day in December 2019 it was much too cold for sightseeing, so I remained ensconced in the Polonia Palace all day, lunching on Russian pancakes, Polish cheesecake and astonishingly inexpensive red wine. That evening's performance had naturally attracted a capacity audience, who by the end of the recital had been whipped into a state of blissful excitement. The Mozart Fantasy & Fugue in C major KV394 became a joyful celebration, along with everything that followed. Quite apart from the amazing clarity there was an arresting visual impression from my vantage point in the balcony, reminding me of an old sepia photograph: the cream coloured interior of the hall gently illuminated by a solitary chandelier, the sturdily scrolled dark wood of the organ housing, and beneath it the endearing figure of Sokolov, modestly going about his business; an image of dignity and wisdom. Outside, there was an unrelenting winter chill, but we fortunates basked in the exclusive microclimate Sokolov carried with him wherever he went.

The Mozart Fantasy & Fugue, Sonata No.11 in A major KV331 and the Rondo in A minor KV511 appeared to be seamlessly bound together as one flawless work of art, and I was deeply moved by this first half of the programme; Sokolov had once again succeeded in persuading me to respect and revere the work of a composer with whom I'd been reluctant to engage, and I was convinced that the Mozart I heard in Warsaw could never be improved upon. Assisted by the wonderful acoustic, the piano gave a very fine account of itself on its first public appearance; another young instrument being sent out into the world by the most knowledgeable and scrupulous of instructors. Sokolov's exquisite variety of touch produced some voluptuous sounds, and the Brahms Op.118/Op.119 programme came from another part of the universe, receiving an equally rapturous reception. Six encores were then hungrily devoured, and the evening ended in unconfined tumult.

Warsaw 2019

The visitor-friendly city of Krakow provided many great musical experiences too. My first visit was in August 2008, when I travelled there by train from Warsaw. The outer environs of Warsaw were grim, but as we travelled further south, the undulating countryside became increasingly attractive. Krakow was heaving with teenagers who'd arrived for some sort of rock festival and as I walked across the old town's main square, said to be the largest market square in medieval Europe, I vowed that the next day I would escape the clamour and visit Auschwitz. The streets were teeming with tourists and I dreaded the noise they might create at night, but my hotel was in a quiet side street and much more upmarket than I'd anticipated.

At seven I took the short walk to the Philharmonic Hall in stifling heat, where Sokolov had to contend with far too much flash photography, passing police sirens, trams rumbling by at the rate of about one per minute and a couple of mobile phone intrusions. The Mozart received a warm reaction, but I had the feeling everyone was waiting for Chopin, whose music was performed on a daily basis all over the city. As Sokolov progressed through the Op.28 Preludes I wondered what this Polish audience would make of them. Some said that his Chopin was an acquired taste, so I was pleased when the entire house rose to its feet at the end. Sokolov received a bunch of flowers from the management and another one from a member of the public. As he stood nursing a bouquet in each arm, I was reminded of an image I'd once seen of the bemused father of newborn twins.

When I discovered the proposed trip to Auschwitz would take one and a half hours each way by minibus I decided against it and instead climbed up to Wawel Castle, explored the bleak former ghetto in the Jewish quarter, wandered round the market square and watched part of a folk song and dance festival which was taking place on a specially erected stage. A troupe of pensionable dancers and musicians in traditional costume took their turn and delivered some good homely stuff - a welcome antidote to the third rate rock and pop being churned out in other parts of the city.

With no concert that evening, I found a music fix at the Bonerowski Palace, where a young Polish piano student was giving a recital. The former palace was now a classy five star hotel with fabulously furnished suites and an attractive little concert room overlooking the main square. The piano wasn't great and the pianist began with a Chopin polonaise which was not quite ready for a public airing, but he continued with a well executed nocturne and in the second half he played Brahms intermezzi, which I enjoyed very much. I spoke to him afterwards, mentioning my reason for being in Krakow, and he said he would love to think that one day someone might travel a great distance to hear him play.

In 2012 Sokolov took his Rameau/Mozart/Brahms programme to Krakow, and the Rameau Suite in D was exquisite, confirming my belief that Sokolov was born to bring this early music into our age using his unique skills, to convince even the most stubborn traditionalists of the validity of these pieces played in modern times on a modern instrument. In the second half, he attacked the Variations & Fugue on a Theme by Handel as if someone had lit a firecracker under the piano stool. It was always a thrilling half hour, but this was positively incendiary. In the lead-up to the fugue he went off like a rocket and I felt thankful I had two more opportunities to embark upon this joyful expedition before saying goodbye to Brahms.

It was good that in August 2016 the final performance of Chopin's 2nd Sonata was to take place in Krakow, and I hoped it would be given a great send-off in the composer's homeland. Before the concert began there was an over-amplified announcement (so loud it made everyone laugh) leaving the audience in no doubt about what to do with their mobiles and recording devices. After that there was little to interrupt the flow of the performance apart from the occasional clank of a passing tram, but in any case, with otherwise ideal conditions Sokolov was unassailable. Equipped with a fine, mellow-toned piano and an acoustic which provided a huge sound, he was destined to produce a larger than life performance. In Bolzano four days earlier, the sound had been more refined; in Krakow it was full-on powerhouse stuff, but I was perfectly happy with either.

Each half of the programme began with an air of tranquillity but soon slid from tenderness into turmoil. The Schumann Arabeske was quickly overshadowed by the emotional havoc of the Fantasy, where the atmosphere was electric. I was totally immersed, hanging onto every note for dear life, while my next door neighbour dissolved into tears. I forgot about the trams; a fleet of Centurion tanks could have thundered past for all I cared. The applause that followed was an oceanic wall of sound and I wondered how much greater the reaction to the second half was going to be. Programmes came and went, and some were much harder to live without than others. This was the last time I would ever hear Sokolov play the Chopin sonata and it seemed like a very big deal. The first two movements were executed with astonishing dynamism and his account of the funeral march was heartbreaking, the sense of desolation and the final cry of anguish painful to witness. The partnership between artist and instrument was formidable, and it was no surprise when this matchless piece of pianism received an immediate standing ovation. In that moment, the platform was Sokolov's kingdom, the piano his most trusted courtier. This Schumann/Chopin programme was pure dynamite. Occasionally my heart was so full at the end of a concert that I felt no need of encores, but on this occasion I was grateful to be diverted from my sense of loss.

A change of venue was necessary in 2017 due to the Philharmonic Hall undergoing refurbishment. The final recital of the season took place in the Opera Krakowska, whose boxlike red exterior reminded me of a fire station. The interior of the auditorium was also predominantly red and somehow lacked atmosphere, but Sokolov provided the necessary counterbalance and delivered the goods to an eager audience who created their own sense of occasion, receiving his final performance of the Mozart programme with enormous warmth.

The opera house's sound quality seemed a little flat to begin with, but the outpouring from the piano carried well and the instrument gave sterling service. It looked extraordinarily sleek and beautiful against a voluminous black backdrop, with just the Steinway emblem illuminated and a small circle of light in which Sokolov held sway. A fine piano looked good wherever it was placed, but this one seemed to have found its true home. The audience was presented with a blank canvas upon which Sokolov created a succession of images, some painted in bold and brilliant colours, some etched in delicate tracery, others executed in much darker hues with rapid and tempestuous brush strokes.

In the second half, at the beginning of Beethoven's Op.111, there was a palpable sense of readiness among those familiar with the music, as if they might be mentally reaching for a safety belt, and by the end of the first movement the audience had all but slipped into a hypnotic trance. Trills of astonishing evenness and fluidity tripped from Sokolov's fingers and the music enveloped us like a cloak as we all travelled together. Towards the end of this sublime journey I imagined Beethoven calling out, "Look what I have shown you! See where I have taken you!" An immeasurable distance was covered in the course of this sonata, and sometimes Sokolov would take me to a place so far removed that I was unable to re-engage until the third or fourth encore was in progress (Rameau usually did the trick).

Predictably, the audience went ballistic and Sokolov left the stage with yet another monument under his belt. As he returned, a young woman followed him up the steps onto the stage, bearing a floral tribute, hovering for a moment and then deciding to walk round the front of the piano to meet him head on. As she skirted round the edge of the platform, hidden from his view by the upturned piano lid, he bowed deeply and swivelled, failed to see her approaching, and walked off. It was a flower-presenter's worst nightmare, and the poor girl did a complete circuit of the piano, trailing behind him, her offering undelivered. She watched mournfully as he descended the steps and disappeared, the audience roared with laughter and

Sokolov must have wondered what was so funny, but as soon as he returned all was quickly resolved.

Security was tight in the building and consequently very few people were allowed backstage. In retrospect I wished I'd given up my place for someone more deserving. I saw Sokolov so often, but others saw him perhaps only once a year or even once in a lifetime. I wanted as many people as possible to discover for themselves that behind the inscrutable expression we saw on stage there lay not only a vast intellect, but also humour, patience and kindness. How I envied Sokolov's younger admirers who would doubtless see him through to the end of his performing days and take pride in telling people, far into the future when his name had joined the pantheon of piano legends, that long ago they'd actually heard him perform live.

8. CZECH REPUBLIC

MY ONLY CONCERT trip to Prague was in May 2003. The quickest way from the airport was by express minibus, a cramped and suffocating journey during which no one spoke, despite a dozen of us being squashed together like bosom pals. We sped through some gorgeous rural scenery before hitting the outer suburbs, and even these were noticeably green and prosperous looking. Notwithstanding the discomfort it was thrilling to have my first glimpse of the famous bridges over the River Vltava and the towers, domes and spires of the city.

It was much warmer than I'd expected and I plodded along a wide street decorated with giant banners announcing the Prague Spring International Music Festival which was then into its second week of events in a host of venues across the city. The crowds became impossibly dense as I approached Wenceslas Square, but close by I found Havelska, the street in which my pension was situated, hidden behind market stalls and a pavement pizzeria. The pension's striking logo was a tarantula, with a particularly large and ugly specimen painted on the outer door and another above the reception desk. The receptionist produced a bunch of keys and took me into a neighbouring building where one key opened a massive wooden door leading to a passage alongside the pizza kitchen and two flights of stairs. The second key opened a heavy wrought iron gate leading to two further flights of stairs ending on an upper landing of bare boards. Unlocking my door with the third key, the girl offered an apologetic, "Is small room", and she wasn't wrong.

Faced with the cheerless prospect of spending two nights in there, my only consolation was that it had cost next to nothing. The carpet was so badly stained it was impossible to determine the original colour, and the contents of the room comprised a single bed without headboard tucked behind the door, a child-sized plastic table and chair and a cupboard with one wire hanger. To accommodate outer clothing a large nail had been driven into the back of the door. There was no washbasin or mirror and the only decoration was a single plastic flower in a chipped vase on the table. A scrap of grubby muslin stretched across the window served as the only curtain, and I made a mental note to switch off the light before undressing. A limp guest towel lay on the bed, blemished with what I hoped was iron mould, and the fourth key gave entry to the communal bathroom, which although superficially clean had some grim corners.

I'd arranged to meet a fellow Sokolov enthusiast from Helsinki and we walked towards the river, admiring the wealth of wonderful architecture along the way. By the time we reached the Charles Bridge the sky had turned leaden and we were enveloped in a blanket of humidity. Something dramatic was afoot in the weather department, but we crossed the river regardless and continued walking until the rain started, diving into a little bar tucked away in an old courtyard, where we drank local beer and watched a spectacular display of lightning through the open doorway. A panic-stricken dog raced in, skidded to a halt on the tiles, took one look at us and was gone again, having decided it was less scary outside. Once it had stopped, we emerged into a deliciously fresh atmosphere, and with the lights of Prague reflected on the wet cobblestones we strolled back across the bridge, the buildings on either side providing a stunning floodlit panorama. Had I been alone I would have spent more time drinking in the scene, but Elizabeth had a long walk ahead of her.

Back in my room there were no disturbances from inside the building, but merrymakers in the surrounding streets shouted, sang and danced the night way, whereupon the market stall holders arrived, dragging crates of fruit and vegetables past my window. When the reception office opened at nine I asked if I could be moved to the rear of the building. The only room available cost twice as much and contained seven beds which had been occupied the previous night by a group of Irish marathon runners. I chose to ignore the spectre of athlete's foot, and by ten o'clock was installed in my very own dormitory.

With a whole day to explore, Elizabeth and I firstly located the Rudolfinum, an imposing neo-Renaissance building beside the river, in which Sokolov would be performing that evening. From there it was a short walk to Josefov, the old Jewish quarter, where more than 100,000 graves were piled on top of one another in the cemetery.

Crossing the river we headed towards Prague Castle, but were drawn by chance into a concealed entrance to the formal gardens of the Waldstein Palace, built by Count Albrecht von Waldstein, in his time the most powerful man in central Europe, who had twenty-six large houses demolished to make way for this showpiece. One of Beethoven's best known sonatas was dedicated to him.

We sat for a while by a fountain enjoying the tranquillity of the gardens before exploring a grotto with thousands of stalactites carved out of stone. A large wire enclosure nearby contained a tree in which two long-eared owls sat together, staring solemnly down at us. The climb up to the castle looked daunting, so we boarded a tram which flew up the hill at astonishing speed. There was much to see on this side of the river: the castle itself, the old Royal Palace, the Cathedral of St. Vitus, the Basilica and Convent of St. George, but we spent most of our time in the cathedral, whose windows were among the most beautiful I'd ever seen, then climbed almost three hundred steps to the top of the tower for marvellous views across the city. Our day of exploration ended with a walk along the Golden Lane, a narrow cobbled alley lined with miniature seventeenth century cottages.

At the Rudolfinum, evening dress was much in evidence and the auditorium was exquisitely decorated. Sokolov was in great demand and looking happy, despite the prospect of a forthcoming two day event in Helsinki at which he was to receive an honorary doctorate from the Sibelius Academy. In particular he was not looking forward to the procession through the streets, for which I undertood he would be expected to wear a ceremonial robe. Luckily for him, the banquet and ball on the second day were too close to his performance, but the actual five hour ceremony could not be avoided.

Elizabeth and I ate supper in an atmospheric old restaurant, and when a group of musicians dressed in peasant costume appeared bearing a variety of traditional stringed instruments, we became excited at the prospect of some authentic regional folk music to accompany our meal. It was something of a disappointment when the leader of the ensemble, flashing us a cheeky smile and waggling his eyebrows, tucked a violin under his chin and launched into 'Smoke Gets in Your Eyes'.

9. FINLAND

IN SEPTEMBER 2000 a brisk tail wind cut my three hour flight to Finland down to two and a quarter, and I landed in Helsinki at eight in the evening. An airport coach stood waiting to provide warmth and shelter from the rain, its immaculately uniformed driver spoke excellent English and the radio on board dispensed Scandinavian folk melodies; an agreeable start to my first Finnish adventure. I disembarked at the city's railway station, crossed a busy square and soon located my pre-booked accommodation. The hotel manager's eager face, framed by an outmoded leonine hairdo, beamed out from the information folder, assuring guests of a home from home in the heart of Helsinki where his staff were ready to attend to every conceivable requirement. Guests were also advised, in the event of a fire, to leave their rooms if possible, or alternatively expose themselves at the window.

On waking I was excited to find the blustery wet weather had given way to a clear blue sky. Fearful that it might not last, I bounded outside after an epic breakfast to find and photograph the nearby South Harbour, from which the pretty tree-lined Esplanadi stretched as far as the Swedish Theatre. En route I discovered the vast expanse of Senate Square and the towering magnificence of the Lutheran Cathedral, gleaming white with green and gold domes, flanked on all four sides by mountainous flights of steps. On the harbour front a bustling flea market was in full swing and fishing boats were selling the morning's catch. There was such an easy atmosphere I was reluctant to leave, but that evening's recital was in Tampere, a hundred miles to the north.

At the railway station a drab green train which looked half a mile long lumbered to a halt on the opposite platform. Unlike the other sleek, modern, brightly coloured ones passing through, this was ancient, with thick dun-coloured net curtains at the windows. I was told it was the train from Moscow, a reminder of just how close I was to Russia. The train to Tampere on the other hand was incredibly luxurious, even in second class, with head and foot rests, reclining seats and lumbar supports. We passed plantations of fir trees, brightly painted wooden houses surrounded by scatterings of silver birch, and shortly before entering the lake region we stopped at the small town of Riihimaki, where Sokolov had performed at a festival earlier in the year. At the time I'd dismissed it as an impossibility, but now I realised how easy it would have been to get there.

Feeling reckless, I checked into the first hotel I saw in Tampere: a rather smart converted granary. The window of my room opened onto a gymnasium full of gleaming apparatus where a multitude of suntanned limbs semaphored to the accompaniment of funky fiddle music. I spent what was left of the afternoon walking through the city centre and out towards the lakeside, lingering beneath the birch trees, exhilarated by the effect of the sun and wind on the water. In every direction I looked there was a factory chimney, but Tampere's factories looked well maintained and productive.

Tampere Hall was a modern and well designed building with a supremely comfortable auditorium. Sokolov was playing Franck's Prelude, Chorale & Fugue for the first time in public, along with ten Chopin mazurkas. It was a unique and personal performance, immensely powerful and deeply moving. At the interval a generously proportioned babushka in a peasant blouse with grey hair scraped into an untidy bun struggled to her feet, arms flailing, to bellow her admiration in Russian, and at the end of the evening a group of small boys came into the artist's room one at a time to be photographed with Sokolov. One of them asked him who his favourite composer was and Sokolov rattled off a long list.

Back at the hotel I ordered tea in the bar and a friendly Finn invited me to share his table. I welcomed the opportunity of some light conversation before retiring, but soon realised my burly companion spoke next to no English and in any case was in an advanced state of amiable drunkenness. With assistance from the hotel receptionist we managed a few awkward pleasantries, but it was hard going. He told me he played a lot of baseball and was employed as a 'footman'. I struggled to picture his muscular frame squeezed into a flunkey's uniform, but further probing revealed that he was a shoe salesman.

On my return to Helsinki the following day I browsed around the quaint old market hall on South Harbour, where every kind of fresh food was imaginatively displayed, then visited the Uspenski Russian Orthodox Cathedral, the interior of which was a treasure house full of precious icons and other religious relics. Combined with the aroma of incense and recordings of glorious Russian voices, the atmosphere was mesmerising and I could have lingered there for hours. In the afternoon I found a tiny church tucked away in a maze of narrow streets and listened to an organ recital of pieces by Bach which provided my daily fix of keyboard music. Returning to the harbour I photographed the sunset from different vantage points, dodging round corners and rushing up flights of steps to catch the final rays. As the sun disappeared behind the city skyline I stood at the end of a wooden jetty feeling profoundly happy to be in such a place.

The next day I wandered further afield into Kaivopuisto Park, originally a health resort complete with a bath house, favoured by Russian nobility. The path led to a rocky promontory overlooking a sandy beach and a sprinkling of small islands. Life-sized wooden reindeer and peasant figures stood at the water's edge, and further round the headland was a marina full of yachts overlooked by a graceful line of pastel coloured art deco villas. On the quayside a small café provided customers with woollen blankets to ward off the cold.

Later I took a boat trip round some of the offshore islands, including the Suomenlinna Sea Fortress, eventually skirting round Uspenski Cathedral, behind which was moored Helsinki's fleet of ice breakers. As we re-entered the harbour we were dwarfed by an enormous Silja Line ferry on its way to Estonia, and the sky was a photographer's dream. Finally, I took a hike across the city to see the monument dedicated to the Finnish composer, Jean Sibelius. Twenty-four tons of steel tube fashioned into a gigantic assemblage of organ pipes produced eerie low-pitched notes as the wind blew through them.

At the Sibelius Academy that evening, the recital was a sell-out, but due to an administrative error no seat had been set aside for me. Forty-five minutes of anxiety ensued, but deep down I couldn't believe I would be turned away. A stream of svelte young blonde females and expensively dressed, meticulously groomed older women drifted past, several bearing tasteful hand-tied bunches of flowers. A crowd had gathered at the box office waiting for returns, and my heart sank at the thought of being forced to sit far away from the piano, but less than a minute before the start, a ticket finally found its way into my trembling hands. A member of the press had failed to turn up and it was a prime position in the front row of the balcony. Overjoyed, I flew up the stairs two at a time.

When I reached the artist's room at the end of the evening, Sokolov's table was piled high with flowers. Mindful of my fear of flying he was surprised I'd travelled such a distance. "It's a three hour flight!" he exclaimed. I told him about the tail wind cutting it down to two and a quarter. "But if the wind hasn't changed it will be three and three quarters going back!" came the reply.

In 2001, shortly after the events of September 11th I returned to Helsinki. In addition to the twin towers disaster there had been a terrible collision on the runway at Linate Airport in Milan, which would normally have been regarded as a major catastrophe, but had received scant attention because of everything else that was going on. I sat nursing the most frightful collywobbles the night before I flew, but as soon as I was on my way I felt ready to face almost anything fate might care to throw at me. Flying via Copenhagen was a nuisance but at least I got fed twice.

On this trip I found cheaper accommodation at a friendly establishment on the top floor of a tall old building close to the station, and although it had a homely feel, my room looked as if it hadn't seen a duster for a while. When I told the manager my reading lamp wasn't working, he yanked the bed away from the wall, tinkered with the trailing wires and assured me it would be fixed the following day. Whilst down there he must have noticed how much dust was under the bed as he reappeared within a couple of minutes carrying a mop and bucket and gave the whole floor a good going over while I stood marooned on a rug. The next morning a cup of tea, a croissant and a yogurt were delivered to my room. Outside, the atmosphere in the city was nowhere near as exciting as it had been the previous year. It was a Sunday, with no market stalls on the quayside, quiet streets and dreary weather, but I sat through a service in the Lutheran Cathedral conducted by a female minister with the voice of an angel.

That year's recital was in the ultra modern lakeside National Opera House, where I had a splendid balcony seat. At the interval, the Director enthused over Sokolov's programme, which included new pieces by Haydn. When I walked into the artist's room Sokolov, who was surrounded by admirers, looked across at me and cried, "Aren't you afraid of flying now?" I admitted to feeling apprehensive, and he said, "Now no one is safe. They need to stay at home and not move around, but I cannot do that. I *must* fly!" I thought, yes, and unfortunately so must I.

In March of the following year I went by train from Helsinki to Riihimaki, fifty miles to the north, where Sokolov's recital took place in the Finnish Glass Museum. There was a lot of snow around and conditions underfoot were treacherous. I'd been advised to take a taxi from my hotel to the Glass Museum but thought I knew better, setting off on foot with plenty of time to spare. Along the way I asked a young man for reassurance that I was walking in the right direction. He was Heikki Saros, a lecturer at Lahti University and a lover of piano music who told me he never missed a Sokolov performance in Riihimaki and would be arriving at the museum later. It was almost dark and the venue was much further away than I'd imagined. I continued struggling along a narrow path inches thick with ice and eventually realised I had little more than fifteen minutes to find the museum and collect my ticket. I began to panic, and in sheer desperation flagged down a passing car, out of which climbed a friendly young fellow who understood my plight, invited me to hop in and delivered me to the recital on time.

The concert room had formerly been the glass-blowers' workshop, the bare brick walls and high timbered roof providing a surprisingly good acoustic, and glass exhibits were displayed on pedestals scattered among the seating. My seat was within a couple of feet of the keyboard, and it was wonderful to watch Sokolov's hands at such close range. To make my night complete, the audience of 250 made not the smallest sound throughout a programme of Haydn sonatas, Komitas dances and Prokofiev's incendiary 7th Sonata.

During the evening I wondered how I could possibly face the long slippery walk back to my hotel, but Heikki told me his uncle would give me a lift. Riihimaki by night generated little in the way of excitement, but the car journey with Heikki's uncle certainly did. I was amazed at the nonchalance with which he and his wife appeared to regard the series of near misses we experienced as we swerved to avoid obstacles, skidded round corners and slewed to a halt at traffic lights. It seemed to be an accepted hazard of winter driving over there; all they could do was fit jumbo tyres at the beginning of November and hope for the best until the end of April.

I went to bed ravenously hungry but rectified matters at breakfast the next morning with several hot potato pasties and a rich egg-based concoction which combined to send my digestive system into overdrive. By eleven o'clock I was back in Helsinki, enjoying the dazzling combination of sun and snow. South Harbour was still frozen over with many boats trapped in the ice. I walked across a series of wooden footbridges linking some of the smaller offshore islands and it seemed that the whole of Helsinki was out walking, muffled against a biting wind.

The recital that evening was scheduled to start at six o'clock in Kerava, a small town half an hour away by train. The venue was listed as the Congregation Centre, which sounded unpromising and conjured up images of a draughty hall, hard wooden seats and a wheezing harmonium. Moreover I'd forgotten to make a note of the exact address, and as I stood outside Kerava's railway station surrounded by a sea of slush, there were no taxi drivers to consult, and the few stray passers-by I approached were unable to help me with directions. Across the snowy wastes of the station forecourt and the main road stood a bulky edifice which could have passed as a concert hall, so I plodded across to take a closer look but found it locked and in darkness. It was already after five and I felt frantic. Eventually I asked a newsagent if he would allow me to look through the local newspaper, from which I gleaned that the recital was indeed in Kerava, and the Finnish word for Congregation Centre was in fact Seurakuntakeskuksessa, so even if I'd known what to ask for I wouldn't have been able to pronounce it.

I found it in the nick of time on the opposite side of town; its foyer was packed, and above the buzz of conversation Sokolov could be heard storming through the final movement of the Prokofiev sonata. The purpose-built hall was tastefully designed, surprisingly plush, and the tiny auditorium contained an admirable Steinway. The concert promoter invited me to choose a seat in the front row, the performance was stupendous, and I felt blessed to have been able to sit so close to the piano on two consecutive evenings. At the interval I was invited up to a balcony overlooking the throng, where open sandwiches, coffee and pastries were laid out. It was here that I met Elizabeth, who drove me back to Helsinki and told me about her involvement in the Kuhmo Chamber Music Festival in the north of Finland where Sokolov performed every year: another challenge for me to consider.

Two years later I was back at the hotel close to Helsinki railway station for an overnight stay before travelling to Lahti. The interior had been walloped over with a coat of emulsion and the breakfast tray brought to my room the next morning contained the same fare as previously, but with the added excitement of a boiled egg. The train journey north to Lahti took an hour and a half, and the city was not at its most alluring, emerging as it was from a particularly long and harsh winter, the roadsides piled high with filthy snow and expanses of yellowish-grey grass looking beyond revival. The main attraction in summer, Lake Vesijärvi, was still frozen solid.

In the compact city centre it was easy to locate the concert hall, and just a few steps away was the Comfort Hotel Lahti, an establishment which had seen better days but suited my purpose. I strolled across to take a look at the hall and bumped into the surprisingly youthful manager, who was belatedly slapping up posters. As soon as I opened my mouth he knew who I was, ushered me inside and proffered my ticket, a programme and a poster, all of which he'd designed and produced himself. He and a colleague were just off to Helsinki to collect Sokolov, who was staying close to the Sibelius Academy.

The Arctic wind whistling across the lake's icy surface deterred me from walking along the shore, and instead I searched out the city's art museum, which amounted to just one room devoted to the work of a contemporary female artist whose preoccupation with male genitalia discouraged any lingering scrutiny. As a consequence, I was soon out of there and supping tea back at the hotel. The evening was a most satisfying one, with an unusually disciplined audience. Sokolov's habit of taking his time to come out on stage sometimes led to a prolonged hubbub of conversation and occasionally a mischievous burst of premature applause, but in Lahti you could have heard a pin drop for at least two minutes before he appeared. He'd played with the highly regarded Lahti Symphony Orchestra on many occasions; indeed they'd only recently completed a countrywide tour, but this was Sokolov's first solo recital in Lahti and it was a resounding success. On my way out I spoke to a young woman who'd been in the artist's room talking to Sokolov. She was a cellist with the orchestra, and although they'd often shared the same platform, this had been her first opportunity to actually speak to him. She told me how impenetrable he seemed in rehearsal with the orchestra, but how greatly revered he was among musicians.

The train journey back to Helsinki was a soothing experience, passing through the classic Finnish landscape of frozen lakes (of which I'd read Finland had a staggering 188,000), vast fields, belts of pine trees and the occasional scattering of wooden houses and farm buildings. At the Academy I sat next to the manager of Lahti Symphony Orchestra, who'd been at the previous night's recital and felt compelled to repeat the experience. The highlights of the evening for me were Bach's Reincken Sonata and the Bach/Brahms Chaconne for the left hand. After the tremendous reception Sokolov received I found him in an especially jovial mood, at one point plucking a bottle of local beer from an ice bucket and knocking it back in what looked like a single gulp.

In the midsummer of 2003 I travelled by train from Helsinki to Kotka, a seaport further along the coast. It hadn't looked very far away on the map, but the journey took more than three hours, travelling a long distance inland before turning back towards the sea. It felt like the height of luxury to be sitting on the shaded side of the railway carriage, foot rest and pillow supporting me, a book in my lap, drifting in and out of sleep as flower filled meadows and sparkling lakes slid by.

Built on an island in the Eastern Gulf of Finland and surrounded by many smaller islands, Kotka catered for outdoor activities such as camping, fishing and water sports. With the aid of one or two locals I found a place to stay which overlooked the harbour. The Hotel Merikotka (Finnish for sea eagle) was blessed with a lively bar/café frequented by good natured locals who consumed vast quantities of beer with enthusiasm, threw darts with gusto and periodically launched into bursts of lusty singing. By contrast, just around the corner on a rocky elevation with a natural grassy depression forming a kind of amphitheatre, a succession of choirs from all over southern Finland performed in national costume throughout the afternoon to an appreciative audience, some perched on wooden seats, others stretched out on the surrounding rocks with their picnic baskets.

Kotka Concert Hall was a modest red brick building with a pale wooden interior and cream décor. I was greeted with enthusiasm as the artistic director of the Kotka Music Festival approached with a broad smile and a huge bouquet of flowers. The smile was for me but the flowers were of course for Sokolov. I was asked a lot of questions and a press photographer took several shots during the performance of me gazing up at my idol, no doubt looking rather foolish. The thought of my gormless features possibly finding their way into the local newspaper was a worrying one.

I caught the train to Riihimaki the following afternoon and arrived in plenty of time to stroll through the Finnish Glass Museum's lofty rooms and admire the astonishing array of colourful exhibits, with the added luxury of hearing Sokolov rehearsing nearby. I'd promised to save a seat for Elizabeth, and when the doors opened everyone rushed towards their favoured seats. I chose two places near the front, and within seconds every surrounding seat had been taken. I was so busy trying to attract Elizabeth's attention as she came in that I failed to notice an unusually tall and heavily built man squeezing his titanic bulk into the seat directly in front of mine. When I turned round to find that the piano had completely disappeared behind his boulder-sized head and massive shoulders I could have wept, and even though Elizabeth offered to change places at the interval, I could sense she regretted the words as soon as they came out of her mouth, so I resigned myself to the inevitable but received from Sokolov's healing hands the kind of solace only great music can provide.

I fared much better at my third recital in Riihimaki in 2008, where the piano was barely an arm's length away and I was directly in firing line with Sokolov's awesome power. Finnish audiences invariably sat in complete silence for those few minutes before he appeared, as if emptying their minds in readiness for what he had to say. He'd been performing in Finland for the whole of his career in so many towns and cities that he'd become a much loved household name. Around 250 people were present; not bad for a comparatively remote place on a snowy night, with another recital scheduled in Helsinki the following evening. As Sokolov delivered the Mozart K280 adagio with sacramental slowness, through the windows I could see lamplight illuminating snow laden trees and fresh snow beginning to fall. Touched by the magic, I became completely lost in the moment and my close proximity to the piano enabled me to fully appreciate every expression, every nuance of finger and pedal work. In the Chopin Op.28 Preludes there was pure lyricism, heartbreaking intensity, dazzling technique. Such an exhilarating journey was going to be difficult to repeat the following evening.

But in Helsinki an even more responsive piano, a suitably fired up Sokolov and the distinctive atmosphere of the Sibelius Academy provided all the ingredients for another great night. It was said that the only pianist who could fill the Academy without even trying was Sokolov, and there were always many musicians in the audience All that could be seen from my seat in the ninth row was a dark silhouette against the Academy's simple cream décor: an iconic image of a great artist in his natural environment. And so this was an occasion to sit back, forget the human element and simply listen. The Mozart alone was phenomenal, bringing forth a spontaneous roar of approval from the audience. This was the real business; Riihimaki had been a mere warm up.

In April 2004 I spent five days in Finland, taking in three recitals, the first of which was in Tampere. The long walk from my hotel to Tampere Hall in new shoes was murderous, but at least my faltering progress prevented me from bumping into Sokolov, who climbed out of a car just ahead of me and entered the building. Recalling a recent radio interview with the English pianist John Lill, who stressed the importance of speaking to as few people as possible immediately before a performance, I was doubly relieved. The Bach/Brahms programme was played sublimely, but anyone wishing to express their appreciation in person found the door leading to the artist's room locked and a po-faced member of staff announcing that Mr Sokolov was in a hurry to return to Helsinki and had no time to see anyone. Two further opportunities lay ahead for me, so it was easy to accept, but two days later in Lohja Sokolov assured me he'd given no such instruction.

At breakfast the next morning the dining room was a sea of shaved heads, beer bellies and black leather and I learned that my visit had coincided with Tampere's annual Hot Rod & Rock Festival. The buffet table looked as if it had recently hosted a chimps' tea party, but my eyes lit up at the sight of a heap of finely diced bacon and potato sizzling in a metal container, a generous helping of which quickly found its way onto my plate.

Returning to Helsinki I pondered the question of how I would occupy myself for the next three days and was tempted to buy a forty-eight hour card entitling me to free transport and entrance to public buildings and exhibitions, but reasoned that I'd need to visit an indigestible number of museums to get my money's worth. In any case that evening Elizabeth drove me to Seurasaari, a thickly wooded island reached by a foot bridge. The woodland paths close to the shore offered marvellous views across the sea to other islands and at the centre was a folk museum where dozens of wooden buildings had been transported from Lapland and outlying provinces to illustrate how the Finns had lived and worked for the past four hundred years. We wandered among tiny peasant huts, cottages and farmsteads, visited a mill and even a manor house, all constructed entirely of wood. Long narrow sheds housed church boats in which islanders had rowed themselves to Sunday services on the mainland. The many activities on the island during the year included folk music and dance events, craft fairs and Easter and midsummer bonfires at which wedding ceremonies often took place. Nude bathing was permitted throughout the year and even in winter when the sea was frozen over an area was cut from the ice to accommodate anyone fancying a dip. At Christmas time, children could follow a trail through the snow, along which Christmas folk tales were re-enacted and Santa's helpers appeared. At the end of the trail there was carol singing, while Santa Claus and his wife handed out bowls of hot rice pudding sprinkled with cinnamon.

The following day I walked along the shore of Lake Toolon and visited the pink washed Hakasalmi Villa, a substantial neoclassical building dating from the 1840s which was exhibiting a collection of Russian underwear from the Soviet era. I was moved by the accompanying photographs of young men and women sunning themselves, bathing in rivers, taking part in sporting activities and gymnastic displays, and I couldn't help wondering if the western world might have turned out to be a better place if we'd all stuck to shapeless vests and baggy bloomers. An accompanying six page text in perfect English without a single spelling or punctuation error was a pleasing bonus.

I joined a midday conducted tour of Finlandia Hall, where Sokolov had given orchestral and solo performances on numerous occasions earlier in his career. Stupendous quantities of Italian marble and travertine had been used inside the building, and in the main auditorium vast wooden panels had been installed in an attempt to provide the best possible acoustics. Sadly this had been unsuccessful, and any number of adjustments had failed to improve matters. We heard about Finland's most famous architect, Alvar Aalto, and his grand scheme for a mammoth arts complex which never got off the ground. Helsinki was nevertheless well blessed with its National Theatre, Swedish Theatre, Opera House and the acoustically superior concert hall within the Sibelius Academy.

In the afternoon Elizabeth and I drove to Lohja, east of Helsinki and close to the Russian border, taking the scenic route through rolling pastureland and tiny hamlets and arriving with time to spare. Scouring the high street for a teashop, we finally resorted to a general store-cum-betting shop where a handful of locals watched horse racing on TV and the good humoured proprietor dispensed undrinkable beverages from thermos jugs.

The recital took place in a remarkably well equipped venue attached to a school. The promoter told us that Sokolov would be the first world-class artist to play the Laurentius Hall's brand new Steinway and I wondered how a concert hall in such a small provincial town could afford the expense. We sat behind a young woman who'd brought along a little girl of about four, probably imagining her daughter might leave the recital fired with enthusiasm and demanding piano lessons. Instead, the child performed silent gymnastics throughout, occasionally turning our way and draping herself over the back of her seat, heaving defeated sighs and staring dolefully at us for minutes on end. This was an irritating distraction, but we still had the rarefied atmosphere of the Sibelius Academy to enjoy two evenings later.

I spent the next day alone in Helsinki, visiting the botanical gardens and the Temppeliaukio Kirkko, known to tourists as the Rock Church. An extraordinary building blasted from a single block of granite, the walls were of unfinished rock, displaying an amazing array of natural colours, and the circular glass roof was topped by a huge dome of beaten copper. I'd read that a piano duo from Vienna would be playing a recital in the church that evening, and with nothing better to do I decided to attend. Harald Ossberger and his younger sidekick, Michael Lipp. executed a programme of pieces for four hands by Bartok, Schubert and Mozart with tremendous verve, although I couldn't help feeling sorry for the earnest young page turner who made a couple of premature moves and had his hand slapped away by a grim-faced Ossberger. The duo turned up at the Sibelius Academy the following evening to hear Sokolov, along with other musicians and wealthy patrons. The quality of Sokolov's playing was extraordinary, indescribable. Elizabeth was sandwiched between two critics, both of whom she knew, and was interested to read their reviews a day or so later. The Finnish critic, who followed the score for the first few minutes but soon felt the need to put the music aside and simply listen, wrote a lyrical piece in Helsinki's daily newspaper, whereas the Swedish critic, who was himself a professional organist, took a different view. Possibly because the organ provided a comparatively limited scope for sentiment, he declared himself uncomfortable with the degree of emotion in Sokolov's performance.

On a subsequent trip to Helsinki I decided to visit Porvoo, one of the oldest towns on the south coast of Finland. A popular tourist attraction in summer, Porvoo was almost deserted, its river frozen solid, and I wandered the narrow cobbled streets lined with wooden houses without seeing another soul. The old town was built around a hill, at the top of which stood a fifteenth century cathedral where a Palm Sunday service was in progress. Among the artisans' workshops I found a traditional Finnish tea room with a cluster of little tables just inside the entrance laden with plates of cakes and buns alongside steaming pots of tea and coffee, from which customers were invited to help themselves. There were several rooms in which to sit and I gravitated towards one decorated in dark blue and gold, containing an old piano and a wealth of Russian pre-Revolution memorabilia with framed photographs of the Romanovs ranged around the walls.

After the recital at the Sibelius Academy, Sokolov was explaining as delicately as possible to the organisers that the Academy's piano was now of a certain age, and by the following year it might have all but expired. He was suggesting that it might be an idea to hire a more robust instrument for his next recital, but as looks of consternation spread across the organisers' faces, he added with an impish grin, "Or maybe not!"

In June 2004 I travelled from Helsinki to Turku on the south west coast. The recital was in nearby Naantali, but there was a better chance of finding a room in Turku, so I equipped myself with a map and headed off to find somewhere to stay as quickly as possible. The first hotel I saw was a charming art nouveau house surrounded by a large garden full of mature trees and adorned with classical statues, a pool and a fountain. As I walked along the garden path I feared this place would probably be out of my league and very nearly did an about turn, but someone inside was making a rather nice job of a Brahms intermezzo and I was drawn like a magnet. A distinguished looking gentleman who turned out to be the hotel's owner was sitting at an upright piano in the entrance hall and stopped playing as I walked in. His wife, a meticulously groomed woman in her fifties, gave me a special weekend rate and showed me into a light and spacious room overlooking the rear garden. It had expensive brocade curtains, fancy bed linen, Persian rugs, a galaxy of mirrors and lamps, classy wallpaper and delicate gilded furniture decorated with flowers. The bathroom was equally attractive with many gadgets and toiletries on offer, including a mysterious sachet of powder with a glass of fizz illustrated on the front but no wording. I couldn't decide if it was intended to relieve indigestion or de-calcify dentures.

Turku was commemorating its 775th anniversary as Finland's oldest city, and it would have been an experience to see something of the celebrations, but Naantali was where I needed to be, and on my way out, the lady of the house mentioned that there was a local music festival. I told her I was just on my way to Naantali to hear Sokolov, and at the mention of his name she clutched her chest, let out a little yelp and told me he had stayed at her hotel on several occasions; he was a wonderful person, and the very thought of him gave her goose bumps. She'd entertained many famous artists over the years, including Sir Yehudi Menhuin, who appeared to have had a similar effect upon her. Producing an old visitors' book in which Sir Yehudi had written a glowing tribute to her hospitality, she recalled an evening when she'd decided to prepare a surprise salad for him after his performance, and he'd rewarded her with hugs and kisses.

It was impossible to imagine Sokolov behaving in such a fashion on account of a salad, or indeed anything else, but he'd clearly made a lasting impression on this lady. As I made my escape she begged me to be sure to tell him that Eva sent her warmest regards.

The bus to Naantali threaded its way along country roads between woodland and lush green meadows, and the town itself was a sleepy old place with mostly wooden houses and unmade gravel sidewalks. A long stretch of waterfront was occupied by an attractive marina in which dozens of small boats were moored, and a boarded promenade provided access to several attractive restaurants. The resort overlooked the Turku Archipelago, whose staggering 40,000 islands made it the world's largest, and on the opposite shore stood the President of Finland's summer residence. The sea was a dazzling sheet of blue and silver and the scent of lilacs danced on the breeze as I strolled along the boardwalk and found Elizabeth sunning herself. Behind us, high on a hill, stood the massive medieval Convent Church of Naantali, which was to be Sokolov's evening venue. We took a quick look inside and were met with the glorious sound of him rehearsing Bach's Partita No.6.

I'd expected the church acoustic to be less than ideal in such a large building, but the number of people crammed inside seemed to take care of any reverberation, and the whole performance was beyond beautiful. During the interval everyone moved outside to stroll among the lilacs and gaze out to sea, while girls in traditional costume served drinks and hot spiced buns. Afterwards we all stood in the sacristy surrounded by fifteenth century wall paintings. The massive door must have weighed tons, and it had correspondingly gigantic keys eighteen inches long. I picked one up to test its weight and Sokolov remarked that it could almost be the key to the city. When I told him where I was staying, his eyes lit up, so I delivered Eva's message. He looked mystified. "Who's Eva?" he asked. Eva would have been very disappointed if I'd told her that he was much more interested in finding out what I thought of Jaakko, the hotel's resident parrot. I said I'd seen no evidence of a parrot and Sokolov looked concerned, telling me that Jaakko had lived at the hotel for many years and was quite a character, entertaining guests with his ceaseless chatter. There was even a story that he'd managed to get himself into the local newspaper some years back when he'd unexpectedly laid an egg. I promised to find out what had happened to him, or her, as seemed more likely.

Elizabeth drove me back to the hotel and we walked in to find Jaakko, large as life, in a cage next to the reception desk. Apparently when I'd checked in earlier, he'd been enjoying his daily recreation period in a room at the rear where there were ladders and swings, a selection of toys and perching places with plenty of space for him to spread his wings. Although we thought the bird looked decidedly out of sorts, Elizabeth called the promoter, who was driving Sokolov back to Helsinki, so that he could be told that Jaakko was still alive and kicking. Sokolov was said to be delighted.

In March of the following year I travelled to Lahti in deep snow, the landscape a uniform dazzling white from the train window. My walk to the concert hall was along pavements of solid ice, largely well gritted but with a few untreated stretches which were terrifying to negotiate. The hall was a warm and welcoming sight and a fine example of Scandinavian ingenuity. Formerly a glass factory and retaining an original brick building as the ticket office and shop, the hall itself was the largest wooden building to be erected in Finland in the past hundred years. Now home to the Lahti Symphony Orchestra, the whole affair was encased in glass and it shone like a beacon at the edge of the lake.

That evening the orchestra was led by one of Sokolov's favourite conductors, Moshe Atzmon, and following a short orchestral piece by Schumann, the piano was wheeled out and members of the orchestra who weren't required for Mozart's Piano Concerto No.23 left the platform and stood on either side of the auditorium to listen. Sokolov's playing was of the utmost refinement and the applause was so prolonged and intense, there was no way he was going to escape without giving an encore. He chose one of Chopin's most seductive mazurkas, and the young female violinist sitting closest to him was visibly moved, eyes closed, swaying in her seat, completely transported. I didn't know it that night, but it was the last time I would ever hear Sokolov perform with an orchestra. I remained in my seat to hear a ravishing account of Brahms' 2nd Symphony, giving myself over to it entirely in the knowledge that this was just the beginning of my four day trip and I would meet Sokolov the following evening.

The temperature in Lahti ranged from minus eight degrees during the day to minus eighteen at night. By ten o'clock the next morning I was walking in brilliant sunshine by Lake Vesijärvi, a huge expanse of water stretching almost to the horizon. It was frozen over with a layer of snow a foot or so deep lying on its surface, through which wide channels had been cleared to accommodate skaters. Climbing a wooded hillside I crunched along happily, intending to visit the Museum of the Railway to St.Petersburg, but when I realised it would involve a steep and slippery descent I settled for the more easily accessible Museum of TV and Radio. That evening, Sokolov gave a solo recital in the Felix Krohne Hall, just across the street from my hotel, and he was in phenomenal form. I told him I was enjoying the experience of real winter, whereupon he began reminiscing about the lowest temperatures he'd ever experienced, finally deciding it must have been minus forty, somewhere in Russia.

A fresh layer of snow fell during the night, and as I sat quietly with a cup of coffee in the deserted dining room before helping myself to some food, I glanced out of the window and saw a coach pulling up outside, from which spilled at least forty men who dumped their luggage in the lobby, came barrelling into the dining room and besieged the breakfast buffet. I sat watching with a sinking heart as kitchen staff raced back and forth replenishing supplies, and by the time I got anywhere near the table, most of the containers were empty. Apparently they were members of a male voice choir from Aaland, a group of islands midway between Finland and Sweden, who were in Lahti to take part in an international choral competition.

The journey back to Helsinki was one of spellbinding beauty. I deliberately chose a slow train in order to take in the acres of virgin snow, the pine forests and lakes, the small wooden buildings set among fir trees, the lazily smoking chimneys and the solitary snowmen gazing out across the winter landscape. I had a ticket to hear an Armenian choir at the Uspenski Russian Cathedral that evening and was excited at the prospect of hearing a choir from eastern Europe performing in such an atmospheric setting. I'd envisaged at least a couple of dozen strapping chaps with combined voices to blow the roof off, so it was a disappointment when just half a dozen willowy young girls filed in and arranged themselves around the altar steps. They sang beautifully, starting with sacred music and ending with folk songs, but there simply weren't enough of them, and I came away wishing I'd stayed in Lahti to hear the coachload of hunks I'd breakfasted with competing in the preliminary round of the competition.

At Sokolov's recital in Lahti I'd thought he looked remarkably well, his usual pallor replaced by a pink-cheeked flush, but in truth he had a high temperature which was to seriously threaten the performance in Helsinki two evenings later. It was a very close call, but thankfully he recovered, and no one in the Sibelius Academy audience could possibly have guessed he'd been ill for the previous forty-eight hours.

My journey to Tammisaari in August 2005 began with a morning flight via Copenhagen, arriving in Helsinki in the late afternoon. Tammisaari was a seaside resort, so I'd had the good sense to pre-book a hotel room, and I was expected there between seven and eight o'clock in the evening. To my dismay the next train from Helsinki wasn't until nine and the journey would take two hours. Afraid that I might arrive to find someone else sleeping in my bed, I confided in a saintly railway employee who willingly rang the hotel to explain, receiving an assurance that my room was safe. After a tedious few hours at the station I was on my way, but storm clouds gathered as it grew dark, and by the time we reached Karjaa, where I changed trains just after ten o'clock, it was raining hard. Very few people left the train in Tammisaari, and those who did quickly disappeared, leaving me standing outside the deserted station building. I wandered through a quiet residential area with no one around to ask for help, but miraculously I was moving in the right direction and ten minutes later I came to a deserted market square, at the far end of which stood the Hotel Gustav Wasa. It was more of a classy B&B than a hotel, and the lady of the house produced a jug of chilled orange juice which I downed in seconds. The décor was stylish, very Scandinavian, every detail carefully considered. My room overlooked the square, which by the time I was ready for bed had been invaded by local youths who revved their motorbike engines for no apparent reason and did periodic circuits of the surrounding streets until the wee small hours, effectively ruining my night.

Breakfast was a DIY affair, but the kitchen provided the makings of every hot beverage imaginable. A huge glass fronted refrigerator contained a staggering array of juices, fresh fruit, cheeses, salad and numerous spreadables. Cereals were also available, along with fish, meat, eggs and warm rolls. I was in my element. Later I strolled along a tree-lined avenue to the seafront, where a stiff wind whipped up the surface of the water. Everything looked scrubbed clean, the air was crisp and clear and I relished being by the sea. The sound of children singing floated towards me on the wind and I came upon a purpose built stage near the seashore on which twenty or so little girls were being coached through vocal exercises by a young woman with a guitar. A cluster of parents stood nearby and they were soon joined by a more substantial crowd, several men in smart suits who kept consulting their watches, and finally someone carrying a TV camera. Something significant was obviously about to happen. One of the mothers told me the President of Finland, Tarja Halonen, was due to arrive at any moment to hear the girls sing some folk songs. It was the President's first visit to Tammisaari, and after the little concert she would be served with coffee at a floating restaurant (built to circumnavigate an alcohol ban in bygone days). A civic reception at the Town Hall would follow, then a lavish lunch, and at three o'clock she would be guest of honour at Sokolov's recital in Tammisaari Church.

I enquired at the railway station about a ticket to Rauma, another coastal town to the north, where I planned to be the following day. I was alarmed to discover there was no rail or bus link, and the only way to reach Rauma by train was to travel all the way back to Helsinki via Karjaa, then north to Tampere and across to the west coast, starting at seven in the morning and arriving at six in the evening. I was horrified, but someone behind me in the queue suggested travelling back to Karjaa and then to Turku, where I would surely find a bus to Rauma, reducing the journey time by several hours. Reassured, I returned to the hotel with a ticket to Turku in my pocket.

At Tammisaari Church, my concert ticket permitted me to sit anywhere in the sixteenth row, and I was early enough to grab one of two chairs placed in the aisle which provided the best view. A group of Swedes from my hotel were there and I also spotted a French girl I'd chatted with on the train journey to Tammisaari. A refined old gentleman spoke to me on the way in and took his place on the opposite side of the aisle. The white and gold interior of the church was dominated by three chandeliers and a handsome model of a tall ship suspended from the ceiling. The President arrived and took her seat at the front, whereupon Sokolov began a particularly impassioned performance. The account he gave of the Schubert sonata was one of surpassing beauty, and the piano sounded wonderful. As we stood at the interval and shuffled outside I noticed the elderly man was in tears. "Sokolov is definitely not of this world", he murmured. The French girl declared that she'd never heard anything so amazing, and the Swedes nodded in agreement. I sat down for the second half feeling as if I were among friends, but the recital was over by six o'clock which resulted in an evening of aimless wandering. The locals in the square threatened another sleepless night, but I fell asleep while watching an English detective drama with Finnish subtitles.

Heavy rain swept across southern Finland during the night and continued for the whole of the next day. By nine in the morning I was on my way to Rauma, and on arrival I was recommended to try a B&B on the outskirts. By the time I found Haus Anna, the only pair of shoes I had with me were completely waterlogged. Hunger drove me straight back out again and I headed towards the old town, which would have looked charming on a sunny day, but torrents of water filled the gutters and gushed from down pipes, swirling across the pavements like the tide. By now my jeans were saturated to mid-thigh and my shoes oozed bubbles of moisture with every step. I sought refuge in a tea room but felt too uncomfortable to sit for long and took a sandwich back to the B&B, where I stuffed newspaper into my shoes in the hope they might dry out a little before the concert.

My kindly hostess insisted on driving me to Rauma Hall and even came inside to ensure I had a ticket. The interior was surprisingly luxurious, and the interval lasted for almost forty minutes, during which time all seven hundred concertgoers were offered hot drinks and slices of cake. I was treated as a special guest and introduced to various local worthies as someone who'd attended more Sokolov performances than anyone else, which made me so happy I almost forgot that my feet were still wet. Back at Haus Anna my travelling clothes were beginning to dry out on their hangers and I woke very early to see sunshine streaming through the curtains. Breakfast was scheduled for seven o'clock, so I had an hour in which to throw on my damp gear and walk along the deserted main street of the old town with my camera. On my way back I passed a narrow stretch of water containing a humorous work of art comprising a small boat with a scary looking bogeyman fashioned out of metal leaning over the side, reaching out towards a terrified trio of matronly bathers in one piece swimsuits and bathing caps, standing waist deep in the water. After breakfast, despite my protestations I was driven to the bus station and waved off like a departing relative.

In Finland the summers were very short and the winters hung around for an awfully long time. In April 2009, when spring had already transformed the English landscape, I remember a dreary two and a half hour bus journey from Helsinki to Kotka, when the unattractive outer environs of the city gave way to waterlogged fields, still frozen lakes and rivers, battalions of morose fir trees and spindly birches. It rained all the way to Kotka and on arrival it turned to snow. With only two choices of hotel at the opposite ends of the price spectrum, I naturally decided on the cheap waterfront option, where I was given an unappealing room at the end of a long corridor. The shower looked unusable, the TV had only three local channels on offer and in the dining room I noticed the cereal containers had been left uncovered. I longed to be at the high end hotel, where for an extra thirty-five euros I would have been considerably more comfortable.

At Kotka Concert Hall my seat was in the eleventh row, but the platform was so low that anyone sitting further back than about row four had no chance of seeing the keyboard. This was disappointing, but Sokolov had been provided with an exceptionally fine piano possessing a bright, warm tone. Kotka was a relatively insignificant venue for Sokolov, but it produced an outstanding musical experience. The Beethoven sonatas were delivered with panache, the articulation razor-sharp, and the Schubert Gasteiner sonata exuded nobility and grandeur. The second movement, which began so primly, developed into something more impassioned each time I heard it. During the playful final movement someone collapsed in the centre of the auditorium, but Sokolov pressed on as if unaware of the drama taking place out there in the darkness. The mostly middle-aged and elderly audience remained silent throughout, even between movements, and three encores were sufficient for them. On the platform, behind the piano, was a free-standing curtained screen behind which Sokolov was obliged to retreat between curtain calls rather than walk off stage. It was a weird sort of arrangement, reminding me of a hospital examination room, where one could easily imagine items of clothing flying over the top at any moment.

Back at the hotel I found the long corridor containing my room swarming with rowdy teenage boys. All the doors to their rooms were wide open and there was a lot of horseplay and shouting. I walked past several shifty looking older men who were standing around looking like gangsters, and although it was almost midnight I sensed that this unsupervised commotion was likely to continue well into the early hours. This prospect, coupled with the tap-tapping of rain on the metal ledge outside my bedroom window, drove me to throw caution to the wind and all my belongings back into my bag. The bar downstairs, which doubled as a reception area, was about to close, and the girl on duty explained that my fellow guests were Greek students living at the hotel for a six week period. She suggested I simply ask them to be quiet, but imagining what might happen in the UK if I told a gang of teenage boys to restrain themselves, I decided not to try it out on this lot. Without even checking that there was a vacancy I left my key in my room and fled across town to the Sokos, shelled out ninety-two euros and was soon luxuriating in a spacious double with every possible comfort. It was exciting to turn up at a new hotel so late at night, whatever the cost, and I was delighted when the next morning the receptionist offered to telephone the hotel I'd abandoned and persuade the manager not to charge me.

For Sokolov's recital the following evening it was impossible to transport the splendid piano he'd played in Kotka, so it was necessary for him to play the Sibelius Academy's resident Steinway. Remembering his suggestion two years earlier that this piano was ready for retirement, it was no surprise when the demands of the Schubert sonata followed by six encores left the instrument in need of life support, and a relief the following year to find that a younger piano had been recruited to replace the geriatric grand.

In April 2012 I visited the architecturally cutting edge Helsinki Music Centre for the first time. Opened in August 2011 and more than twice the size of the Sibelius Academy's hall, the 1,700 seat Music Centre auditorium had already proved popular with orchestras, who valued the additional space and the fine acoustics. It was the first major piano recital to take place in the hall and a greatly anticipated event. Sokolov had been performing in Helsinki since 1969, chiefly at the Sibelius Academy to capacity audiences of 650, but now so many more people would get a chance to hear him. The new auditorium was steeply raked with a remarkably audience-friendly seating configuration, separated as it was into small, easily accessed areas (ideal for seat-hopping). Unfortunately for Sokolov, his preference for minimal lighting couldn't be met here, and he was also surrounded by permanent seating. I feared my place in the second row would be too close, but when the first bars of Rameau's Suite in D floated into the atmosphere with such purity and roundness of tone, I knew I was entering piano heaven. Sokolov brought so much fine detail to each piece, every ornament a tiny work of art. I was particularly struck by the delicacy of Les Soupirs, the glorious dexterity of Les Tourbillons, and I loved the sheer nonchalance with which he strolled into Les Cyclopes; I'd listened to many other versions of this piece and no one did it quite like him.

Helsinki Music Centre

The next day I travelled to Hameenlinna, birthplace of Sibelius, a hundred kilometres to the north, for a performance in the Verkatehdas, a former clothing factory which had been converted into an attractive 700 seat auditorium. There were no seats behind the platform, and characteristic of Finnish audiences, there was very little conversation as we settled into our seats. Everyone had been handed a free programme sheet on the way in, so there was an alarming amount of paper rustling as we sat waiting, but this was soon silenced when we were enveloped in a comforting blanket of darkness, leaving just a glimmer of light on the platform in which Sokolov could distance himself.

My second visit to the Helsinki Music Centre was in June 2018, when again I was in an excellent position to view the keyboard, and as the first fledgling notes took to the air they seemed to hover overhead, sweet and clear, almost liquefied. Sokolov proceeded to unfurl an immaculate Haydn programme: subtly accented, incisively articulated; an irresistible blend of dignity and humour much admired by the audience. The jewel in the crown that evening was Schubert's Four Impromptus Op.142. Sokolov's eloquently expressed reading of the first impromptu already had a special place in my heart, but in Helsinki I felt I was hearing the music from within, viewing its finer workings, grasping its true meaning. Then there was the visual spectacle of Sokolov's left hand crossing and re-crossing with mesmerising fluidity and grace. In his eternal pursuit of perfection, Sokolov placed every small detail before the listener with reverence and respect for the composer's intention. In the second impromptu those noble triple chords framed a middle section which could only be described as heroic, and Sokolov's artistry transformed both of these pieces into anthems for all that remained good in this life.

My soul having been thoroughly searched, there was something therapeutic about impromptu number three, but then the witching hour arrived when, at the wave of a magician's wand the hall held its breath, rational belief was suspended, and we allowed Sokolov to propel us into Schubert's fairy realm. How adroitly he described this land of make-believe with its mischievous game of hide-and-seek; the impudent little silences broken by forest murmurings, the twitch of greenery as the players attempted to conceal themselves, bright eyes darting among the foliage. Predictably, the final mad gallop generated a clamorous reaction from the audience. Unquestionably, these sublime forty minutes came from another galaxy in which Sokolov appeared to spend much of his time.

Standing outside the artist's room I glanced back along the corridor and it looked as if half of the audience had ventured backstage. Heaven knew how long it would take him to receive them all, but in the same way that he paid scrupulous attention to the very last notes of his performance, he would remain kind and courteous until the last worshipper had left the room.

10. SWEDEN

IT WAS SEVERAL years before I returned to Stockholm following my first Swedish adventure back in 1998. In October 2006 I heard Sokolov's first performance of a new Scriabin programme in the impressive neoclassical Konserthus: a monumental feat requiring massive energy and great technical skill. Sokolov opened with the romantic Prelude & Nocturne for the left hand Op.9, which I found disarming; likewise the powerful and passionate 3rd Sonata. Two playful poèmes preceded the 10th Sonata and the mesmerising and unsettling poème Vers la Flamme brought the programme to a turbulent conclusion. Most of the programme was new to me and there was certainly a lot to digest, but I leapt out of my seat at the end, along with the rest of the hall, to welcome this challenging newcomer.

I was drawn back to Stockholm many times in subsequent years, always in October, when the city's green spaces glowed with Autumn colour, and I spent many contented hours exploring the waterfront, following footpaths leading to some of the offshore islands and photographing the seasonal splendour. On the island of Skeppsholmen, I was jubilant when by pure chance I happened upon an exhibition of part of the Terracotta Army in an underground tunnel beneath the Museum of Far Eastern Antiquities: a subterranean setting ideal for the purpose.

I especially enjoyed roaming round the Nobel Park with its glimpses of blue water between the trees, and on the rare occasions when the weather was unfriendly I would visit the National Museum and spend time revisiting the works of my favourite Swedish artists, Carl Larsson and Anders Zorn. Half way through my progress around the gallery I always longed for a cup of coffee, but I was strangely intimidated by the museum's vast echoing atrium in which people queued for classy open sandwiches and mysterious fishy concoctions. Once served, they sat at large communal tables, and I could never quite pluck up the courage to join in.

The 2,370 seat Konserthus was routinely sold out whenever Sokolov was in town and he always received an ecstatic welcome. I remember hearing Chopin's Op.28 Preludes in 2007, when I sat close to the platform and watched two young men sitting behind the piano whose faces bore expressions of rapture throughout. Occasionally they exchanged glances and slowly shook their heads. They obviously knew the preludes intimately and it was evident that their expectations had been more than met. The following year, Sokolov played as an encore the daredevil Prelude Op.28/16, which caused pandemonium. Amid gales of laughter I got the feeling that had there been room enough to do so, the audience might have left their seats and danced round the auditorium, and it occurred to me how ridiculous was the claim by some that Sokolov showed little sense of humour in his playing. On a personal level, anyone acquainted with him could attest that he was full of fun, and he certainly generated plenty of it in Stockholm that night.

In 2015 the only seat available anywhere near the piano was in the front row, a little to the right, which would normally be considered much too close and on the wrong side of the keyboard, but by a stroke of good fortune the piano was positioned slightly off centre, my seat was aligned with the piano stool and the instrument was set well back from the platform edge. Suddenly everything was perfect. The piano sounded rich and velvety, nicely balanced, and remained in this blessed condition until the very last note; in fact such a reliable and steadfast instrument might have encouraged the tuner to go home long before the intermission, job done.

Taking Schubert's Sonata D784 firmly in hand Sokolov took every risk in the book, and the whole evening became an epic journey on which he barnstormed ahead and the rest of us followed in willing submission. We now had a finely balanced programme with a mighty sonata at either end, with shorter Schubert pieces and Chopin nocturnes providing a period of respite in between. Both sonatas were played with huge sustained power and uninhibited passion. Chopin's 2nd Sonata arrived like a tsunami, the first movement in particular played with a fearsome degree of attack, but the sound was never overpowering. I thought I already knew exactly what Sokolov was capable of, but this performance left me speechless. The sixth encore was Debussy's enigmatic Canope, played with delicacy and poise, at the end of which Sokolov, as if in slow motion, withdrew each hand separately from the keyboard and remained, head bowed, for several seconds before slowly rising from his seat. Even then, the audience seemed reluctant to break the spell.

In 2016 I sat behind a giant of a man whose head moved relentlessly from side to side like an inverted pendulum despite his perfectly clear view of the platform. Every other seat appeared to be occupied so I closed my eyes and accepted my fate. Sokolov opened his programme with Mozart's Sonata K545, which he might well have tackled at the age of four, but he displayed a stunning variety of touch and a captivating degree of playfulness with no hint of clockwork. The K475 Fantasy arrived rather like the bogeyman creeping into the nursery and Sokolov accentuated its darker corners with more than a hint of menace. During the K457 Sonata that followed, I realised that I didn't actually experience the Mozart; I simply stood back and admired it. Schumann, on the other hand, demanded to be lived.

Throughout the first half in particular, Sokolov was up against some stiff competition in the shape of heavy duty coughing from a couple of people who appeared to be competing with one another. I felt depressed as I took the same seat for the second half but hoped that Schumann would transport me. The hall's acoustic produced a supreme sound quality and the Arabeske washed over me like a soothing balm. As the heartbreakingly poignant ending approached, I prayed that Sokolov would be allowed to deliver it uninterrupted, and saints be praised, each final note was released into a blessed silence. Within seconds, a remarkably muscular Schumann Fantasy began its eventful journey, my eyes remained closed and I threw back my head to drink in this musical miracle, note by glorious note.

It was in Stockholm that I first heard the new Haydn programme in 2017. This time I was sitting up in the balcony, where the first notes were clad in a cathedral-like bloom as they ascended into the hall's cavernous and dimly lit interior, as if the audience might be in some lofty place of worship. With unwavering purity of tone the piano fulfilled its vital role, and the Haydn sonatas were as great a delight as I guessed they would be. There were plenty of opportunities to show off but none were taken; there was no over-embellishment, no unnecessary pressure applied. Sokolov displayed an admirable lightness of touch and delicacy of expression; even the darker accents were softly textured, as if touched by a velvet glove. Haydn's music was a succession of inescapably catchy melodies, sometimes tumbling over one another, vying for attention. The infectious Sonata No.47 presto, which I expected to be delivered at a moderate pace, was driven along at a deliciously fast tempo, but not too fast.

In the second half, the spirit of Beethoven's Op.111 Sonata burned as fiercely as ever. It had already achieved monolithic status, and one of Sokolov's jaw-dropping performances had already been captured on video for posterity. To deny his admirers the opportunity to own a recording of this unparalleled masterpiece would have been an act of lunacy at every level; there were too many people out there who never got to see a live performance. This was a musical journey like no other, and from a marketing viewpoint it would undoubtedly fly off the shelves. There were so many moments in this sonata that I devoured, savoured and dwelt upon long after the event: the sudden gear change towards the end of the first movement, the subsequent wondrous exploration of the heavens, the long succession of exquisite trills. Sokolov was in overdrive in Stockholm and the rapturous reception confirmed the unifying force he engendered. It was a memorable start to my autumn spree and a shining testament to Sokolov's one abiding goal in life, to faithfully serve his chosen (and for him still very much alive) composers.

In the following season Sokolov brought another winning programme to Stockholm, beginning with Beethoven's Sonata No.3 Op.2/3 which began and ended in the sunniest of moods. The vivacious final movement was thrillingly executed; the superabundance of lively runs and trills a delight to the ear, and for anyone lucky enough to watch those flying fingers, a dazzling sight to behold. As the music hurtled along, the articulation remained perfectly intact, and even in the swiftest passages time was allowed for subtler shadings. Conversely, the Eleven Bagatelles Op.119, with which the sonata was paired, began and ended in a more genteel fashion, but for the moment my main focus rested on the exquisitely drawn landscapes of the Schubert Impromptus Op.142. An amalgam of tenderness and passion pervaded the first two, and the opening bars of the final impromptu filled me with the sweetest anticipation, not only on account of the enchanting nature of the piece, but also the effect I knew it would have upon the audience. In the closing bars, as the music stopped in its tracks momentarily before Sokolov began the final chaotic scramble down the keyboard I held my breath and waited for the outcome, and sure enough the hall erupted. The encores received similarly wild acclaim and I was so happy that Sokolov included two Rameau pieces, which always seemed to be enormously popular with audiences. I hoped that he might one day revisit some of the other baroque treasures he'd played in the past. He had no real need to go in search of new encores to play; there was already a vast reservoir of show-stoppers in his back catalogue he could dip into if he wished.

The 2019 recital was stupendous, and from where I sat in the middle of the eleventh row, the sound quality was amazing. From the very first notes of Mozart's Fantasy & Fugue K394 the music soared untrammelled into the vast space above us, and a part of me went with it. As for Sonata No.11 K331 which followed, I should have known it wouldn't take long for Sokolov to enable me to view this work in a more favourable light. I realised I was already coming to terms with the first movement variations which I'd hitherto found tedious. Suddenly they began to distinguish themselves as separate entities, and I found myself rejoicing in their subtle variety. The alla Turca was perfectly balanced, and the Rondo K511 encapsulated everything I loved about Sokolov's playing.

Stockholm 2019

Brahms Op.118/Op.119 were nothing short of sensational: two collections of the most arresting pieces of music imaginable, by turns loosely woven, tightly bound, with passages of heart-melting fragility and titanic force. Although part of a whole, each segment was an individually wrapped priceless gift. It was another of those occasions where I felt Sokolov had gone 'beyond'. What I heard that night filled my heart to overflowing and fed my soul with a special kind of nourishment.

One of my earliest Swedish trips was to Gothenburg in 1998 for two performances of Brahms' 1st Piano Concerto with the city's symphony orchestra. On the flight from Heathrow I noticed a photograph of Sokolov in my neighbour's Swedish newspaper, and not only did he translate the most interesting bits of the accompanying article for me but gave me the paper to keep.

I'd set my heart on staying at a hotel described in the Rough Guide to Sweden as 'mediocre but amazingly cheap', but it was undergoing external repairs and surrounded by scaffolding and cement mixers, so I turned instead to a nearby establishment where a grand piano stood promisingly in the reception area. I asked to see their cheapest room and was shown into a gloomy little cell overlooking a brick wall. Three nights in there would surely have led to some sort of meltdown, so I opted for an equally dreary room at the front overlooking a square, across which trolley buses rattled at frequent intervals. I was warned that they ran all night and things could get pretty lively out there at the weekends, but I was tired of searching and took the room regardless.

The concert hall was situated at the far end of Avenyn, a fashionable shopping street. There was a mix-up with my ticket which resulted in me sitting in the middle of the front row, a less than ideal position from which to listen to an orchestra. Nevertheless, at seven-thirty, seated at the foot of the conductor's podium I heard a superb account of Ralph Vaughan Williams' Fantasia on a Theme of Thomas Tallis. A short Beethoven symphony followed, and after the interval I returned to my seat to find the piano had been positioned at the very edge of the platform and the piano stool was in direct line with my upturned face. As the unusually long introduction to the Brahms concerto began, Sokolov sat gripping the corners of the piano stool, waiting for his entrance, and apart from the occasional split second glance at the conductor, he kept his eyes firmly closed. His hands eventually came to rest in his lap but the fingers twitched with tension until it was time for him to lift them towards the keyboard and start playing. The music touched my heart and it was an experience I'll never forget.

In the artist's room I was lost for words, wishing I could think of something to say to him which hadn't already been said a thousand times. At that point, the conductor – a well-known name in the UK and someone with whom Sokolov enjoyed an excellent working relationship – appeared in the doorway. Sokolov introduced me to him, announcing that I'd come all the way from Birmingham especially to attend the two concerts, which the conductor initially took to be a joke. I assured him it was indeed the case and so did Sokolov, but he showed very little interest in speaking to me.

Sokolov asked about my hotel and I told him how ghastly it was, whereupon he asked the concert promoter's representative if she knew of any decent budget accommodation nearby. She mentioned a hotel on the waterfront where performers at the opera house enjoyed reduced room rates and suggested I try there next time I was in Gothenburg, but Sokolov insisted she telephone the hotel straight away to see if they had a room available. A few moments later I was fixed up with a double room overlooking the harbour for the following two nights at an amazingly low cost. I asked if I needed to masquerade as an opera singer and Sokolov gave his impression of me walking into the hotel singing arpeggios. I was anxious about escaping from my current hotel but he told me to simply tell them that my plans had changed.

Moving my belongings to Victor's Hotel the next morning was immensely satisfying. My new room was spacious and flooded with light; the furnishings were expensive, the bed was fit for a queen and the huge picture window provided a panoramic view of the harbour and canal. Uplifted by this unexpected turn of events, I wandered towards the cathedral and was drawn inside by the sound of a piano. An elderly Danish pianist was celebrating his 80th birthday by giving a recital of Chopin pieces, and the equally elderly Steinway sounded so wonderful that I stayed until the end. I continued walking, stopping to look round a handsome three masted barque which had been converted into a hotel, all the while wondering how I was going to occupy my time the following day, when I would be alone in Gothenburg with no concert to attend in the evening.

I had a more sensible seat a few rows back for the second concert and again it was an overwhelming experience. Sokolov knew how much I hated the prospect of staying over for an extra day, and when I told him I'd had all the pleasure but now came the pain, he looked sympathetic. Somehow I got through the final day, lingering over breakfast, walking through the city and along the canal, searching out all the green spaces I could find, listening to groups of children making music along Avenyn and to a full orchestra outside the concert hall. As darkness fell and the harbour lights came on, I stood at the window and acknowledged my good fortune, silently thanking Sokolov for using his influence to transform my living quarters and for making my world such an agreeable place.

It was four in the afternoon in November 2002 when I arrived at Västerås Airport, ninety kilometres west of Stockholm. The terminal building resembled a shed the size of a modest garden centre and space was at a premium, so all one hundred and eighty of us were obliged to form a queue out in the open and somehow I managed to be at the very end. It was almost dark, bitterly cold and starting to snow. Behind a glass partition stood another planeload of passengers waiting to board, and long before I got anywhere near passport control they were stampeding across the tarmac to grab the seats we'd just vacated. The one Ryanair flight per day in and out of the airport was apparently the main event, with just a handful of internal flights using smaller aircraft.

The majority of my fellow passengers boarded waiting coaches for the one and a half hour journey to Stockholm, but I on the other hand was exactly where I needed to be, and I felt rather smug as I watched them pulling out into the darkness. A short bus ride into the city took me to the splendid newly built Konserthus, which had been operational for just three weeks, and I was soon settled into the nearby Arkad, a charming, traditional hotel in a peaceful leafy square. It was so quiet that I wondered if I might be the only guest, but the next morning I found the breakfast room full of ladies of all ages who were using the hotel's conference facilities to discuss women's issues. It made a refreshing change from the usual couples, families and lone businessmen, and I enjoyed being surrounded by female chatter, whatever the language.

Muffled against the cold I set out for a wander, exhilarated to be in Sweden on such a bright morning with the prospect of another Sokolov experience before the day was over. Complimentary hot drinks and cookies were on offer at the hotel throughout the day, so I returned for a mid-morning treat and sat in the big bay window sipping coffee, dunking cookies and listening to Bach, while outside the hotel the finest fairylike flakes of snow fluttered gently through the trees. This was another of those intoxicating moments when I recognised what riches Sokolov had unwittingly brought to my door. Savouring these thoughts for as long as the coffee lasted, I turned to more practical matters, searched out an extra layer of clothing and set off with the intention of staying out for the rest of the day. I headed straight for the Svarta river and took a narrow winding path along the bank. The water was frozen over in places and a multitude of wildfowl sat huddled in patches of sunlight between the trees. A decorative dusting of powdery snow made everything look magical, and I felt like the luckiest person alive.

Across the river stood the 13th Century Domkyrkan, the final resting place of King Erik XIV, who reputedly died after eating pea soup laced with arsenic and whose feet were allegedly amputated because his coffin was too short. Behind the cathedral was the best preserved part of the old town: the Kyrkbacken, or church village, a homely hotch-potch of rough stone cottages and tiny rust-coloured wooden houses. Shortly before midday forty-seven bells rang out from the tower of the city hall, beginning with a sacred piece which contained beautiful harmonies and a surprising degree of expressiveness. The deepest bell then chimed the hour and there followed an incongruous selection from Phantom of the Opera. I continued towards the harbour front and the vast waters of Lake Malaren. In a lacerating wind I explored the lakeside in both directions for photographic possibilities, but my face became so contorted with the cold that I was forced to turn away from the water and seek refuge in the first building with public access in order to rearrange my frozen features.

At the Konserthus that evening, youthful and enthusiastic ushers were lined up in the foyer and the whole place buzzed with excitement. Sokolov was the first world-class artist to perform in the new hall, and many who had heard him in Stockholm earlier in the season had come along for a second helping. Shortly before the performance was due to begin I glanced at the monitor in the foyer which should have shown an empty platform, apart from the Steinway silently waiting to begin its work. Instead it revealed the keyboard lifted out of position, the tuner elbow deep amongst the instrument's innards, several people anxiously looking on, and in the foreground Sokolov, hands on hips, pacing back and forth, occasionally peering over the tuner's shoulder. Whatever the problem was, it delayed the start of the recital by twenty minutes.

The piano behaved remarkably well considering its newness and Sokolov's programme of works by Beethoven, Komitas and Prokofiev was received with enormous enthusiasm. Rhythmic handclapping and squeals of delight abounded, and a very happy concert manager escorted me to the artist's room as if I were a visiting royal, where I had a short but happy exchange with Sokolov.

Before leaving the Arkad the next day I sat in the bay window watching people arrive for the hotel's popular buffet lunch. They came in from the cold stamping their feet and were soon ladling out hearty soups, hacking away at crusty loaves, piling plates with fish, baked vegetables, salads and sauces. Had it been more affordable I might have joined the queue, but I contented myself with the tantalizing aromas drifting in my direction until it was time to re-engage with Ryanair.

In October 2008 I heard Sokolov play in Vara, a sleepy little Swedish town north-east of Gothenburg. The rail journey was a delight, passing lakes and forests, brightly painted summer homes among trees clad in autumn glory. There was no station as such in Vara, merely a halt, and Hotel Grepen was just a few minutes away. The town was surrounded by farmland, and the hotel logo showed an ancient rustic in a flat cap and wellies perched on a ladder leaning against a haystack. I expected converted stables or outhouses but the hotel consisted of four red brick single storey buildings, each containing six holiday apartments with huge kitchens. One of these was assigned to me, and my bedroom could have accommodated six people with ease.

On my walk to Vara Konserthus I passed large wooden homes, many painted dark red and ochre, with candles in the windows, glowing lanterns hanging outside, gardens crowded with heavily laden apple trees and late flowering shrubs. The hall was surprisingly plush with a restaurant and lecture room in which enthusiasts were receiving a talk about the works Sokolov was to perform. The auditorium had 540 seats and just twelve rows on the ground floor. My place was located on the right side of the eleventh, but shortly before the recital began I managed to exchange it for a seat in the middle of the front row. If anything, it was too close for comfort, but on balance I was much happier there. The piano produced some odd sounds when certain notes seemed unable to die away naturally, but the performance of Mozart Sonatas K280 & K332 followed by Beethoven Sonatas Op.2/2 & Op.27/1 topped with a string of sensational Chopin encores left the audience reeling.

Perhaps my favourite small town experience in Sweden came in October 2011, when I travelled to Gävle, 250 kilometres north of Stockholm, to hear Sokolov's new Brahms programme for the first time. The town possessed an attractive 800 seat concert hall beside a rushing river, but only 350 tickets had been sold. Apparently very few piano recitals took place there, which explained the pre-concert announcements in Swedish and English highlighting not only the importance of switching off mobiles and refraining from the use of cameras, but also suggesting the audience do their best not to cough, to reserve their applause until the end of each half of the programme and, if they wished, to show plenty of appreciation at the end of the recital in view of Mr Sokolov's famously generous supply of encores. It felt rather like being addressed at a school assembly, but my goodness it had the required effect, and I would have been happy to sit through something similar at the start of every performance I attended.

The entire Bach programme was now honed to perfection, the second movement of the Italian Concerto having taken on a beautiful burnished quality, the outer movements tackled with renewed vigour, and the French Overture giving a clear impression of having been finely tuned. At the start of each new season, despite Sokolov having invested much time and energy on his new material, the long standing element of his programme never became routine.

After the interval came the long awaited Brahms Variations on a Theme by Handel, which I knew would be remarkable, but the reality was even greater. After the bell-like beauty of the opening theme we were gradually caught up in a whirlwind, momentarily brought back to earth and finally swept away by a tornado. During the ninth variation I mused upon one of my impossible dreams and wondered what kind of monumental experience it might have been to hear Sokolov play Mussorgsky's Pictures at an Exhibition. The tension built steadily, and by the end of the fugue my excitement had reached the kind of level I experienced on first hearing Sokolov play Prokofiev's 7th Sonata when I felt in need of a defibrillator. In Gävle I felt an urge to clap, shout, jump out of my seat (someone directly behind me groaned with pleasure) but we had to contain ourselves on account of Sokolov's requirement to press on with the Op.117 Intermezzi without seeking applause.

Stockholm 2017

11. NORWAY

FROM THE AIR, Norway's offshore islands were partially obscured by a layer of thinly teased out cotton wool cloud, through which I glimpsed what looked like waterways with amazingly tight twists and turns winding their way along narrow velvety green valleys towards the sea. The local bus service from the airport meandered through several villages and into the suburbs of Stavanger as if it had all the time in the world, providing ample opportunity to admire the scenery on what must have been one of the most picturesque journeys between airport and city I could ever remember. Vast stretches of water were never far away, edged with woodland and astonishingly green hillsides dotted with brightly painted dwellings.

The bus dropped me alongside the city's central lake which separated the business quarter from the main shopping area and harbour. I was soon swept into a heaving mass of Saturday afternoon shoppers surging along the narrow streets and spilling out onto the waterfront. A colourful assortment of ferries and fishing boats bobbed in the harbour and a cluster of market stalls on the quayside displayed some of the most robust looking vegetables I'd ever seen. All of this had me reaching for my camera before I'd even thought about finding somewhere to stay. I could already sense a relaxed, jolly atmosphere and couldn't wait to dump my bag somewhere, make myself look less like a visitor and become a part of it all for the next twenty-four hours. At the Tourist Office a prominently displayed poster announced to the citizens of Stavanger that one of the world's greatest living concert pianists was in their midst, but as I was later to discover, the poster had made little impact.

The Rough Guide to Scandinavia had warned that the only budget accommodation in Stavanger was close to the harbour, where all the bars and clubs remained open until two in the morning and were frequented by roistering sailors, fishermen and oil refinery workers. I decided to avoid this lively option and chose instead to spend my one night at the Grand Hotel, which hardly lived up to its name but nevertheless provided a good breakfast, free tea and coffee and a DIY waffle making facility which I tried and failed to come to terms with.

I walked to the far side of the harbour where, behind a row of 19th century storehouses, lay Old Stavanger, a network of narrow cobbled lanes containing an area of clapboard housing originally inhabited by seafarers and cannery workers, now immaculately preserved as a quiet residential quarter. Each house was painted white, with a gas lamp hanging outside and a pretty terraced garden where orange nasturtiums ran riot around picket fences. In every suitable spot there was a bench from which to enjoy a view of the harbour, and apart from a couple of low key antique shops hidden away in side streets and one or two artisans' workshops, there was no other hint of commercialism. It was good to discover such a peaceful place so close to the bustle of the quayside.

Beyond Old Stavanger lay Bjergsted Park, in whose gardens stood the Konserthus. On arrival that evening I met the Norwegian concert promoter who had accompanied Sokolov on his two week tour of the country, performing to packed houses in seven cities as far north as Trondheim. Stavanger was the last engagement of the tour, and although Sokolov had received tumultuous receptions wherever he'd played, unfortunately in Stavanger the recital had been omitted from the Konserthus calendar. The original intention had been to use a more intimate venue and the decision to switch to the larger hall at short notice had not been followed up with the necessary publicity. Apart from displaying a few posters here and there, little else appeared to have been done and this was reflected in the embarrassingly small audience. The hall's 1,060 seats looked barely a quarter occupied but the public could not have been more attentive or enthusiastic and the recital was a resounding success.

A Russian lady related to Prokofiev was in ecstasies in the artist's room and asked the director to take a group photograph of herself and younger members of her family with Sokolov. The director suggested they all say 'cheese' in Russian, but Sokolov pointed out that the Russian word for cheese would not produce a suitable facial expression. As soon as they'd gone, Sokolov tackled the director head on and asked how many tickets had been sold. "About two hundred I think" came the sheepish reply. In an attempt to lighten the atmosphere I joked with Sokolov, "Aren't you glad I came along to make up the numbers?" "Oh yes!" he laughed. "Two hundred and *one* – big deal!" I left the room to find the promoter patiently nibbling a pear and he invited me to help myself from the fruit bowl. Sokolov followed me out and chose an apple. I slipped a banana into my handbag to supplement my breakfast cereals the next morning.

I encountered no badly behaved sailors on my walk back to the Grand, but a large number of Stavanger's younger generation had gathered on the harbour, already well tanked up. Back at the hotel, apart from the occasional burst of hysterical laughter from the next room and a few random screams, I had a reasonably peaceful night. Before leaving for the airport on Sunday I took a final stroll round the harbour, and at eleven o'clock I joined the throng making their way into the 12th century Domkirke. The church bells played the first few bars of the opening hymn as we filed in, and in stark contrast to the Konserthus the night before, the church was packed to capacity. The choir and organ sounded marvellous, the responses were beautifully sung by the congregation and the service was interspersed with uplifting musical interludes, including a lovely cello solo. The sermon was delivered by a female minister with such a compelling voice and hypnotic delivery that an understanding of the words seemed irrelevant.

At the airport later that afternoon as I sat reading in the departure lounge near the window, Sokolov came and stood beside me, watching the aircraft manoeuvres outside. He hadn't noticed me and I decided not to invade his privacy, but as he moved away he spotted me and confirmed that he too was flying to Copenhagen for a connection to the Czech Republic, where he was to play in Brno the following evening. Our flight was delayed and he plodded impatiently back and forth, now and then glancing my way and shrugging. From time to time he leant both elbows on the departure desk and stared intently at the empty space behind it, as if deep concentration on his part might result in the appearance of a member of staff. In the meantime I'd struck up a conversation with someone who was asking what had brought me to Stavanger. I wanted to say, "Well, you see that man over there by the desk? That ordinary looking man in a raincoat.....?" but I resisted the temptation.

All of the subsequent Norwegian recitals I attended were in Oslo, starting in 2015. I'll never forget the moment I turned a corner and saw for the first time the Opera House, an extraordinary building designed to resemble an iceberg, standing in late afternoon sunlight beside a glittering blue waterfront. As I walked across the harbour I was fired up with the usual blend of elation at simply being there and anticipation of what was to come. Inside the oak lined auditorium, behind the piano was a huge black backdrop overlaid with rippling grey cloud shapes. Emphasised by the dimness of the lighting throughout the hall, Sokolov's silver hair shone in the semi-darkness and he seemed to take on an almost godlike presence, perched among the clouds, transmitting directly from the firmament.

A brand new Steinway was put through its paces that evening, and it acquitted itself admirably. The already well established Schubert programme came first, and in the second half there were Chopin Nocturnes and the formidable 2nd Sonata, which Sokolov had played and recorded in the distant past, but on witnessing my first live performance I found the whole piece took on another dimension, and I was riveted from start to finish. The precision with which he tore through the final flurrying presto was astounding. During the first half I wondered if the audience might be hard to please, but I'd forgotten how remarkably generous Scandinavian audiences can be and the response couldn't have been warmer.

Oslo Opera House

The performance ended at nine o'clock so there was plenty of time to encourage a group of young Norwegian admirers to meet Sokolov for the first time. But anyone hoping to shake the celestial hand was in for a disappointment. Apparently there was no procedure in place to allow public access to performers and so we were directed to the outside stage entrance, which was in fact locked and unmanned. A great pity, but for those unfortunates who didn't get to shake that hand, the Sokolov mystique remained intact for another occasion.

The following year's recital in Oslo was the beginning of the new season for me. I longed to hear my beloved Schumann Fantasy again after the summer break, but I felt less enthusiastic at the prospect of the new Mozart programme. Contrary to expectations it turned out to be a delightful experience, and from the opening bars of the K545 Sonata I was intoxicated, not so much by the music itself but by what Sokolov actually did with it. The wealth of subtlety and nuance he brought to this comparatively simple sonata exceeded all imaginings, and my lack of emotional involvement allowed me to focus purely on the beauty and refinement of the playing. He certainly knew how to create an atmosphere in the K475 Fantasy which followed, and together with the K457 Sonata, all three pieces blended together seamlessly. The audience reaction was swift, immense, with many up on their feet, and a surge of heartfelt cheering rang out across the auditorium. By now I was eating my words, indeed choking on them, in the certain knowledge that much pleasure would be derived from Sokolov's Mozart in the coming months. In the second half I became happily immersed in the glories of Schumann and the encores ended with a gorgeously rendered Canope by Debussy. I heard someone remark that hearing that piece alone had been worth the cost of his ticket.

In 2017 the cloudlike projection behind the piano had disappeared, leaving the audience with a blank canvas and no distractions. Haydn's music poured out like a succession of courtly dances, in the midst of which came the suggestion of a spirited sailor's hornpipe which provided a comic touch. The B minor presto sounded faster than ever as Sokolov hurtled off like a getaway driver, but there were no blurred outlines and every note was distinct. It was a foregone conclusion that Beethoven's Op.111 would be stunning. The opening bars suggested a gladiatorial thrust, as if Sokolov was striding into an arena to face some kind of formidable challenge. I was always so forcibly drawn into each distinctive part of this sonata that only when it was over could I step back and marvel at the architectural grandeur and the sheer scale of this splendid creation. The closing moments of the first movement were never far from my consciousness; the grinding bass notes which heralded the final few minutes of this heavenly voyage haunted my dreams. The entire audience rose to its feet at the end of the main programme and continued to do so after each encore. I was reminded that twenty years before this night, as I watched Sokolov walk towards the piano for the first time, my impression had been that he seemed aloof, detached, but as soon as he sat down to play I realised he had no need to even flutter an eyelash to encourage his audience to sit up and take notice.

A year later a friendly, animated audience with an unusually high percentage of young people and musicians were gathered in the Opera House to hear what Sokolov had brought for their delectation that season. At some venues the piano would sit resplendent at the edge of the platform, its illuminated surfaces gleaming, as if poised to knock everyone's socks off. Some pianos lived up to expectations but others didn't always sound as good as they looked. The unassuming instrument in Oslo that evening remained modestly in the shadows with just a glimmer of light directed at the keyboard, but oh boy did it deliver the goods!

I'd heard Sokolov's Beethoven Sonata No.3 Op.2/3 on numerous occasions in 1998/99 and I expected few surprises, but as the first movement unfolded I could almost imagine it to be something quite new. Sokolov projected the full quota of youthful exuberance yet seemed to temper it with an occasional restraining hand. In the second movement he created a mysterious, at times almost sinister quality which lingered like incense, and the dramatic bass notes were accentuated as only he knew how. There was so much to love about this sonata: the short but luscious waltz sequence at the heart of the third movement thrilled me to the bone, and the closing movement was an expression of boundless joy which Sokolov captured to perfection.

The Eleven Bagatelles Op.119 were new to Sokolov, and I could well understand why he'd chosen to include them. Despite one or two possessing a deceptively childlike simplicity, they covered a lot of ground and were far from being inconsequential trifles. The final piece had an air of thanksgiving about it, prompting me to give silent thanks to him for revisiting a great sonata and adding this set of bagatelles, which doubtless he would hone, refine and subtly reshape as the season progressed.

As he worked his way through a diverse collection of encores it struck me that he could travel from Rameau to Scriabin with a couple of intermediate stops along the way, seamlessly entering each distinctive soundworld as if he'd been playing works by that particular composer all evening, and what we were hearing was merely a part of the whole.

12. DENMARK

IT WAS CLOSE to midnight when I arrived in Copenhagen city centre for my first concert experience in Denmark. I met with the usual collection of inebriates clustered round the railway station entrance but soon found the Hotel Centrum in a neighbouring street. Dismayed to find the reception area crowded with teenagers, I explained to the receptionist that it had been a long day and I needed a quiet room, so she sent me up to the top floor, which was so eerily quiet I got the feeling I was the only one up there. My room had an unfinished look about it, having plain white walls and bed linen with no adornment of any kind, but I slept undisturbed.

The next morning I found the breakfast room occupied by a gang of noisy schoolboys sporting back-to-front baseball caps and trailing bootlaces, together with a similar number of cocky teenage girls with strident voices. The accompanying teachers looked barely a year or two older than their charges and appeared to exercise little control. Amongst all the shouting and showing off, every trip I made to the buffet table required an iron will, nimble footwork and the skilful employment of elbows.

Happy to escape into the fresh air I wandered along the waterfront and through the botanical gardens before preparing for Sokolov's recital at the Louisiana Museum of Modern Art, which was situated in a small coastal town twenty miles north of Copenhagen. I caught a train and arrived in Humlebaek shortly before dusk. The museum was a ten minute walk away, and at the box office I discovered that my ticket had been overlooked. After a few tense moments I was given one of three remaining unsold places at the very back of the concert room. The ticket provided free admission to a temporary exhibition of works by René Magritte, which seemed like a marvellous stroke of luck and kept me occupied for an hour or so. With time still to spare I contemplated the restaurant, where concertgoers were enjoying candlelit meals, but instead I took my home-made sandwiches outside and sat in the sculpture garden, gazing out across the water and relishing the prospect of the evening ahead.

As soon as the concert room opened I looked for my place and was so disappointed that I dashed back to the box office in the hope of an unclaimed seat in a better position. I had to retrace my steps through the restaurant, the museum shop and countless exhibition rooms and was rewarded with a premium seat in the middle of the second row. Overjoyed, I hurried back but took a wrong turn and got hopelessly lost. Mindful that the recital was about to begin I begged a member of staff to point me in the right direction. He looked at his watch, shook his head doubtfully, grabbed my hand and yanked me through a glass door out into the pitch black night, hauling me through a belt of trees surrounding the sculpture garden and across a long stretch of rough grass. He was considerably older than me but remarkably sure footed, and the dear man delivered me into the concert room within seconds of Sokolov's entrance.

The piano was stationed at the foot of a huge and hectic abstract painting in primary colours by the American artist, Sam Francis. I was beside myself with relief and the programme of works by Froberger, Brahms and Ravel was a complete *tour de force,* generating a wild response from the audience. The concert director handed me a generous glass of red wine as I entered the artist's room and I quickly knocked it back for fear of missing my train.

After such an enjoyable experience at this distinctive and atmospheric venue, I'm not sure why I waited another twenty years before returning there in 2019. It was my first concert of the autumn and I'd had mixed feelings about Sokolov's choice of Mozart to accompany Brahms for the new season, however I'd done some homework on YouTube and discovered that the Prelude (Fantasie) & Fugue KV394 sounded intriguing and quite unlike Mozart, and the Rondo KV511 was a work of immense beauty. I was already familiar with Sonata No.11 KV331, so I arrived in Louisiana feeling confident that Sokolov would work wonders.

At eight o'clock he descended the staircase in a corner of the room and the 267 seat setting was so intimate, it was as if a group of friends had gathered there for an impromptu soirée. Sokolov proceeded to reveal the wealth of surprises contained in Mozart's Prelude & Fugue in C major, and as the music took its first dramatic turn, the exuberant colours of the backdrop became muted in the presence of such power and urgency. The swift transition from the mighty fugue to the sweetly expressed opening bars of the sonata provided such a stark contrast, it was as if the piano had somehow been replaced by a completely different instrument. The alla Turca was played with delicious bite, and as for the Rondo, it sounded as if Mozart had written it especially for Sokolov to play. The Brahms was predictably stunning and the combination of silent audience, excellent piano and fine acoustic provided everything I needed. In the knowledge that I'd hear it all again in Stockholm two evenings later, I left Denmark with a contented heart and a renewed sense of anticipation.

In October 2010, I heard Sokolov perform in Copenhagen itself. I travelled there directly from Stockholm, and instead of flying I took the six hour train journey which took me across the Oresund bridge, said to be the longest road and rail bridge in Europe. Crossing vast stretches of water, we passed blue lakes, pine forests and belts of fir trees, the Autumn landscape clad in a thin mantle of snow.

The recital took place in the city's newly built ultra modern Danish Radio Concert House, a massive glass-roofed cube clad in mesh which glowed brilliant blue at night and contained three recording studios in addition to the 1,800 seat auditorium. The interior was vast and impressive with blocks of seating completely encircling the platform. Sokolov's programme was a continuation of Bach's Partita No.2 and Brahms Fantasies Op.116. The newcomer was Schumann, with his hugely entertaining Humoreske Op.20 and Four Piano Pieces Op.32, ending with the Fughette: furtive, almost sinister but ultimately emerging into the light.

13. NETHERLANDS

I SET OFF for Amsterdam in March 1999 with a room booked for the second night but not the first, so it was necessary to join a long queue spilling out of the tourist office in the city's Central Railway Station. It took forty-five minutes to reach the desk, where I learned there was no budget accommodation available in Amsterdam that night, the nearest option being Rotterdam, over an hour away by train. I had no choice but to take it, and by the time I arrived in Rotterdam it was already dark. A local man cautioned me that the area was notorious for pickpockets and it would be safer to take a tram rather than walk to my hotel. I was touched when he also reminded me to look left when crossing the street; valuable advice in a city of 800,000 bicycles.

As the tram snaked along shabby windswept thoroughfares strewn with litter and graffiti I had visions of spending the night in a den full of drunken sailors, but fifteen minutes later I found the hotel beside a quiet stretch of canal, where the friendly manager greeted me with a pot of tea and a cosy chat. He seemed delighted that the Tourist Office had sent someone civilised to stay at his establishment, telling me that all manner of undesirables crossed his threshold on a nightly basis. This was confirmed when at three in the morning a crowd of noisy guests came thundering up the stairs like a herd of buffalo and continued partying in their rooms.

By eleven the next morning I was back in Amsterdam, and I found my hotel very close to the famous Concertgebouw. I'd booked a suspiciously cheap room without facilities, but it was so conveniently situated I was prepared to overlook any shortcomings. I rang the bell and was greeted from a second floor window by a smiling Afro-Caribbean face framed by a shower of dreadlocks, the owner of which came bounding downstairs to greet me. It soon became apparent that his laid- back establishment was ideally suited to back-packing types. Rucksacks were piled on every landing, young people wandered from room to room in varying states of undress, and the freshly laundered bedsheets were draped over the bannisters to dry in the stairwell. I was ushered into a room containing an iron bedstead with a beastly mattress, a painted wooden cupboard with two wire hangers, a rickety old table and chair which would have looked more at home in a skip (probably where they came from in the first place) and a horribly stained washbasin with a large piece missing. The walls were bare apart from a small rectangle of mist and mottle which at some stage must have been a mirror. It was certainly not a room in which to linger for very long, but I was content; I could see the concert hall from my window with Sokolov's name plastered across the front and that was good enough for me.

A single bulb in the middle of an extraordinarily high ceiling gave out nothing more than a reluctant glimmer, so I was obliged to apply my make up in a laundry-cum-shower room in the company of two good-natured teenage girls with flawless complexions and lustrous hair who stood around in their underwear, their finely toned limbs displaying not a single blemish. I felt as old as the hills.

Later, across the street in the Concertgebouw the auditorium was full to bursting, ready for Sokolov's programme of works by Byrd, Beethoven and Ravel. In order to reach the platform he had to descend twenty-six steep red-carpeted stairs in full view of the audience of just under 2,000 and climb back up again each time he

Concertgebouw Amsterdam

left the piano. For someone who'd already expended a vast amount of energy in his performance, this was an additional workout which he repeated countless times to receive applause and deliver his customary six encores. He was in magnificent form and the audience was on its feet at every possible opportunity. Afterwards, the big cheese in Dutch concert promotion expressed his satisfaction with the evening by entertaining the public waiting in the corridor outside Sokolov's room with a burst of spirited yodelling which rang round the building.

There was no dining room at my hotel, so breakfast was served on a tray, and I was agreeably surprised to receive a pot of freshly brewed tea, warm toast, jam, cheese, ham and a lightly boiled egg. There was even an embroidered tray cloth and a silver cruet, and I wondered if these refinements were standard issue or merely set aside for stray pensioners.

The following year I arrived in the city on a dreary, wet Sunday afternoon in November, and as I stood outside the station trying to fathom the complicated tram zone system, a tall, well turned out young man of African extraction offered to help. He also invited me to drink a cup of coffee with him, so as it was raining and I had nothing better to do, I accepted. What a lark, I thought. Haven't been in Amsterdam more than five minutes and I've pulled already! As we made for a nearby coffee shop I expressed the hope that I'd be able to smoke in there, which in one of the major drug capitals of Europe meant only one thing. He offered to procure some kind of substance on my behalf, but I quickly explained that all I needed was an innocent cigarette. As we drank our beverages he told me that in African culture, drinking coffee with a member of the opposite sex had significant meaning, which seemed rather far-fetched, and he went on to suggest we locate my hotel and spend the afternoon getting better acquainted. Inwardly splitting my sides I primly reminded him that I was English and old enough to be his mother, to which he countered, "But this is Amsterdam, and in any case I love old people". Back at the tram stop he demanded a goodbye kiss, but I told him we didn't go in for that sort of thing in England, and without assistance I soon found my hotel, a friendly place run on informal lines and just a short distance from the concert hall.

Some venues always seemed to be charged with a special kind of excitement and anticipation before Sokolov's performances began, and Amsterdam's regal Concertgebouw was the perfect example. Its gilded interior and acres of red carpet added to the sense of occasion, and I had the privilege of being allocated the seat which Queen Juliana occupied whenever she attended concerts there, right in the centre of the balcony with an expansive view of the proceedings. As Sokolov appeared at the top of the staircase the tremendous surge of affection which swept through the audience and onto the platform was enough to inspire anyone to give a sensational performance. His programme comprised Schumann's Arabeske, Three Novelettes and the Geister Variations, Franck's Prelude, Chorale & Fugue and ten Chopin Mazurkas, which his adoring audience received with immense gratitude.

The next morning I moved on to Arnhem, the centre of which looked bleak and uninteresting, the market square deserted and all the churches locked. I took a bus ride out to the village of Oosterbeek, walking from there to the Airborne War Cemetery, a peaceful place in a rural setting where it felt appropriate to be, so close to Remembrance Sunday. In the evening, Sokolov filled Arnhem's Musis Sacrum with an infinite variety of tonal colour and content, from exquisite miniatures to broad canvases, transforming Franck's Chorale, Prelude & Fugue into something close to a religious experience.

In February 2003 I travelled to the Netherlands for two concerts, and although I'd recently recovered from a chest virus I was still plagued by an irritating cough. I was terrified that I might cause a disturbance during one or both of the performances and spent a terrible first night in a cold room with just a cotton sheet, a summer duvet and a brute of a pillow. My room was not only positioned next to an ancient elevator and creaky staircase, both of which were in frequent use during the night, but also directly above the hotel bar which was open round the clock.

The next day was sunny, but a biting wind drove me into the Rijksmuseum, whose not inconsiderable entrance fee was a complete waste. I could scarcely haul myself from room to room, my eyes refused to focus on the paintings and I suffered several embarrassing fits of coughing. That morning I'd complained about the lack of heating and unsatisfactory bedding, and when I returned to the hotel at lunchtime I found a selection of pillows, an extra duvet and a noticeable increase in temperature in my room, so I crawled into bed and pondered the question of where I might be sitting that evening.

I'd hoped my seat would be at the end of a row, with ease of exit in the event of a sudden urge to cough, but again it was in the centre of the front row of the balcony; normally a seat to die for but in my state of health out of the question. At eight o'clock I stood in the balcony clutching a bottle of water and a bag of cough pastilles, waiting for the front row to assemble. I could see that my empty seat half way along was sandwiched between the big Dutch cheese and Leif Ove Andsnes, Norway's number one concert pianist, and in happier circumstances I would have been honoured to sit there. As soon as everyone was seated I quietly explained my predicament to the man on the end of the row and asked him to pass the message along the line in the hope that the eleven people to the left of where I should be sitting would each move along one place so that I could take the end seat. In the manner of Chinese whispers, by the time the message reached the promoter it had probably been reduced to the bare bones of a random female wishing to sit at the end of the row. This was the one row of seats in the hall reserved for promotion personnel, members of the press, invited guests and royalty, so there was understandable reluctance to allow the spare seat to be taken by some unknown straggler, in case Sokolov's guest arrived at the last minute. I hovered in the gangway until the lights were dimmed and finally they all shuffled along, allowing me to sit down.

At the interval, on his way out of the auditorium the promoter told me I was extremely lucky to get that seat and it had only been possible because a guest of Sokolov's hadn't turned up. When I told him who I was he almost fell over. "Ah, so YOU are the friend of Grisha's?" he exclaimed, shaking my hand energetically. "You will come and speak to him afterwards, yes?" I responded casually, "Oh, I expect so" but thought just you try and stop me, sunshine.

The evening was a phenomenal success, my cough was effectively suppressed, the artist's room overflowed with admirers and I was invited to join the promoter and a group of colleagues for a celebratory meal in a nearby restaurant, leaving Sokolov to return to the tranquillity of his hotel room. As soon as the promoter and his entourage entered the restaurant, the staff stood to attention.

A balcony table had been prepared for us, from which we were in a position to survey the other diners. It was almost midnight and I'd eaten little since breakfast, but for once I ordered something sensible and drank only water, unlike the rest of the party who began consuming trays of oysters, washed down with copious quantities of vodka. I looked on in amazement as they all ploughed through colossal main courses and the promoter, the only one among us capable of facing a dessert, polished off a towering creation scattered with chocolate, vanilla and strawberry hearts: a gesture to Valentine's Day.

I reminded the promoter of his impromptu yodelling performance outside the artist's room four years earlier and he looked mortified. "Oh my God, you heard me yodelling?", he cried. "Do you think Grisha heard me?" I said I wouldn't be surprised if the whole of Amsterdam had heard him, and as if to reassure himself that he'd not lost his touch, he tentatively brought forth a melodious peal of notes redolent of alpine pastures, drawing a ripple of applause from the tables below. Encouraged by the warm reception and emboldened by the vodka he leapt to his feet, launched into a full-throated bravura performance and had the restaurant in uproar.

The gathering broke up at two-thirty and I was untroubled by the lateness of the hour after such a memorable evening; in any case I was in no rush to get to Utrecht the next day. When I did arrive there I noticed far fewer British tourists, and the sunken canals, narrow streets and quirky little shops were most agreeable, rather like Amsterdam in miniature. On the downside, the central hotels were very expensive, and unless I was prepared to sleep in a hostel dormitory I needed to go further afield to find anything remotely affordable. I settled for a two star B&B on the edge of town, a half hour trek from the centre, occupying two old properties facing a railway line. My billet was in the house next door to the main building and I climbed the stairs feeling dispirited. The contents of my room were shabby and in poor repair; an undersized and carelessly made bed was wedged beneath the window. The house was silent and I feared I might be the sole occupant. With a sinking heart I noticed the washbasin was smeared with someone else's soap and toothpaste and I dissolved into tears.

In the late afternoon I did a trial run by bus to the Musikcentrum to see how long it would take, drank consoling quantities of tea and shopped around for comfort food to take back to my room. As I ate, the house began to show signs of life, and despite much banging and crashing around in the neighbouring rooms I climbed into my junior sized bed at eight o'clock and slept for a glorious ten hours without coughing. As a consequence I awoke feeling positive, and spent the day strolling through the museums quarter and along the canals.

That evening at the Musikcentrum, the piano and acoustic were not as luscious sounding as in Amsterdam, but the performance was a dream. Thankfully I'd managed to organise an end seat and a few minutes into the second half it was necessary to hasten outside for a fit of coughing in the foyer. After about ten minutes I was ready to return, and a member of staff let me through the first of two sets of double doors. When I applied pressure to the second set, the rubber seals made a horrible squelching noise and Sokolov was in the middle of a slow movement. I readied myself to barge through during the fortissimo on which the movement ended, but realised I didn't know whether to push or pull and was so afraid of forcing the doors in the wrong direction and making an even more disgusting noise that I decided it was best to remain where I was until the end of the recital. It was frustrating but I could just about hear and there was a porthole window to peer through. Sokolov had been less than happy with the piano that evening, and when I told him where I'd spent the last forty minutes of the performance he laughed and said, "Oh well, maybe that was the best place to be!".

As I made my way to Arnhem in May 2007 there was nothing to see but billowing black clouds stretching to the horizon and rain streaking across the train windows: a far cry from my recent sun-kissed idylls in Switzerland and Germany. I stayed at a mid-range hotel which provided a small complimentary bottle of Rioja which I drank with a sandwich lunch in my room. After a refreshing nap I set off for the Musis Sacrum with plenty of time to spare. The seats for the recital were unreserved so it was imperative to arrive early. I spent almost an hour in the hall's own restaurant, waiting to stake my claim at the appropriate time. Avoiding tea or coffee for fear of being taken short before I got inside, I compromised with a refreshing cold dessert comprising several scoops of lemon sorbet smothered in a foaming cream sauce and surrounded by pink grapefruit segments soaked in vodka: a choice I was later to regret.

Outside the entrance to the auditorium I stood talking to a small group of Dutch concertgoers, including a young couple who were both professional pianists. As the foyer became crowded, a larger group seemed to gather around me and I found myself fielding questions from all directions. When the doors opened I dived into the fourth row and the two pianists sat directly behind me. It was a relatively small hall with an audience of perhaps four hundred. The piano was in excellent shape, the lighting almost non-existent, with no recording equipment and no pressure. I couldn't remember ever seeing Sokolov look so relaxed and free, simply enjoying himself, gaining momentum as he went along. This extraordinary evening again confirmed my theory that the best performances didn't necessarily occur in the major concert venues. At the interval I turned round to find the two pianists looking completely stunned; they told me they had no idea such things were possible.

During the second half, my inner workings began to gurgle horribly and I was seized by an overwhelming desire to rush to the nearest exit, but I was trapped in the middle of a row. The combination of the wine, the sorbet, the mysterious foaming sauce, the vodka soaked grapefruit and possibly a warm sausage roll I'd eaten at lunch time, threatened to bring about an unthinkable catastrophe. After the initial wave of ghastliness had passed I was able to appreciate the incredible force and passion with which Sokolov tackled the Scriabin programme, at the end of which the audience flew out of their seats with deafening shouts. As soon as I stood up my stomach turned to water and I was obliged to sit down again very quickly. There were still six encores to endure which would last for possibly twenty-five minutes and I had no idea how I would survive. At the end of each piece everyone around me leapt up and cheered, but I could only remain seated, feeling more uncomfortable and desperate by the minute.

Finally my ordeal was over, Sokolov disappeared for the last time and I sat tight until everyone had moved out of the row and my path to the blessed WC was unimpeded. Fortunately it was empty, and a few minutes later I emerged feeling like a new woman. I'd persuaded the pianists to visit the artist's room, and as I arrived they were coming out, looking awestruck. Two friends from Italy appeared and the Italian concert organiser, who also taught piano at the local conservatory, asked them to join her and a group of students for drinks in the restaurant. I was also invited, and while the Italians chatted in their own language the Dutch students fired questions in my direction about Sokolov's repertoire, my experience of his performances and my favourite venues. I found myself holding court once again, and I rather liked it.

Later the same year I heard Sokolov perform at De Doelen in Rotterdam, where the hall was modern, massive and only half full, but the audience responded to Schubert's Sonata D958 and Chopin's Op.28 Preludes with enormous excitement. The following day I took a train to Nijmegen, where I had two days to kill and hoped I would find enough of interest there to occupy my time. Outside the railway station I saw several smoking factory chimneys and braced myself for a disappointment. The next thing I encountered was a sea of bicycles; thousands of them, parked up in what appeared to be a hopeless jumble. The underpass beneath the busy road outside the station was entirely taken up with more bicycle stands, a shop selling what else but bicycles, a workshop repairing and building them and a puncture mending service. My fears about the town quickly evaporated and everything fell into place when I discovered that the tourist office, the concert hall and the admirable Hotel Apollo were all situated within yards of one another. A route map from the tourist office guided me through an undulating park bursting with late autumn colours, along a river bank and into the old town with its fascinating architecture and charming cobbled squares.

I was by no means the first to arrive at the Concertgebouw de Vereeniging but sufficiently close to the front of the queue to ensure a satisfactory place. The 1,800 seat hall was a mixture of art nouveau and art deco, famed for its exceptional acoustics and considered to be the best in the Netherlands. Within half an hour of my arrival the corridor was heaving, and with Sokolov rehearsing inside the auditorium a member of staff made a vain attempt to quieten everyone down. One of my Italian friends was there, and also the two pianists I'd met in Arnhem earlier in the year, bringing with them a party of friends who were new to Sokolov.

The performance was overwhelming, powerful, poetic. I left the auditorium feeling ravenously hungry and as luck would have it, my Italian friend was invited to an informal reception by the chairman of the foundation responsible for organising classical events at the Vereeniging. I was also asked to join the gathering, handed a glass of wine and invited to help myself to a selection of hot and cold delights, which hit the spot perfectly. I bluffed my way through a musical conversation with the chairman, did justice to the refreshments and returned to my room feeling musically and gastronomically replete.

Sokolov's Amsterdam recitals were said to be one of the highlights in the Concertgebouw's calendar. The Grote Zaal's 2,000 seats were routinely sold out, the Dutch audiences appeared to adore him, and experiencing his performances in that electric atmosphere became an annual event. In 2008 I was relieved to see that apart from his initial entrance at the start of each half of the recital when he descended the staircase behind the piano, Sokolov was able to retreat and re-enter through a side door. His Mozart sonatas and Chopin preludes had a rapturous reception that night and in the artist's room a lady from Rotterdam presented him with a charcoal sketch she'd begun working on during his performance in Arnhem the previous year which captured him perfectly.

I stayed in a small hotel run by a Chinese family where there was no lift and the staircase was almost vertical with narrow treads: a treacherous climb and an even more terrifying descent with size eight feet and a suitcase. The food laid out in the dining room on the morning of my departure looked very tempting but I had to leave an hour before breakfast time. As I clattered down the stairs with my luggage feeling rather deprived, a cheerful family member waited in the hallway and handed me a carrier bag containing bread, cheese, fruit, yogurt and a drink for my journey.

My 2009 trip to Arnhem and Amsterdam coincided with my 65th birthday. By the end of the Arnhem recital the piano was hopelessly out of tune but it hardly mattered, and another audience went home enriched. In Amsterdam the next day there were endless queues outside the museums, but on an evening stroll in search of a cup of tea I noticed the Van Gogh Museum was still open with no one waiting outside. The exhibition featured a number of his night paintings and the accompanying audio guide included a selection of letters Van Gogh wrote to his brother Theo. The combination of the paintings, the readings and the background music left me feeling quite emotional.

Breakfast at the Zandbergen Hotel was not only ample and stylishly presented but accompanied by classical music as opposed to local radio, which seemed to be standard fare in most budget hotels. The manager gave me a pair of china clogs filled with sweets to mark my birthday, and at his suggestion I visited the Keukenhof Gardens by bus. There was very little in bloom outside but I saw magnificent displays of giant freesias, lilies, hyacinths and other spring flowers in the hothouses.

That evening, as Sokolov descended the staircase in the Concertgebouw, I wouldn't have wished to be anywhere else on earth to celebrate the occasion. His recitals were consistently brilliant, but sometimes he managed to pull something out of the bag which exceeded all expectations, and this was one of the nights when he produced a performance of indescribable magnitude. From the first note to the last he gave everything. The standing ovations began at the interval and continued until the final encore. This was Sokolov at the very zenith of his powers. The divine second movement of the Schubert Gasteiner sonata, echoed so sweetly in the middle section of the third, never sounded better. At the beginning of the year, in preparation for hearing Sokolov play this sonata I'd listened to other versions and wondered why he'd chosen to play it, but now I understood.

On a Sunday evening in April 2010 Sokolov began his mission in the Concertgebouw with an exquisitely played Bach Partita No. 2. From the grandiose announcement through to the measured beauty of the sarabande, the scurrying notes of the rondo and the joyful climax, I was lifted into another dimension. Prolonged applause brought him back to the platform to express the more earthly anguish of the Brahms Op.116 Fantasies. The message behind these pieces grew more powerful and poignant with each performance, and the desperate conclusion produced a complete standing ovation. I was sitting next to a pianist friend who confessed that although he'd played the fantasies himself, he had never fully understood them. Sokolov's performance had been a revelation to him. "Now he has explained everything", he said at the interval. A short walk around the balcony's communal areas brought me face to face with Dmitri Alexeev, Dmitri Bashkirov, Evgeny Kissin and several other familiar figures.

There were many refinements in the Schumann sonata and the encores were divided equally between Chopin and Scriabin, after which the artist's room was besieged, firstly by a succession of illustrious visitors and finally the lower orders, all of us received with the same degree of affability. I often thought about the many hours, days, weeks and months that Sokolov spent studying, practising and perfecting each piece he chose to play, and the thousands of people who went along to his concerts, the majority of whom heard those pieces only once. I mentioned this one evening and said I hoped it meant something to him that those of us who heard these pieces many times noticed the differences, the subtle changes he made, the gradual progressions. He responded with a smile and told me it did.

The following evening's recital took place in Leiden's Concertgebouw before a smaller but equally enthusiastic audience. The piano's purity and sweetness of tone were perfect for the Bach and again I was transported to a joyful place. On the third evening I was back in the Vereeniging in Nijmegen, where a seat in my favourite spot beckoned and Sokolov's mastery was absolute. It was one of those occasions when the night seemed to belong to whichever composer one happened to be listening to, but by the end of an astonishing Schumann sonata I decided that Bach, Brahms and Schumann had stepped aside, and this night belonged to Sokolov.

The closest I could get to the piano in Arnhem's Musis Sacrum in 2016 was up in the balcony, but the piano rang out beautifully, soaring freely above and around us. Under Sokolov's hands this admirable instrument sang, danced, strutted, raged and wept. From up above I watched as members of the audience literally jumped up and down with excitement as six encores poured forth, ending with an achingly melancholy Griboyedov Waltz.

Two evenings later in Amsterdam there was warm applause as Sokolov descended the stairs, swelling to twice the volume as he approached the piano. The front row of seating on stage was so close to him he almost had to edge his way past, and I wondered how his concentration might be affected by the close proximity of other humans with their many and varied noises and movements. Luckily, those immediately beside him were instantly transfixed and remained so throughout. The main events were the Schumann Fantasy and Chopin's 2nd Sonata. It was a revelation to hear a human volcano produce such weightless pianissimi, and always a privilege to share in the amazing voyage he embarked upon each time he began a recital. Whenever I attended two successive concerts, one of them usually had the edge over the other, but each of these two miracles perfectly exemplified Sokolov's enduring supremacy.

De Oosterpoort in Groningen looked from the outside like the last place on earth one might expect to witness historic pianism, but that's exactly what happened on a Friday evening in May 2017. Although the auditorium wasn't full, a highly receptive audience knew exactly what they were listening to and silently absorbed every moment. I was very close to the piano but unable to see Sokolov's hands making contact; however it was fascinating to watch them occasionally floating high above the keyboard before gently reconnecting, sometimes hovering as if about to pounce on some unsuspecting prey (a friend once compared Sokolov's hands when on the attack to a bear catching salmon in a river). The sublime quality of the playing quickly propelled me into a parallel dimension and the opportunity to watch so closely the sheer physicality of Sokolov's artistic process seemed like the greatest of all privileges. He played with the kind of joyous freedom one might expect from someone much younger, but in addition to the technical assurance of youth, he brought with him decades of experience and earnest study, a deep understanding of the music and its creators, and the skill of the grand interpreter.

An evening with Sokolov was always a shot in the arm, but this felt more like a blood transfusion. The Beethoven in particular spoke volumes; the Op.111 arietta was executed with gravity-defying slowness but the momentum was never lost. Sokolov was sometimes criticised for his slow tempi but he surely had his reasons. Every bar of Op.111 was imbued with such a weight of significance and the piece itself was one of such incredible beauty that I never wanted it to end. During the final set of trills Sokolov produced some amazing otherworldly sounds from the piano, as if a gathering of angels had brought along their celestial instruments to join in with the music-making.

From Groningen I transferred to Amsterdam for the annual recital at the Concertgebouw and two days after that a third miracle occurred in Nijmegen's Vereeniging. Three opportunities to embark with Sokolov on Beethoven's journey into the great unknown, every step of the way expressed with eloquence and humanity.

The following year I chose to attend another three performances in quick succession, this time in Utrecht, Amsterdam and Eindhoven. The Utrecht recital took place in the Herz Zaal, a well-proportioned recital hall on the seventh floor of the Tivoli Vredenburg, a large entertainment complex with numerous performance spaces. The hall had just 543 seats, two small balconies and a panoramic view of the city from its attractive foyer. The audience was an ardent and respectful one, manifestly thankful to be hearing an artist of Sokolov's calibre in such intimate surroundings. It was ideal for the purpose; the sound was exceptional, the piano velvet-toned.

The Haydn sonatas sounded very much at home in this smaller than average space, by turns measured, aristocratic, delicately wrought and full of elegant swagger. After the break came the four Schubert impromptus, each with a different character and tale to tell. Sokolov reminded me of the proud parent of four equally adored children, who wished to present each of them to the world in the best possible light, extolling their individual virtues as only a father knew how. The final impromptu took us deep into the forest, and it was as if at any moment a gathering of other-worldly creatures might come stealing out of the shadows. Suddenly the Herz Zaal was transformed into a mystic realm where prolonged airy trills spoke of magic spells and extended scale runs suggested darker incantations. At the conclusion there was a commotion of cheering and ear-splitting whistles as a young girl bearing flowers got caught up in a comical circle dance with Sokolov around the piano before completing her task.

In Amsterdam, for the first time I sat on the platform just behind the piano, which provided an intriguing close-up of what happened down at the bass end of the keyboard and a golden opportunity to witness the balletic beauty of that dancing left hand. Microphones were in evidence, the performance was flawless and the piano sounded sumptuous. The programme as a whole, including six enticing and diverse encores, would amount to an intoxicating cocktail with huge commercial possibilities if the recording was successful. It was thrilling to be on stage in that great hall watching the reaction of the audience exactly as Sokolov saw it: hundreds of people flying out of their seats, voicing their gratitude, begging for more; eager faces radiating pure joy. At some performances there came a moment when I imagined I was hearing the most lovely piece of music ever written, and on that particular night it came when Sokolov played Schubert's emotive Hungarian Melody, a recent addition to the encore collection which had immediately joined my list of all time favourites. If it were possible to feel homesick for somewhere I'd never been, this piece encapsulated just such a sense of longing.

The Muziekgebouw in Eindhoven was the third venue: modern, attractive, with a medium-sized auditorium, another fine piano and an excellent acoustic. At the conclusion of the Schubert impromptus the audience emitted the most extraordinary sound I'd ever heard in a concert hall: a kind of unearthly ecstatic wailing which came in perfect unison as if it had been rehearsed, rising and falling like a tide; an amalgam of heavenly choir and Greek chorus.

On the afternoon of Sokolov's 2019 recital in Amsterdam the audience had the opportunity to hear a short recital by a young Russian pianist, Alexandra Dovgan, for whom Sokolov had predicted a bright future. With remarkable composure this diminutive, fragile looking 11-year-old descended the stairs and took her place at the piano. Designed to illustrate her prodigious technical skills and versatility, her programme included pieces by Chopin, Debussy and Rachmaninoff, followed by a Bach encore. Her performance was one of straightforward dignified application, amazing technique for one so young and a musical understanding way beyond her years.

Later it was Sokolov's turn, and again I sat on the platform, very close to the piano. This was a colossally powerful performance and the public were ecstatic. Strangely, the evening didn't pass as quickly as it sometimes did; in fact it seemed to stretch into infinity and the striking image I had before me, almost within touching distance, and the sublime sounds Sokolov produced, would be etched in my memory for ever. He seemed to have the universe at his fingertips and for the duration of this blessed evening, he and his chosen composers – Beethoven and Brahms - combined to provide a vital link between the human and the divine.

14. BELGIUM

MY FIRST IMPRESSION of Brussels Central Railway Station was that it looked in need of a facelift, and an hour or so later in Ghent, I watched fascinated as a lavatory attendant sat at a table behind piles of coins, regarding her clientele as they came and went, whilst ploughing through a mountainous plate of steak and chips with salad on the side, seemingly untroubled by the wafting miasma pervading her domain.

The twenty minute tram ride into the city through drab streets full of seedy shops with perfunctory window displays did little to whet the appetite, but the centre was crammed with towering historic buildings, and despite the overpowering smell of drains I was impressed. In the crypt of the old belfry I found the tourist office, where a girl with infinite patience ran through all the accommodation options. The central hotels were too expensive, most of the B&Bs too far from the centre, and I drew the line at a dormitory bed in a youth hostel. I settled for a room in an ancient hotel in a noisy street with a bar and tea room on the ground floor. The bedrooms were accessed through a curtained recess behind the bar which led to a creaking wooden staircase, so dark, steep and narrow I dreaded negotiating it late at night or in the event of a fire.

I visited the massive Saint Bavo's Cathedral, home to Ghent's most prized possession, Jan van Eyck's altarpiece depicting the Adoration of the Mystic Lamb, and admired the tall merchants' houses beside the canal. As the sun was setting I made my way to the newly built Handelsbeurs concert hall which was just a couple of months into its first season. A battalion of bushy-tailed young staff stood poised to fulfil their duties and the foyer overflowed with outlandishly arty outfits, quirky hats and geometric haircuts. The start of the recital was delayed by almost an hour due to a last minute retune of the piano, and after a couple of clunky opening bars the Beethoven flowed magnificently. The interval came at ten o'clock and half an hour later I wandered back to my seat and saw that the piano had been dragged to the rear of the platform behind a curtain, where the recalcitrant middle C sharp was being tuned to within an inch of its life. The audience seemed remarkably patient, although I did overhear one or two grumbles about so much fuss being made over just one note, from people who failed to grasp the concept that one note could be struck thousands of times in the course of an evening. By eleven the piano was back in position and the remainder of the programme by Komitas and Prokofiev took its triumphant course; an inspired performance under stressful circumstances, ending happily for all concerned.

The next day I returned to Brussels and secured a special weekend rate at one of the central hotels. Just around the corner was Grand Place, the city's most imposing square, overlooked by the magnificent Town Hall and an array of richly decorated guild houses. The square was filled with Christmas trees, the pavements swarmed with visitors and a carnival was in progress with marching bands and floats progressing through the streets. As I mingled with sightseers in the Town Hall courtyard we were swept aside to make way for a yuletide procession headed by the most diminutive Father Christmas I'd ever seen. Looking more like an undernourished pixie, he strode with great ceremony through the portals and out into Grand Place, followed by a band of cohorts dispensing festive sweetmeats to the throng.

Many different events were taking place simultaneously at the Palais des Beaux Arts that evening including a major art exhibition. In order to promote a Restoration comedy due to begin a Christmas run the following week, three male members of the cast dressed as Regency fops mingled with the assembled gathering in the entrance hall wearing full costume, make-up, beauty spots and periwigs. Their falsetto voices jarred as they pranced and pirouetted amongst us and it was a relief when we were allowed into the auditorium. As the lights were dimmed, the air of hushed expectancy was disrupted by the same three pranksters fumbling their way through the side curtains onto the platform and capering around the piano, speculating as to the possible whereabouts of Mr Sokolov. Off they scampered, only to return twice more to repeat the routine, leaving the audience in a state of bewilderment and Franco Panozzo with his head in his hands. It was a perplexing start to the evening, but soon forgotten as the music took over. Sokolov was due to begin a tour of Spain the next day with solo recitals in six cities and two performances with orchestra in a seventh. Now that the year was almost at an end we touched on the prospect of his change of programme in the new year and when I said it was a foregone conclusion that he would come up with something remarkable he picked up a litre bottle of water and took a long guzzle, rolling his eyes as if to say, "Let's hope so!"

A year later in November 2007 I had a comfortable and peaceful rail journey from Luxembourg to Brussels, passing dank fields, remote farmsteads and endless belts of fir trees wreathed in mist. My first night was spent on the outskirts of the city but on the day of the recital I transferred to a central hotel close to the concert hall which claimed to have two stars, despite my room being a virtual cupboard on the top floor facing the busy square, with no facilities and a broken window. The WC was on a different floor, the bed springs were struggling to escape through the fabric of the mattress, the curtains were filthy and the ancient TV had appalling reception: an absolute bargain at seventy-eight euros.

I visited the city's famous shopping arcade, the Gallery of St. Hubert, and plunged into the surrounding narrow alleys crowded with sumptuous fish restaurants outside which elaborate displays of shellfish mounted in ice-filled cabinets were decorated with fruit, vegetables and flowers. Each restaurant glowed invitingly but most passers-by were more interested in photographing the produce.

At the Palais des Beaux Arts it was pleasing to find that the 2,200 Henry le Boeuf Zaal had been extensively refurbished since my last visit, with comfortable seating and an even better acoustic, achieved by replacing the carpeting with a gleaming parquet floor; an infinitely more agreeable environment in which to soak up Schubert's Sonata D958 and Chopin's Op.28 Preludes.

In 2010 I heard Sokolov's Bach/Brahms/Schumann programme in Brussels, and this time I chose to stay in an apartment in the outer suburbs which was infinitely cheaper than the city centre options. It wasn't easy to locate, and as I climbed two flights of steep wooden stairs I was greeted by a rather laid-back individual who invited me into her kitchen in order to explain the rules of the house. Whilst doing so she absently opened her fridge and took out a pack of ham from which she proceeded to peel off slice after slice and fold them into her mouth. I had my doubts as to what her breakfast would be like, but to my surprise the next morning she delivered to my door five warm rolls, a brioche bun, an assortment of cheese slices, a whole pack of ham, two tomatoes and a couple of kiwi fruits.

It would be a further seven years before I found myself back in Brussels, this time to hear Mozart and Beethoven. I understood perfectly Sokolov's preference for playing the works of each composer without pause, but in Brussels the audience applauded warmly at the end of Sonata K545, and who could blame them? Sokolov's wealth of expression had transformed what was sometimes regarded as a beginner's party piece into a miniature masterpiece.

There was an array of CDs and DVDs in the foyer and the new Deutsche Grammophon recording of Mozart and Rachmaninoff concertos teamed with Nadia Zhdanova's thoughtful documentary "A Conversation that Never Was" had been released for sale a week ahead of schedule and was selling like hot cakes. After the interval, as the pastoral calm of the second half of Beethoven's Sonata Op.90 washed over us like a breath of summer air, I was already anticipating the darker territory we would soon be entering; the stellar odyssey at the heart of Op.111 was always a momentous event. When I heard it for the first time it was impressive, a few times more and it became sensational, and after that it crept into my bones and never left me.

In 2018 the Haydn sonatas and Schubert's Four Impromptus Op.142 received a response bordering on hysteria in Brussels, when Sokolov, in blistering form, radiated warmth and generosity through the music without the need of a single word or gesture. The following year the response was even greater for Beethoven's Sonata No.3 Op 2/3 and the eleven Bagatelles Op.119 teamed with Brahms' Op.118/Op.119. This was a staggering performance; the atmosphere was electric, the excitement uncontainable, and at the end of the scheduled programme it seemed there might be a riot. I'd not heard such a deafening response in a very long time; all of this commotion generated by an unassuming figure, so far removed from any kind of self-promotion or extravagant behaviour, calmly attending to his business with priestlike devotion, fulfilling his solemn duty to the composer. The final encore came like a benediction as Sokolov began Bach's Chorale Prelude Ich ruf zu dir, Herr Jesu Christ, and on this night, as sometimes happened, the motion of the world seemed to be suspended until time and place re-established themselves.

15. LUXEMBOURG

THE FIRST RECITAL I attended in Luxembourg was in January 1999 in a small town twenty-five kilometres from the city in a converted shoe factory machine shop, where Sokolov played his Byrd/Beethoven/Ravel programme. In the autumn of that same year he returned to perform works by Froberger, along with the Brahms Op.117 Intermezzi & Chopin's 3rd Sonata, this time in a compact hall beneath the Bank of Luxembourg, where I had the privilege of being allowed to attend the evening rehearsal.

In 2002 Sokolov's recital was enjoyed by a much larger audience at the Luxembourg Conservatoire, where he gave a mesmerising account of the Haydn/Komitas/Prokofiev programme. In the artist's room Sokolov was invited to join a party of Conservatoire music patrons for a late supper but understandably he declined, having exerted himself to the limit on stage and worked up a raging thirst that only vast quantities of mineral water could satisfy, quite apart from which he appeared to have a strict routine when it came to mealtimes. The man who extended the invitation was very disappointed, but when he turned to me and asked if I would care to join the gathering I nearly bit his hand off, eager to prolong the pleasure of the evening and possibly have the opportunity to discuss the performance.

The appointed restaurant was in the middle of nowhere down a dark country lane, and the kind of place I'd never had the opportunity to sample. It was small, very French, with a relaxed, rustic atmosphere, and the smiling owner, clad in a huge apron, together with his wife and an assistant, stood waiting to cook, serve and attend to our every need. Glasses of champagne were lined up on the bar as we walked in and I lost count of the number of bottles of wine that were opened. The food was wonderful, starting with heaps of tender buttered asparagus served with crusty French bread. We were then invited to choose between steak or lobster for the main course, and my stomach lurched at the thought of either. Asking for a plain omelette seemed out of the question so I opted for the steak. Then there was a choice of steak cordon bleu or steak with foie gras, a much easier decision for a lapsed vegetarian. My cordon bleu comprised generous amounts of cheese and ham sandwiched between thick slices of steak the size of tea plates, smothered in a rich chanterelle gravy. Bowls of salad, pasta, rice and French fries were passed round the table and although everything tasted like heaven I anticipated a night of raging indigestion.

I sat opposite an interesting man who was something big at Lux-Air, and his wife, an aspiring pianist. The conversation flowed as easily as the wine, and I flopped back in my seat feeling ready to explode. I was just about to light a cigarette (our host had already smoked four during the meal) when in came the dessert, borne aloft on a huge platter. As the Aproned One rolled up his sleeves and set fire to a mountainous creation enveloped in meringue which looked similar to baked Alaska, a fanfare would not have come amiss, or at the very least a modest accordion flourish. Once the flames had subsided it was hacked into massive portions, and despite the amount of food I'd already consumed, it slipped down with ease. The bill must have been enormous but I doubt it could have sent our host's blood pressure soaring any higher. Judging by the amount he'd eaten, drunk and smoked that night it was probably already on triple bypass alert.

The following year's recital at the Bank of Luxembourg was my 100th Sokolov performance, and again I was welcomed into the hall in the early evening to hear his last minute run through. As I was ushered into the basement of the bank, the scurrying notes of a Bach presto filled the corridors. I peered tremulously round the door closest to the platform and was greeted by an endearing rear view of the Sokolov bulk crouched over the keyboard just a few feet away. His wife greeted me and we sat together through the remainder of the new Reincken Sonata, during which she glanced at me occasionally to gauge my reaction. I'd never heard it before and was overwhelmed. Sokolov moved swiftly on to the Bach/Brahms Chaconne for the left hand, a piece by turns massively powerful and heartbreakingly poignant. Sokolov's right hand rested in his lap throughout, and at one point he looked up from the keyboard, gazed at the ceiling, then casually glanced across at his audience of two, rather like a youth on a bicycle showing off by letting go of the handlebars.

The seats were unreserved so there was a mad scramble for the keyboard side, and although I'd been allocated a perfect place from which to see the chaconne, at the last minute everyone in my row was required to move three places to the right in order to accommodate VIP guests who'd been invited by the bank without the organiser's knowledge. Not only were the three people on the far right evicted from their seats and forced to find somewhere else to sit, but I was effectively shunted beyond the point where I could see the keyboard. I was extremely disappointed, but a gallant volunteer offered to change places with me. Photographs were taken in the artist's room to mark my special occasion and Sokolov wanted to know when I'd first heard him play so that he could calculate how many performances per year I'd attended.

Luxmbourg 2003

From 2005 onwards, Sokolov's Luxembourg recitals took place in the city's newly opened and rather magnificent Philharmonie, a vast white otherworldly edifice whose outer contours comprised over eight hundred steel columns and which looked as if it might have been shipped in from a distant planet overnight. Its public spaces were cavernous, but at the heart of the building lay a reassuringly traditional auditorium with excellent acoustics.

At the 2015 recital, as the Schubert sonata came to an end there were gasps from the audience and unusually prolonged applause, even though Sokolov had sat down after a perfunctory nod and was poised to begin the Moments Musicaux. But something even more exceptional was waiting in the wings in the shape of what was for me the most earth-shattering and technically accomplished performance of Chopin's 2nd Sonata to date. Firstly there were the Op.32 Nocturnes, providing a period of tranquillity before Sokolov plunged us into the sonata's dark interior. As the drama of this great work played out, I felt a sense of jubilation. It was executed with an awesome degree of abandonment but remained technically rock solid. Sokolov nailed the Chopin sonata firmly to the wall and left me in no doubt that it would produce some historic performances over the next nine months.

After such an experience I was ready to leave, but of course the usual six encores materialised. A heartfelt "Merci!" rang out as Sokolov sat waiting to begin his third Chopin mazurka, followed by a loud "Spasiba!" from another part of the hall, triggering a burst of applause. Sokolov waited patiently and then delivered. The audience allowed each piece to breathe out before responding, and at the conclusion of Debussy's Canope which ended the evening, there was a long moment of quiet reverence as Sokolov sat with head bowed. His was a mark of respect for the composers he had served so lovingly; ours was almost certainly for him alone.

Twelve months later the Luxembourg recital was Sokolov's last of the year, and my final opportunity to hear the Schumann programme. In the first half every crystalline note of the three works by Mozart sang out, and after the break came the amazing Schumann Arabeske with its tender and eloquent closing bars, leading on to the Fantasy's dramatic radiance, the grand entrance of the second movement and the subsequent exhilaration of the triumphal march, bursting with pomp, banners streaming. Sokolov had already harvested so much from this piece, forever reminding the listener that beneath the grandiose exterior of Schumann's greatest keyboard composition there beat an all too human heart.

As the languid dreamlike sequence in the third movement wound its way into our consciousness it drifted out across the auditorium like a trail of sensuous vapour, and as Sokolov approached the final grand declaration he again exceeded his boundaries, as if we needed a further reminder of how perfectly equipped he was to guide us through the complexities of Schumann's masterpiece. As the second half drew to a close I felt as if I'd lost a beloved friend. At the end of the encores and numerous curtain calls, Sokolov seemed to walk off stage at twice his usual speed as if to say, "That's it, folks – my work here is done".

In November 2017 the Luxembourg audience gave an object lesson in self-restraint, especially in the first half when there was not so much as a murmur. The public were there to listen, and those familiar with the second half of the programme were soon to discover that Sokolov was the best possible helmsman to steer them to the furthest corners of Beethoven's final keyboard sonata. But firstly we were to visit environs of a more domestic nature, although Haydn's sonatas could never be described as commonplace or everyday. Certainly they were closer to home than Beethoven's celestial wanderings but they overflowed with ingenuity, charm and wit. In Luxembourg Sokolov dipped into his paintbox and introduced so much colour and detail into Haydn's imagery that it seemed as if everything I'd heard up until that evening had been a mere outline.

After the break Beethoven's kaleidoscopic Op.90, a gem of a sonata, prepared the way for the majesty of Op.111. Now nearing the

Philharmonie Luxembourg

end of its triumphal reign, the challenges of this great work had been met by Sokolov with the highest degree of technical and intellectual mastery and he had taken his audience on a journey into the unfathomable enormity of the universe. On this night the piano responded admirably to the stringent demands made of it, but towards the end of the evening it began to show signs of fatigue. Sokolov showed no mercy, however, and drove on into the teeth of the wind, finishing on his own terms with a beautiful Chopin Prelude Op.28/15 and a particularly robust Op.28/20.

16. UNITED KINGDOM

FOLLOWING MY FIRST experience of Sokolov in Birmingham and again in London in 1997, the next UK performance I attended was a lunchtime concert at Wigmore Hall in London in January 1999 which was again broadcast live on BBC Radio, and Sokolov played works by William Byrd and Beethoven. Later in the year there was another live broadcast from The Queen's Hall in Edinburgh featuring the same programme but with the addition of Ravel's Le Tombeau de Couperin. The interior of the hall was in any event rather dreary, in addition to which Sokolov's preference for subdued lighting had been amply accommodated, and shortly before the second half began, someone in the balcony stood up and complained very loudly that the hall was much too dark, comparing it to a mausoleum, and insisting that no one should be expected to listen to music in such disgraceful conditions. I understand the Director of the Edinburgh Festival was in the audience that day and chose not to respond, but someone else suggested that if the complainant wasn't happy then he should feel free to leave, and leave he did, to a burst of applause and hearty cheering from the rest of the audience. At that point Sokolov reappeared and I wondered if he'd heard the commotion. Apparently he had, but as ever took it in his stride and concentrated on the job in hand, which was to execute the collection of pieces by Ravel. By the end of the performance his right index finger had split and was dripping blood.

Afterwards he was in high spirits, very talkative and full of travel tales, measuring out the size of a minuscule bedroom he'd once occupied in a Siberian hotel and describing a long haul journey from Moscow, where it was minus thirty degrees, to his final destination where it was plus thirty. He'd arrived severely jet lagged with little time to recover, rehearse or adjust to the change in temperature. Someone asked about his next programme and he spoke about Froberger, predicting that there was much for him to do and remarking that the exploration of these works was like travelling to the deepest part of an ocean.

The 2000 Wigmore Hall recital was in danger of cancellation when Sokolov arrived in London feeling unwell, but with a period of rest, less than adequate preparation time and a hasty choice of piano, he soldiered on with his Froberger programme followed by Schubert's Sonata D664, and no one would have guessed that anything had been amiss. Four days later I was in Manchester's Bridgewater Hall to hear Chopin's 2nd Piano Concerto with the Halle Orchestra conducted by Moshe Atzmon. The orchestra was in fine fettle, Atzmon's conducting was incredibly sympathetic and Sokolov's performance was masterly.

Afterwards we spoke about his illness, his recent tour of Spain, the piano he played at home. I lamented that I'd been unable to find an affordable flight to Munich the following week but Sokolov attempted to console me by predicting bad weather in Germany at that time, and in any case it would be the same programme as he was playing a week or so later in Lucerne, where I planned to be. I said, "The programme may well be the same but the performance never is" and he smiled. "Yes", he said, "it's always different."

In April 2000, again in Manchester, Sokolov gave a miraculous account of Beethoven's 1st Piano Concerto with the Scottish Symphony Orchestra conducted by Osmo Vanska. It was shortly before Sokolov's fiftieth birthday, a subject upon which he was reluctant to dwell, but nevertheless I gave him a greeting card, and despite his apparent unwillingness to acknowledge the approach of his half century, we laughed about being fifty and I told him I'd stuck at forty-nine for as long as I could get away with it but had now decided to start claiming to be much older than I was, in the hope that people might think how good I looked for my age.

In addition to a Wigmore Hall recital in the spring of 2001 Sokolov also performed in Aldeburgh, whose festival was founded by Benjamin Britten in 1948. The recital took place in the Maltings at Snape, a former malthouse with such an excellent acoustic that the opening bars of the first Couperin piece sounded like delicate fairy music. It was one of Sokolov's five star performances, also including works by Mozart and Franck, and was recorded by the BBC for future transmission.

Two evenings later he played at a music festival in the market town of Arundel. It was a perfect English summer's day, the town was garlanded with flowers, a band was playing in the market square, and I hoped Sokolov would enjoy this glimpse of rural England in contrast to the cities he normally visited. He performed in the Barons' Hall of Arundel's medieval castle, a lofty room with plank flooring and an English oak hammer beam roof, massive fireplaces, numerous gilt framed portraits and a minstrels' gallery. It was an impressive setting, but the audience, unlike the discriminating one in Aldeburgh, appeared to consist mainly of county types and local gentry who were there purely to be seen and to support the festival. At the end of the main programme the lights came on immediately and there was a mass exodus in the direction of a much vaunted festival supper, leaving Sokolov with no opportunity to play even one encore. It was the first time this had ever happened in my experience and I was appalled that this slap in the face should occur in my home country.

Worse still, when I walked into Sokolov's room, which was separated from the hall by a long portrait gallery, I found him standing alone in a corner with no one from the festival management at his side. He'd given a stupendous performance which had been all but wasted on a largely unappreciative audience, and when he remarked that he'd had no opportunity to see anything of Arundel or the castle grounds and was staying at a chain hotel far from the town, I felt terribly sad, realising just how solitary life must sometimes be for solo artists, however famous. It also triggered a memory of Pebble Mill Studio back in 1997 where I first discovered Sokolov. One of the other soloists in the piano series had been the great Russian pianist, Lazar Berman, and after his performance I walked past the open door of his dressing room, where he was sitting alone at a table. He looked up and smiled at me, but I was too shy to go in and tell him how much I'd enjoyed the explosive pieces by Liszt he'd just delivered, especially the cataclysmic Funerailles. I'd regretted it ever since.

Sokolov went on to give many more UK solo recitals and orchestral performances, in Birmingham's Symphony Hall, in London (at Wigmore Hall, Queen Elizabeth Hall, the Barbican), Edinburgh's Usher Hall, Manchester's Bridgewater Hall, Leeds Town Hall, Reading Town Hall, Wyastone Concert Hall in Monmouth and

Victoria Hall, Stoke-on-Trent, but I preferred to hear him in other countries. When his visits to my homeland ceased on account of a change in visa regulations, my disappointment was nowhere near as great as it must have been for the strong following he'd acquired since his first UK appearance in 1990.

At the 2007 Wigmore Hall recital, which was to be the last one in my country, I sat next to a man with a vaguely familiar face who appeared to live every note of Sokolov's superlative performance of works by Schubert and Scriabin, and when it was over my neighbour remained slumped in his seat looking physically exhausted and emotionally drained. Realising that Sokolov's UK agent was sitting directly behind me, I turned round to thank her for organising such a marvellous seat for me. She responded by telling me that no one deserved an excellent seat more than I did, at which point the man sitting beside me sat bolt upright, possibly imagining I might be someone worth knowing. Offering his hand, he introduced himself and then I remembered he was the English conductor who'd shown so little interest in speaking to me back in Gothenburg in 1998 when Sokolov had introduced us. I couldn't resist pointing out that we'd already met and reminding him of the occasion.

17. GERMANY

GERMANY WAS THE country I visited most often, taking time to explore the diverse landscape, cultivate numerous friendships and soak up performances in a wide variety of venues, from the simple to the spectacular. In the summer of 1998 my first German concert trip was to the spa town of Bad Schwalbach where I stayed in a traditional family-run hotel whose jovial owner ushered me into a characterfully furnished room, its windows bedecked with ancient creeper.

Strolling through the town in the afternoon sunshine I came upon a large expanse of parkland where tables were set out beneath the trees and groups of musicians in traditional costume sat with tankards of beer and plates of sausages smothered in mustard, waiting to compete in a regional band contest. The atmosphere was light-hearted and festive, and I sank onto a bench to listen to one or two entries and watch a demonstration of alpine horn playing.

My hotel sported a classy restaurant, of which the owner was very proud. He and his wife were busy preparing dishes for a special Rheingau Festival dinner in the banqueting room of the nearby Kurhaus later that evening. On arrival at the Kurhaus I was pleased to find myself sitting quite close to the platform to hear Sokolov's Rameau/Beethoven/Brahms programme, and at the end of the evening I was invited to the festival dinner. I proudly took my place at the top table in the banqueting room, where from time to time people came across to congratulate the director on the success of the performance. There was much talk of music, artists and venues, but I was unashamedly preoccupied with the food. I'd missed the first two courses but there were still three to come, ending with a rich chocolate mousse liberally coated with vanilla sauce and decorated with dark chocolate treble clefs. As we finally left our seats I realised that the entire gathering had been waiting for us to finish before making a move, as if they were subject to some sort of protocol.

Six months on, I landed in Düsseldorf on a December afternoon to find a light dusting of snow, and the further north I travelled on the

Hamburg train, the thicker it became. It was exciting to be streaking through the darkness towards a strange destination, passing small towns trimmed up for Christmas, with no real idea of where I'd be spending the night. As I emerged from Osnabrück railway station with rough directions to a reportedly cheap hotel near the Stadthalle, an icy blast took my breath away. After a half hour trudge through heavy snow to the other side of the city I found the Dom Hotel tucked behind the huge Romanesque cathedral. I was soon installed in a cheerful little room overlooking the Dom and went straight back outside to explore the Altstadt, which contained elegant half-timbered houses, a Gothic town hall, an ancient market place, glittering arcades and narrow streets lined with twinkling Christmas trees. In front of the floodlit cathedral a Christmas market was selling gifts and handicrafts, hot punch, sausages and fried potatoes. Snow was still falling, the church bells began chiming and I was completely captivated, happy to have a cosy room to return to and a free day ahead of me to wander further afield.

At the hotel bar I chatted with a guest from Munich who told me that back in the seventies he'd spent three years living in London in a Chelsea bedsit and mentioned a fascinating individual who'd occupied the flat above his, with whom he'd been invited to take afternoon tea once a week. When he began describing his neighbour's elaborate mauve hairdo I said, "Oh, that sounds very much like the writer, Quentin Crisp", and he almost fell off his chair.

It was still snowing steadily the next morning and I was in no hurry to go out, sitting at my window watching a succession of passers-by, including three nuns who emerged from the Dom and sped away on some errand, perfectly sure-footed. At eight o'clock a deep, sonorous bell clanged out and I half expected Boris Godunov to put in an appearance on the cathedral steps. By eleven o'clock I was wondering if I would need to stay in my room all day, but suddenly the sun came out and the market began stirring into life, so I ventured outside to visit the Dom and walk through the Altstadt again before preparing for the evening.

The Stadthalle was a modern building with an unattractive auditorium and the piano was surrounded by four straggly potted plants to depressing effect. My seat was so far removed from the platform that I couldn't properly engage with the performance and as a consequence the evening was a disappointment. Afterwards I mentioned to Sokolov my short visit to Nice following the recent concert in Monte Carlo and with a cheeky grin he asked, "Was it nice, in Nice?" I remarked on the high frequency of flights from Birmingham to Düsseldorf and he recalled that when he first started performing abroad, the only flights to Europe were from Moscow, involving long and arduous train journeys from his home in St.Petersburg.

I visited Frankfurt for the first time in February 1999 and I'd been given a reduced room rate at the newly opened Frankfurt Hilton. The impresario I'd met in Monte Carlo was going to be there, and not only had he promised to try and get me admitted into the afternoon orchestral rehearsals but also undertaken to engineer an invitation for me to eat breakfast with him and Sokolov. The idea terrified me, but I resolved to be grown up about it and set off with high hopes. But as soon as I walked into the hotel lobby I lost my nerve. The ground floor was largely open plan and contained vast lounges, a cocktail bar with grand piano, a huge dining room, a hair salon, beauty parlour, gymnasium and swimming pool. Three glass sided elevators rose and descended silently, serving the hotel's twelve floors, and it looked as if the doors to all three hundred bedrooms might be visible from the reception area. I'd never felt so out of place

Alte Opera Frankfurt

nor experienced such luxury; my room was soundproof, pristine and expensively furnished, but moving through the hotel's cavernous public spaces left me feeling exposed and inhibited.

I received no message regarding the rehearsal and at seven o'clock I walked to the Alte Oper and heard Sokolov perform Brahms' 1st Piano Concerto with the Frankfurt Radio Symphony Orchestra conducted by Hugh Wolff: a heart-melting performance which was over much too soon. Afterwards Sokolov told me he was recovering from 'flu and had been unable to play two recent concerts in Hanover, where John Lill had replaced him. He also confirmed that the impresario had cancelled his trip due to a rail strike, so any hopes I may have had were dashed. In truth I was relieved to have been spared the breakfast experience but disappointed about the rehearsal.

Walking back to the hotel I felt inexplicably downhearted at the prospect of the three days stretching ahead of me. There would be a second concert in Frankfurt the following evening and a third in Marburg the evening after that, but the days would somehow need to be filled. Back at the Hilton, in jarring contrast to what I'd just heard, an ageing male pianist was casually tinkling cocktail tunes in the foyer, accompanied by a female in a slinky frock who swayed back and forth, plucking the odd note here and there on a double bass. I drank a quick cup of tea at the bar and hastened away to the sanctuary of my room.

The next morning I awoke in a cocoon of silence and gloom thanks to the soundproof door, the triple glazing and the heavy curtains. I lay immobile for what felt like a couple of hours, only to discover it wasn't yet seven o'clock. The thought of emerging from my room into that vast space and stepping into the glass lift filled me with terror. When I eventually summoned the courage to approach the dining area I was told exactly where to sit, in a spot directly facing the reception area surrounded by businessmen talking on their mobiles between forkfuls of smoked salmon. There was no sign of Sokolov, and in a state of suppressed panic I remained glued to my seat for half an hour, drinking tea but unable to swallow anything solid. As I was about to leave, in he walked looking fresh-faced and ready to begin his day. He chose a table on the far side of the buffet bar and as he stood sawing away at a crusty loaf I breezed across and wished him good morning. He asked if I'd eaten my breakfast yet and I assured him I had indeed finished and was off to see what Frankfurt had to offer. I was desperate to go to the rehearsal but too shy to ask, so I bounced off with a spring in my step and an ache in my heart.

That evening my seat was up in the balcony, and from there the orchestra and piano sounded glorious. I sat next to a former cellist with the orchestra whose thirty year career had been cut short by a recent stroke. The heart-rending passages for strings, and for the cello in particular, were especially poignant, and the cellist was visibly moved. It was painful to watch him leaning forward as if willing himself back into his position in the orchestra, now occupied by someone else.

By mid-morning the next day I'd taken my leave of the Hilton and caught a train to Marburg, an old university town north-east of Frankfurt, where I hoped to find somewhere homely to stay, as an antidote to the vastness and sophistication of the Hilton. It was a gloomy overcast day, the streets were almost deserted and most of the shops were closed. I had details of a small guest house on the opposite side of town which necessitated trudging into the centre and out again, lugging a bag which grew heavier by the minute. Eventually I realised I was straying much too far away from the concert hall, so I took a bus back to the railway station and started again, this time looking at several rooms in central hotels, all of which were either too expensive or too dark and dispiriting. In desperation I decided to return to the original option, which I found wedged between two shabby apartment buildings. It looked unpromising to say the least, with a tub outside the front door containing the withered remains of a small Christmas tree, from which dangled three rusted baubles. That tree looked exactly how I felt, and when I stepped inside the grubby hallway I decided it was definitely not for me, but I'd been in Marburg for over three hours now and needed to find somewhere fast.

Back in town I tried my luck at an old three storey guest house which could not have been a greater contrast to the Hilton and was like stepping into another age. It was packed full of treasures and every piece of furniture would have set an antique collector's heart racing. The owner was an incapacitated elderly lady who lived on the first floor. All of her guest rooms on the floor above were unoccupied that night and she invited me to go upstairs and choose one. They were all shapes and sizes, containing oddments of very old furniture and ornaments, faded rugs and primitive plumbing, and were every bit as depressing as the rooms I'd just rejected. I went back downstairs and tried to explain to her that I was undecided, in low spirits and feeling emotionally fragile, whereupon she offered to look after my luggage while I went in search of somewhere more uplifting. She seemed to understand my state of mind so readily that I immediately decided to stay with her and I took the most expensive room, which was in any event ridiculously cheap.

She told me something of her family history as she pointed out portraits of her ancestors lining the walls of her sitting room. The only child of wealthy parents, she'd never married and was last in the family line. Marooned on the first floor due to a heart condition she was unable to reach the other floors; students cleaned the house and helped with breakfast and most of her guests were university lecturers. The house, a listed building, had been occupied by the Nazis for an eight year period and Marburg's oldest church had been used as the local SS headquarters, where the town's Jews were taken before deportation.

At the Stadthalle that evening a sizeable crowd had gathered at the box office in the hope of last minute opportunities, and I felt fortunate to be elbowing my way through to claim my ticket. After the performance I had a long and leisurely conversation with Sokolov, during which he showed keen interest in my accommodation in Marburg, spoke about the beauty of his birthplace, St. Petersburg, and talked about the constant travelling, recalling a period in 1969 during which he'd played something like nine recitals on consecutive evenings, travelling to a new city each day, and the occasion when his luggage had been mistakenly transported to St.Petersburg in Florida.

The next morning I walked along the river and through the picturesque old town, climbing up to the schloss and reflecting on my trip. When I considered the trouble-free journeys to Frankfurt and Marburg, the luxurious room at the Hilton, the three wonderful concerts, the undisturbed meetings with Sokolov and the usual quota of kindness I'd received, I wondered how on earth I'd managed to extract so much misery from the experience.

On a sweltering Saturday morning in July 1999 I arrived in the elegant city of Wiesbaden. Once settled in a hotel room I located the

Casino-Gesellschaft where the recital was to take place the following evening and strayed into a nearby park where I paused to change the batteries in my camera. It was here that I encountered Bernhard, an affable man somewhere in his forties, who offered to take a picture of me against a floral backdrop, after which we began a conversation which lasted for eight hours. We strolled back across the city and took the funicular railway up to Neroberg, a local beauty spot where a Russian-Byzantine chapel with five golden domes could be found, along with forest walks and extensive views. As soon as all the photo opportunities had been exhausted Bernhard suggested we walk back down the hillside rather than take the funicular, and it wasn't until we were half way along a particularly dark stretch of deserted woodland track that it occurred to me I might be in the company of a serial killer.

Safely back in the centre we sat in a terrace bar beside the lake at the rear of the Kurhaus and consumed copious quantities of beer and pretzels until after dark. Bernhard was a good conversationalist who welcomed the opportunity to practise his English, and he was keen to discuss, amongst other things, history, politics and current affairs, subjects on which my ability to sustain even the briefest chat, let alone several hours of deep discussion, was woefully inadequate. I was surprised to find myself coping reasonably well, hoping the language barrier might disguise the worst of my inaccuracies, but at a crucial moment when he asked for my opinion on some matter and leaned back in anticipation of an intelligent reply, I was completely lost for words and at the same time blessed with a genuine attack of cramp necessitating a swift exit from my seat, which created a timely diversion. As the evening wore on it dawned on me that Bernhard might be expecting more than a goodnight handshake. By half past midnight he'd missed the last train home and it became obvious that he was angling for an invitation back to my room. I made it clear that this was definitely not on the cards so he quickly announced that as his next train wasn't due until four in the morning he would go dancing.

A thunder storm woke me around dawn and I spent much of the day walking in the Kurpark, drinking in the aroma of damp earth and the freshness of greenery after the rain, while counting the hours until I would hear Sokolov's Byrd/Beethoven/Ravel programme again.

A recording was being made of that evening's recital and Sokolov's recording manager, Yolanta Skura, was supervising the setting up of equipment and placement of microphones. The audience behaved impeccably during the first half and the performance was flawless, but as soon as Sokolov touched the damper pedal after the interval it gave out a loud groan which persisted until the end and ruined the second part of the recording. He tried moderating the pressure but it was still a distraction for the audience and presumably a nightmare for him. At the inquest afterwards it was decided to try and capture another performance two days later in Essen if the conditions were right.

A post-concert supper had been arranged at the Kurhaus's Terrace Restaurant and I was invited to join the entourage. I produced some English newspaper cuttings about Sokolov that no one had seen before and they were passed eagerly round the table. There was I, sitting beneath the stars with Fourth of July fireworks exploding in the distance, dining and conversing with Sokolov's colleagues. I could hardly believe I was living such a life.

My next destination was Munich, where Sokolov gave two consecutive evening performances of Tchaikovsky's 1st Piano Concerto with the Bavarian Radio Symphony Orchestra conducted by Vladimir Fedosseyev. A special room rate was available at a classy hotel right next to the Gasteig concert hall, but mindful of my unhappy experience at the Frankfurt Hilton I opted for something cheaper, far away on the other side of town. I knew nothing about Munich and had imagined it to be a bustling metropolis, choked with traffic and dominated by tall office blocks, expensive department stores and swanky hotels. It was therefore a revelation to discover that the walk from my hotel to the Gasteig was almost entirely along a wide pedestrianised thoroughfare dotted with pavement cafés and flanked by imposing and beautiful buildings.

Hidden from view by a screen of trees, the Gasteig was an extensive modern cultural complex housing two theatres and an enormous concert hall. The first performance was a disappointment, primarily because the orchestra sounded as if they'd been up all night, opening the programme with a lacklustre Capriccio Italien, in addition to which the piano tuning left something to be desired. When I spoke to Sokolov afterwards I told him that even after two years of flying, each time I boarded an aircraft I was certain it would crash. I tried to convey to him – just in case anything happened to me - how much I valued those two years, and he said, "I don't think anything will happen to you". He then placed his hand on top of the practice piano and declared, "We are all under God".

The next day I explored the city, stopping to watch a group of old men playing chess in a park with pieces as big as traffic cones. I meandered across cobbled squares, gazed at the architecture and climbed to the top of one of the Frauenkirche towers for a marvellous view across the city. There was much to see in a compact area: the old and new town halls, the opera house, numerous churches, theatres and museums. Shortly before midday I stood with a crowd of tourists in Marienplatz, waiting for the glockenspiel to come to life in the Rathaus tower. As the hour struck, thirty-two revolving figures enacted a jousting tournament and a group of twirling coopers celebrated the end of the plague. A few minutes later I was stopped in my tracks as I turned a corner into Max-Joseph Platz and discovered an outdoor platform on which the orchestra and chorus of the Bavarian State Opera were rehearsing Mahler's 2nd Symphony under the baton of the great Zubin Mehta, in preparation for an evening performance in their series *Oper für Alle*. How fortunate I felt to stumble upon such ravishing sounds, and I stood transfixed until the end of the finale. My wanderings continued through the elegant courtyards of the Residenz, Munich's royal palace, and the famous Viktualienmarkt, one of Europe's great food markets, where a stunning array of produce was artistically displayed. In the afternoon I explored the extensive Englischer Garten with its expanses of green, wooded walks and gurgling river.

The second night at the Gasteig was a totally different experience. I sat closer to the platform with a view of the keyboard, the piano sounded splendid and the orchestra had become enlivened overnight. When I remarked on the contrast between the two evenings, Sokolov threw up his hands and said, "Yes, I know! Last night was terrible! Everything was out of tune!" As I left the building I caught sight of the Sokolovs ambling contentedly away towards their hotel, arm in arm, laden with flowers, and I rejoiced in the knowledge that Sokolov, far from being the archetypal solitary musician, was so often accompanied by a devoted wife with whom he appeared to share a singularly harmonious and loving relationship.

Later that year I went to Berlin, and on account of various delays I found myself elevated to business class. After a further delay on account of one loose screw which I would have preferred not to know about, we were off. A splendid four course meal was included in my upgrade, and I chatted with a German businessman who invited me to share his taxi into the city, instructing the driver to take us on the scenic route passing Schloss Charlottenburg and finally dropping me off at the Hotel-Pension Imperator, an elegant old establishment run by an artist whose ancient rooms were filled with artwork and books on art history and architecture.

I quickly located the Konzerthaus, where Sokolov was to give two performances of Chopin's 2nd Piano Concerto with the Berlin Symphony Orchestra under Walter Weller. At the box office I learned that only one ticket had been allocated to me and it was for the next evening. Both concerts were sold out, so my only hope of hearing that night's performance was to be back at the box office by six-thirty in the hope of a return, or alternatively wait for Sokolov to arrive and ask for his assistance. I decided to try the latter but on arrival found he was already installed in his dressing room. I was reluctant to disturb him, but a member of the orchestra took it upon himself to go and explain my predicament. Within minutes I was handed a ticket enabling me to sit in a box reserved for the director's guests. The gentleman sitting next to me announced very proudly that he had once heard the great French pianist Alfred Cortot play the Chopin concerto conducted by Furtwangler. He'd not heard Sokolov before but by the end of the performance he was in raptures.

The next morning I walked in the grounds of Schloss Charlottenburg, through the vast Tiergarten, then on to Unter den Linden and the iconic Brandenburg Gate. On the walk back to my side of the city I was targeted by a skilled trio of pickpockets who stole my purse as I stood waiting to cross the street. It wasn't until I'd sat down in a café and ordered tea that I made the discovery and remembered being jostled at the kerbside. I'd lost a considerable amount of cash and had no means of paying for the tea but a sympathetic waitress told me it was on the house.

To add insult to injury, on the long walk back to the Imperator I tripped and fell in the street right next to a crowd of people waiting to board a bus. Two young men helped me to my feet and within seconds my knee became so stiff that I had difficulty in walking. It was late in the afternoon when I limped into the hotel and related my tale of woe. Without hesitation the manager gave me enough cash to get me through the evening, added it to my bill and told me I could settle matters when I got home. Despite feeling less than my best, I was soon on my way back to the Konzerthaus, exhilarated at the sight of the Gendarmenmarkt with a floodlit cathedral at either end. It had been my intention to leave the hall after the concerto, but I decided to stay for Mendelssohn's Scottish Symphony and give the artist's room a miss. The next morning I left the Imperator feeling touched by such understanding. My return flight was overbooked, and had I not been so tired and uncomfortable I'm sure I would have taken up the airline's offer of 600 deutsche marks in exchange for taking a later flight. I regretted my decision all the way home.

The Rough Guide to Germany described the accommodation I'd set my sights on in Münster as old-fashioned, and at first glance it seemed they were spot on. Arriving on a May evening in 1999 I found the hotel in a forlorn looking street close to the station, and I was received by an elderly lady who spoke no English. Despite the unpromising exterior there was evidence of recent refurbishment and everything in my room looked brand new. The next morning I breakfasted alone, apart from the aged manageress who chain-smoked in a corner. I was attended by a maternal ancient in a flowered overall who chattered non-stop about who knew what, brought second helpings whether I wanted them or not, showered me with leaflets and joined me at the table in order to spread out a street map and direct me to everything worth seeing in Münster.

The city centre reverberated with a commotion of church bells as I walked along the Prinzipalmarkt and crossed Domplatz where people were flocking into the cathedral for the morning service. I soon came to the schloss, an elegant eighteenth century building now used by the university, behind which were botanical gardens densely planted with azaleas and rhododendrons in a multitude of colours. From there I took to the cool, tree-lined promenade which encircled the city centre and continued around Münster's large boating lake, the Aasee, where locals and visitors sailed, strolled and cycled. As I reached the far end of the lake and drew level with a nondescript concrete building, the unmistakable sound of Sokolov playing Schubert drifted out of a nearby window. I spent the next forty-five minutes perched on a cool stone ledge listening to his practice session, enjoying the luxury of extra rations.

That evening I was greeted enthusiastically by the concert organiser who had to be restrained from whisking me straight into Sokolov's room before the recital had even begun. Housed as it was in such an unattractive building, the auditorium looked surprisingly smart. There were a few empty places in the front block reserved for subscribers, presumably on account of the six o'clock start, the unusually hot weather and the fact that it was Mothering Sunday. I planned to move forward after the interval, but the unexpected appearance of Mrs S in the seat next to mine put paid to that idea. She seemed pleased to be sitting with me, but her sense of anxiety throughout the performance was palpable. Each time the audience rose to its feet I hesitated, but she encouraged me to do likewise if I wished. In her shoes I too would have spent the entire duration praying for all to go according to plan, which of course it did.

The second time I visited Wiesbaden I pre-booked a room at a chain hotel recommended by Bernhard, whom I'd met on my previous visit. On the afternoon of my arrival he was keen to show me where he lived, so we took a short train ride to his home town where he had a studio apartment. I remember nothing about it other than one wall of his room being almost entirely occupied by a massive monochrome poster of a famous Helmut Newton photograph showing four perfectly proportioned models striding towards the camera wearing nothing but make-up and stilettos.

Back in Wiesbaden Bernhard suggested we drink some beer in my room, which I agreed to do, having sent out plenty of signals that our connection was to be purely platonic. To my dismay, he walked in, plumped up the pillows on my bed, switched on the television and made himself at home by stretching out full length. I sat on a chair and primly sipped my beer until I could summon up the courage to ask him to leave, suggesting we meet the following afternoon. I took a bus the next morning to Schloss Biebrich, a baroque palace on the Rhine, and in the afternoon I had tea with Bernhard in the palatial Kurhaus restaurant. The sight of so much cake reminded me of my mother, and as I sank my teeth into a generous wedge of torte I wondered what she would have made of the amazing turn my life had taken.

That evening the festival director looked hot under the collar as he stood in the foyer of the Casino-Gesellschaft instructing his staff and dispensing complimentary tickets to the favoured few. Sokolov was still rehearsing just five minutes before kick-off, and the director must have been wondering how to eject the man of the moment from the piano stool in order to get the restless multitude seated. Several people who remembered me from previous recitals came up and greeted me, Mrs S blew me a kiss from the back row, and I felt very much at home. The recital was stupendous and the director could have won first prize in a Mr Smug contest.

In the middle of having photographs taken with the Sokolovs to mark my fiftieth concert I remembered my coat was still in the cloakroom. The director's wife, who was looking resplendent in electric blue, bustled off to retrieve it for me. It had been raining when I'd set out so I'd been forced to fling on a cheap nylon cagoule, which she soon reappeared with, suspended from one finger and held at arm's length. I seriously considered disowning it, having just learned that I was about to be driven to the sumptuous Nassauer Hof, reputedly the most expensive hotel in Germany at that time and one of Europe's truly grand hotels, for a glass of champagne to celebrate the occasion.

Arriving in Hanover on an Autumn evening in 2000 I found the Expo trade fair was in full swing, rendering budget accommodation virtually non-existent. I put in a good two hours of pavement pounding before I found a room in an outlying hotel with quite the most extraordinary reception area imaginable. It was decorated in primary colours with a few abstract paintings scattered about, an incongruous collection of antique grandfather clocks, a wind-up gramophone with a large horn, three massive mirrors with extravagant gilt frames propped against the walls which looked too heavy to hang, half a dozen painted statues of religious figures and, in a garage-sized alcove opposite the reception desk, a white Rolls Royce Silver Cloud motor car.

On my ramblings the next day I learned that little of the old part of Hanover remained, but inside the Rathaus were four scale models of the city: one as it looked in the seventeenth century, another in the twentieth century, a third immediately after the bombing and one showing how it looked currently. I decided to visit one of the city's major attractions, the Grosser Garten, which could be reached by tram or alternatively by walking through a series of three other royal gardens. I chose to go by tram and found a baroque showpiece on a grand scale with geometrically arranged flower gardens, dozens of statues, pools and fountains, an Italianate cascade, a grotto and a maze. At the rear, Europe's second highest fountain rose to eighty-two metres, from which radiated a series of tree-lined walks, each of them leading to another fountain. There was also an amphitheatre where Handel's music and plays by Molière and Racine had been performed for the royals and their guests.

In the NDR Funkhaus that evening Sokolov gave an exceptional performance of Schubert's Sonata D664, Franck's Prelude, Chorale & Fugue and Ten Chopin Mazurkas. I was told that at a recent recital in Luxembourg, a sub-standard Steinway had not taken kindly to the Franck fugue, during which two notes had jammed and an extended interval had been necessary in order to resuscitate the piano. The mazurkas which had followed were executed with caution, after which Sokolov let rip with some explosive encores, as if in an attempt to put the ailing instrument out of its misery.

In November 2000 a series of delays resulted in a late arrival in Berlin, and I finally walked into my hotel room at two in the morning. The Hotel Charlot provided an uninterrupted flow of classical music, mainly piano concertos, throughout the communal areas all day long, which for me was a source of constant pleasure. Furthermore, a bus went from the end of the street directly to the Philharmonie, which housed not only the Kammermusiksaal, Sokolov's recital venue, but also a museum of musical instruments, where I spent all morning enjoying an exhibition of period keyboard instruments to mark three hundred years of piano building in Germany.

Later, at the Kammermusiksaal Sokolov's performance was warmly received, and just before he disappeared for the final time following the fourth encore, a bearded boho leapt onto the platform proffering a large box of chocolates. Sokolov smiled and held out his hands, assuming he was being presented with the whole box, but the young man merely whipped off the lid and invited him to choose one. A bemused Sokolov duly made his selection and carried it into the wings.

Earlier that afternoon I'd called in at a tobacconist's next door to my hotel to stock up with cigarettes at less than half the price I paid at home. The shopkeeper had only five packs left of my favourite brand, so I bought them all. Early the next morning as I passed the shop on my way to the airport she came rushing out waving a pack of Silk Cut. "I found another one!" she gasped. As I reached for my purse she told me to put it away and accept them as a farewell gift. I found it hard to imagine such a thing happening to a German tourist in England.

February 2001 brought reports of Arctic conditions across Europe, prompting me to don specially purchased all-weather footwear and leave home at five in the morning with a bag full of thermals, spare sweaters and thick socks. The taxi to the airport was rocked by vicious gusts as flashes of lightning snaked across the sky, but by the time I took off it was daylight, the wind had dropped and the sun was on its way. Before I knew it I was in Munich, queueing for a rail ticket to Bamberg, a journey necessitating four changes. As I might have expected, Bavaria was basking in a balmy thirteen degrees, the boots proved unnecessary and the thermals never saw the light of day.

Bamberg was a captivating place, full of architectural gems, exquisitely decorated houses and glorious churches. The Tourist Office booked me into a small hotel in the centre, run by a stylish lady who was waiting out on the pavement to welcome me. The five hundred year old building groaned with age, and its ground floor was occupied by a spacious shop selling luxury gifts and designer label clothing. Just around the corner in the cathedral tea room I had several opportunities to witness the solemnity with which German ladies applied themselves to the ceremony of afternoon coffee and cake. Firstly the overcoats were hung in the cloak cupboard, although hats generally remained in place. Then came the serious business of deciding which cakes to order: never less than two and often accompanied by generous swirls of cream. Finally, the sacred moment arrived when the cake fork was taken up and the silent ritual began.

To reach the Konzerthalle that evening I walked along the river bank, passing a row of pretty fishermen's dwellings known locally as

Little Venice, where a gondola was moored outside one of the cottages. As the brightly illuminated hall came into view I positively fizzed with excitement. This was to be Sokolov's first public performance of a programme of pieces by Mozart - the Fantasy KV475 and Sonata KV457 - which he delivered with consummate elegance. On my way back, the intricately decorated Altes Rathaus straddling the rushing river Regnitz and the Concordia Water Palace looked so enchanting by night that I could scarcely tear myself away.

I moved on to Nuremberg the next day, where I snapped up an unmissable special offer at Le Meridien Grand, one of the city's smartest hotels. When I opened the door to my room and viewed the opulence within, I feared I may have been given the wrong key and returned to reception just to check. Making good use of the time available, I firstly took a tram to see the site of the Nazi rallies, Hitler's monstrous Kongressbau which was modelled on the Colosseum. There was also time to stroll through the city, climb up to the Kaiserburg for a wonderful view across the rooftops and enjoy coffee and cake in the pretty little square at Tiergärtner Tor.

Another great evening unfolded at the Meistersingerhalle, and the next day I took a train to the tiny island town of Lindau on Lake Konstanz for one more performance. Beyond Augsburg the landscape changed and we began passing alpine villages, frozen lakes and vast drifts of snow. On the island I found a cosy guest house just a minute away from the concert venue. The recital wasn't until the following evening and there was much to see and photograph on the island, but for the moment it was shrouded in mist. Finding something uncomplicated to eat also proved difficult and I spent an age trudging from restaurant to restaurant peering at menus. Long after dark, on my umpteenth circuit of the town centre, I walked along the promenade feeling increasingly hungry and dejected. Lindau was much too classy to entertain a Pizza Hut, sausage stall or chip van, all of which I'd utilised in Bamberg and Nuremberg. Passing the deluxe Hotel Bayerischer Hof I could see guests dining by candlelight and spotted a couple I knew seated at a table in the window. I scuttled away for fear they might glance out to admire the lake and see me staring in at them. Within minutes I'd found a splendid little bistro hidden away in a narrow alley which became my regular haunt for the remainder of my stay.

Sun streamed through my curtains the next morning and the empty square beneath my window was now full of market stalls. It was a perfect day for walking round the island: crisp and clear with unspoiled views across the water. I also took a bus to the mainland as far as the village of Hoyren, where a footpath climbed to a vantage point with a breathtaking vista across the lake towards the Alps. Later in the day I sat on a bench near the water and counted my blessings. The lake was like glass, the snow on the mountain tops tinged with pink, and as the sun went down the entire scene was bathed in a soft roseate glow.

Sokolov performed in a converted 700 year old Franciscan church, where charcoal sketches of him at the piano were displayed in glass cases in the entrance hall. As we congregated in the artist's room after the recital Sokolov was presented with a set of studies in miniature and the manager came in with beer and pretzels all round. Sokolov's performance had, for a number of reasons, been marginally less than his best, but the recital in Lindau was merely a reminder that he was human, which made the truly great performances even more remarkable.

A month later I was back in Germany for concerts in Stuttgart and Munich. At Birmingham Airport my sandwiches were confiscated due to the recent outbreak of foot and mouth disease, which wasn't a good start. In Stuttgart I checked into a moderately priced hotel next door to a lap dancing club, then located the unremarkable Liederhalle building and took a brisk walk to Schlossplatz, a wide open space overlooked by the stately baroque Neues Schloss, the neo-classical Konigsbau and the Renaissance Altes Schloss with its beautiful triple-tiered courtyard, where summer concerts were sometimes held. In the Liederhalle's Beethovensaal the concert organiser apologised for the fact that the best seats were allocated to subscribers. He'd been listening to the rehearsal of pieces by Couperin during the afternoon and remarked that there seemed to be about two hundred of them (in fact there were twenty-three). Personally I loved the abundant ornamentation but could imagine anyone less enthusiastic leaving the recital with a strong desire never to hear another trill as long as they lived.

The next day I moved on to Munich, and with an empty evening to fill I scanned the listings for some musical entertainment, but in fact there was no need. A wealth of talented musicians were performing along the main thoroughfare against a backdrop of majestic floodlit buildings and city gateways. Many shops were still open, the streets teemed with people, and I was content to mingle with them until bedtime. Much of the following day was spent in the Residenz building, where a number of royal apartments and galleries were open to the public. The building also contained two concert halls, including the Herkulessaal, where Sokolov performed that evening. Facing the former royal park, the Hofgarten, the hall's foyer contained larger than life golden statues of Bavarian royalty and the auditorium was lined with tapestries. Sokolov was in top form and a large gathering clamoured to speak to him afterwards. His wife was at home recovering from 'flu and he was unaware at the time that she'd already passed on the infection to him, which was to result in the cancellation of two recitals in the Netherlands I'd planned to attend the following week.

My next trip to Germany came in May 2001 when I first sampled the delights of Schwetzingen, a town not far from Heidelberg, whose major attraction was its baroque palace and gardens. Within the palace were a number of chamber music salons and a theatre, and the combination of the beautiful gardens with world class theatrical and musical performances attracted many visitors to the Schwetzingen Festival every summer. It was a fine evening and I couldn't resist taking a quick look at the schlossgarten, which was in a different league to anything I'd seen before. The setting sun provided wonderful contrasts of light and shade and I looked forward to exploring every square inch of the garden the next day. No wonder it took thirty years to complete the layout and construct the many intriguing features: fountains and statues, hidden pavilions, Roman temples, a Turkish mosque, a fort and an aqueduct, a bath house with beautifully decorated water pipes and a jewel encrusted inner chamber.

In Schlossplatz I ate supper beneath the trees. A pile of pasta, cheese, fried onions, potatoes and a flagon of beer went down nicely but did its best to come back up again during the night. All was well by morning and I returned to the gardens for a thorough exploration. At lunchtime I subsided onto a seat in the shade of the palace building. Somewhere inside, a chamber orchestra was rehearsing, blending perfectly with the splendour of the French formal gardens spread out before me. As I plunged into a plastic carrier to make a start on the food I'd brought with me, who should appear from behind an ornamental tree but Sokolov, accompanied by a young man wheeling a bicycle, presumably someone detailed by the festival management to accompany him to the venue. How thankful I was that I'd not just stuffed a sandwich into my mouth, or worse still kicked off my shoes and lit a cigarette. He stopped in his tracks when he saw me, put his hands on his hips and expressed amazement at seeing me there. He was of the opinion that Schwetzingen was an awkward place to find but I could have told him that compared to many of my other concert journeys it had been a doddle. "Nice garden", he observed with a smile, then warned me it was going to be extremely hot at the recital and continued on his way.

I was disappointed that he wasn't playing in the Rokokotheater on account of an opera currently being staged there. The theatre was closed to the public during the day, but I sneaked round the back of the building, ran into someone with access and persuaded him to let me have a quick look inside. Attached to the main building in the 1750s for the performance of French comedies (Voltaire was a regular visitor) the beautiful little auditorium was lyre-shaped and the stage exceptionally deep. I was thrilled to have seen it and glad I'd summoned up the courage to ask.

Walking to the outer reaches of the gardens I passed an orchard and the inevitable English garden with acres of woodland crammed with wildlife and untamed open spaces full of orchids and a host of other wild flowers. Skirting round a vast lake guarded by statues of river gods representing the Rhine and the Danube, I walked through the colonnades of a Turkish mosque. There was something Disneyesque about the English garden, where I came upon a pool with herons standing motionless at the water's edge, while groups of ducks clambered out and waddled across carpets of daisies. Squirrels frolicked and scampered beneath the trees like puppies, and peacocks paraded up and down like supermodels, needing no encouragement to show off their finery, turning this way and that for better effect. As the afternoon grew hotter I retreated to the woodland walks, where even more amazements lay in store. At one point I stood on a narrow path between the trees, looking down at two red squirrels as they sat up and begged at my feet. A tiny field mouse came to join them and gazed up at me expectantly. As if that wasn't enough, a cluster of tiny blue birds with black caps appeared from nowhere and fluttered round my head. I held out a hand and one of them settled on my finger. If at that moment seven dwarfs had come hi-ho-ing round the bend I wouldn't have been in the least bit surprised.

The Konzertsaal in which the recital took place that evening was almost as beautiful as the Rokokotheater, complementing the delights of Couperin, Mozart and Franck. Beside the piano were urns cascading greenery and giant pedestalled candelabras; the huge windows were uncurtained and so Sokolov began his programme in daylight and reached its conclusion by moonlight. A magical experience to end a remarkable day.

Konzertsaal, Schwetzingen 2001

In July of 2001 I returned to Wiesbaden and on the day of the recital I walked in the Kurpark, where the regular Sunday morning fitness fanatics jogged past me, some of them bursting periodically into vigorous sprints or pausing to stretch hamstrings. By contrast I took a long time to cover very little ground and spent the afternoon resting my unhappy feet, a lifetime of long distance walking having rendered them less than fit for purpose.

That evening I made a special effort with my appearance in order to impress the festival director's wife, but she was at home recovering from eye surgery. Sokolov approached the piano with a pained expression, as if he'd been promised a damned good hiding if he dared play a wrong note, but the evening ended in celebration and the director was obliged to make four attempts to present him with a box of wines. Approaching the platform from various directions, he narrowly missed catching Sokolov's eye before the elusive figure turned away and walked off stage or returned to the piano for another encore. Desperate to fulfil his mission, the director hovered on the sidelines for the duration of the final encore and then scrambled indecorously onto the platform to deliver the goods at last.

In the artist's room an attractive young woman stood waiting to speak to Sokolov, clutching a single rose which perfectly matched her outfit. When her turn came she handed him the rose, gazed into his eyes and began pouring out her heart. As usually happened in such circumstances Sokolov hastily introduced Mrs S into the equation. He must have dashed quite a few hopes over the years with those four little words, "This is my wife". In my particular case, back in Bordeaux in 1998, I already knew that he had a wife and was fully prepared for the brush-off.

Wandelhalle Bad Kissingen

The next day I went by train to Bad Kissingen, a gem of a spa town in northern Bavaria, which was like stepping into another dimension where all my favourite things were assembled in one place and there was a complete absence of everything I found irritating. Elegant buildings stood alongside traditional old world charm; the town was pervaded by the scent of flowers, the splash of fountains and the sound of music. There was an air of gentility and refinement, with nothing to offend the ear or eye. Bad Kissingen seemed to be populated predominantly by the middle-aged and elderly. It was one of those places where wealthy Germans went either to be cured of their ills or to expire, and they appeared to have a splendid time in the process.

I chose a small hotel along the narrow river promenade overlooking the Kurpark, where a huge expanse of green was dotted with dozens of reclining chairs provided for public use. These could be placed out in the sun or moved into the shade of the trees, where rustic picnic tables were randomly scattered. In a distant corner of the park a discreet beer garden was set up and a Tyrolean band oompahed gently from mid-afternoon until sundown. Along the promenade were the thermal baths, a gambling casino and the Wandelhalle, a lofty building of glass and marble in which thermal waters bubbled. Nearby was an enclosed garden with rows of benches under the trees where residents and visitors gathered three times a day in spring and summer to listen to a live orchestra. I attended the afternoon concert and was intrigued to see women in their seventies and eighties sashaying along the rows of benches, dressed in floaty chiffon numbers, expensive accessories, full make up; some with picture hats, bare legs, strappy high-heeled slingbacks and painted toenails. Equally fascinating was the orchestra, who launched into the first half of the concert with tunes from operettas and lilting gypsy melodies. The grim-faced pianist looked like one of Hitler's henchmen, but after the interval when the violins were cast aside and replaced by saxophones and trumpets for a lively medley of big band swing numbers, he was transformed.

Beyond the garden stood the grandiose Regentenbau, completed in 1913 in neo-baroque style to entertain European nobility on their visits to take the waters. The building also housed several concert halls, the largest of which, the Max-Littmann-Saal, was Sokolov's recital venue. The Regentenbau overlooked a large rose garden in full bloom, the centrepiece of which was a fan shaped fountain, illuminated at night in rainbow colours. This was the dreamlike backdrop to my first experience of Kissingen's Summer Festival. Sokolov had already told me he enjoyed performing at this annual event, and it was evident in the Regentenbau that evening. He gave his all to an affectionate audience and I came away feeling that this was just the start of a long love affair with Bad Kissingen.

Regentenbau Bad Kissingen

My final German concert destination that year was Bremen's splendid Die Glocke, with its striking interior of dark mahogany and luminous pale green ceiling. Just about everything was perfect that evening: my seat, the audience, the acoustic, the piano and above all Sokolov's playing. The audience stamped and cheered after the Haydn sonatas and by the time Sokolov had delivered the Mozart pieces and powered his way through the Franck, the place was in uproar. His first encore, Couperin's Le Tic-Toc-Choc, brought the house down, and he followed up with the volcanic Ravel Toccata, which elicited screams of delight from an exhausted but very happy audience.

On my next trip to Munich in the spring of 2002 I arrived at the Herkulessaal sufficiently early to examine more closely the towering gilded statues of European royalty and other notables in the foyer, including Duke Ludwig the Severe, my secret nickname for the concert organiser, whom I found rather intimidating. My seat that evening was a disappointment, situated on the extreme left hand side in the front row, resulting in a stiff neck and a distant view of Sokolov's rear. Afterwards Mrs S asked in German how I was, and at the very same moment I asked her the same question in Russian. I replied to her question in English and, rather confusingly, she did the same in Italian. (I often cast my mind back to the night I turned up out of the blue in Bordeaux and she generously pushed me in the direction of her husband to have a photo taken with him, imagining it might be a once in a lifetime opportunity for me, little realising how much of a persistent fly in the ointment I was destined to become.)

Eight years later I was to change my opinion of the Herkulessaal concert organiser, when the Icelandic volcano erupted and the resultant ash cloud closed the air space between Birmingham and Munich. On this occasion I'd agreed to pay for my ticket on arrival, but he offered to dispose of it at the last minute on my behalf, which now I come to think of it would have been a simple matter. The major halls often had waiting lists for Sokolov's performances.

One of my favourite German adventures was a trip to Bonn and Braunschweig in May 2002. The Bonn recital took place in the Beethoven Haus, a historic building consisting of two large houses, one of which was now a museum containing over a hundred exhibits, including the last piano Beethoven possessed, a bonnet he wore as a baby and a sad collection of ear trumpets. It was a profound experience to stand in the room in which he came into the world. The Kammermusiksaal, a charming little auditorium inside the building adjoining the museum, was created specifically for chamber concerts and solo recitals. It seated two hundred people and was designed in such a way that behind the audience was a large window overlooking a garden, and this view was reflected onto an expanse of black marble behind the platform just above the soloist's head. As night fell, the reflection slowly dimmed.

Just three weeks had elapsed since Munich but it could easily have been six months, and the performance almost reduced me to tears. Sokolov brought such freshness to every piece and so many subtle changes in tempo, dynamics and phrasing, it all seemed brand new.

Afterwards he modestly attributed any credit to the different acoustic and piano, but when I insisted that he must have played some part in this miracle, he grinned and shyly conceded, "Well yes, I expect so". I mentioned that I was going to the recital in Braunschweig the next day and he warned me that the venue was in the small village of Bisdorf, miles away from the city and impossible to reach by public transport. Giving one of his characteristic shrugs he said, "I don't know what it will be like; it's a kind of agricultural place, to do with horses I think". Actually it was sheep, but he certainly gave me food for thought and I began to suspect that some sort of challenge lay in wait.

Outside the artist's room I chatted with a friendly threesome who were fascinated by my commitment. Although musically knowledgeable, this was their first Sokolov recital and they were overwhelmed by what they'd heard. They went in to see him first and invited him to supper, received the standard polite refusal, withdrew reluctantly and left me to have my precious few moments. On my way out of the building I was surprised to find them waiting for me in the street, where they asked if I was alone in Bonn and invited me back to their house for a late supper so that we could discuss the events of the evening. My hosts were an elegant man in his fifties, his attractive wife and their extraordinary son. Probably in his late twenties, he was heart-stoppingly handsome, gentle in the extreme and softly spoken with a mesmerising delivery.

We were soon purring along in their Mercedes, heading for the old spa town of Bad Godesberg, and as the front door of their palatial house opened, so too did my mouth, such was the magnitude of their home and the lavishness of its contents. I'd never set foot in such an enormous private dwelling in my life. Beautiful period furniture adorned the main room, much of it exquisitely inlaid, along with an impressive collection of French clocks and several statues. A huge antique cupboard stood against each of the four walls, one of which had been part of a dowry, painted and inscribed with the bride's name and the date of the wedding in the early 1700s. The room's centrepiece was a handsome Steinway grand which took up no more space than a small occasional table would in an average suburban home. The family held regular chamber music soirées there, and the organisers of Sokolov's recital had asked them if he could spend the previous evening practising on their piano, but because they'd heard about his formidably powerful playing and knew he was currently performing Prokofiev, they'd feared their elderly Steinway might not recover from such a trauma. It seemed a Steinway was almost as common a household accessory as a lawn mower in Bad Godesberg, for they were able to direct Sokolov to a friend round the corner who possessed a much more robust instrument. As it turned out, he'd played only Haydn, so my hosts were determined to be first in the queue for him to lay hands on their piano next time he was in Bonn.

I was shown what could be seen of their essentially English garden, which had been planted painstakingly with specially selected trees and shrubs. Climbing a steep grassy bank to see Bad Godesberg's moonlit castle complete with mountain backdrop, I thought of dear Robert Schumann, whose life ended so tragically at the age of forty-six in nearby Endenich. We ate a leisurely supper and it pleased me no end when they told me they usually found the English rather cold but that I was different. Before leaving, I was asked to sign their visitors' book, and I couldn't resist pointing out that they could have had Sokolov's signature in there, just above mine, had they been prepared to take a risk with the piano.

I moved on to Braunschweig the next day and found a cheerful room filled with sunshine, birdsong, the distant thwack of tennis balls and a fire escape garlanded with wisteria. A swift excursion by tram revealed that the city was blessed with many historic buildings which would ensure plenty to occupy me the following day. My euros were disappearing fast so I set out the next morning with the aim of spending as little as possible. Miraculously it was the one day of the year when admission to all museums and places of interest was free, and one of the museums was dispensing coffee and cakes at give-away prices, so I took advantage of everything on offer, breezing through several museums, lingering in the sumptuously decorated Rittersaal in the Castle of Henry the Lion and visiting the city's botanical gardens, arranged along the bank of the river Oker.

I decided the best way to get myself to Bisdorf was to catch a train to the nearest railway station and take a taxi from there. The recital started at seven, and at five-thirty I'd reached the small town of Helmstedt, outside whose tiny station there was a choice of four taxi drivers, none of whom had any idea where Bisdorf was located. Two of them leafed through road atlases, another radioed his headquarters to seek guidance and the fourth lay prostrate across his front seats beating his head with his fists. It was agreed that I should go in search of a cup of tea and return at six o'clock, by which time hopefully someone who knew the whereabouts of Bisdorf would be waiting for me. There were no cosy teashops in evidence so I swept through a beaded curtain into a small bar where an assortment of locals were enjoying a quiet jar. They looked startled to see a stranger in their midst, somewhat overdressed for a sleepy Sunday afternoon in this most modest of watering holes. I ventured to ask if anyone had heard of Bisdorf but was met with a collective shaking of heads.

At six I hastened back to the station and a taxi drew up immediately, containing an alarmingly muscular lady driver who spoke no English but leaned across and barked, "Bisdorf!" The journey took thirty agonising minutes but was wonderfully scenic. With no hedgerows to obscure the views, the long, straight, gently undulating roads allowed the distinctive pastoral landscape of Lower Saxony to unfurl, but the rural idyll was somewhat dampened when I noticed the meter reading was perilously close to exceeding the amount of cash left in my purse. My heart sank as we passed through countless villages with no signs pointing to Bisdorf, but at last I spotted a Braunschweig Classix Festival banner, and there at the side of the road was a massive barn with an awning, beneath which a prosperous looking crowd were knocking back pre-concert drinks. I had no idea how I was going to get back to Braunschweig with no cash, but I soon met up with two representatives from the German concert promoters, who offered me a lift.

The auditorium was in the upper half of a building that resembled a giant hay loft. A substantial capacity audience piled in and despite less than perfect conditions it was a terrific performance. As I sat wondering what would happen if a fire broke out I acquired an extensive collection of insect bites. Goodness knows how many times Sokolov had been bitten since he arrived in the afternoon, but performing in a glorified cow shed was bound to have its drawbacks. So, with horse flies dancing attendance around his head, he battled courageously against a multitude of birds gathered in the nearby trees, whose evensong could be heard quite clearly through the roof of the barn. For much of the first half they had the advantage, but

Prokofiev succeeded where Haydn had failed and eventually the birds admitted defeat. When asked how he'd enjoyed performing in Bisdorf, Sokolov's face reminded me of a small boy being encouraged to eat his greens.

That summer, Sokolov's Wiesbaden recital was moved to the Christian Zais Saal inside the Kurhaus. The festival director reigned supreme in the spacious reception hall, distributing tickets which might have been sprinkled with gold dust, surrounded by a sleek and manicured gathering who sipped champagne and eyed each other's outfits. As I walked out into the gardens at the rear where it was cooler, I collided with the director's wife, who looked stunning in a perfectly accessorized figure-hugging oyster brocade dress and jacket, with a haircut to die for, expertly applied make-up and gleaming dental work. She'd been unable to attend the previous year's recital, having undergone a treacherous sounding procedure on her retina. Greeting me with enthusiasm she held me at arm's length and exclaimed, "Mrs Truman! You look so elegant this evening, and *very* pretty!" giving rise to the suspicion that the eye surgery may not have been entirely successful.

The Christian Zais Saal was cool and comfortable with its marble pillars and gilt framed mirrors behind the piano, and I found myself clinging to every note of the Haydn sonatas in the certain knowledge that this was the last time I would hear them. Outside, a group of people I'd seen at previous recitals invited me to have a drink with them in a nearby bar along with a few others, all of them musicians or music teachers, one a musicologist. They showed great interest in my passion for Sokolov's live performances and I felt lucky to be holding my own in such elevated company, realising all too well that I could never hope to pull off such a feat in my own country.

Everyone drifted off around one o'clock apart from the musicologist, who was only just getting into his stride. With several language degrees already to his credit he was currently studying for a doctorate and preparing a dissertation on an obscure nineteenth century Russian composer. Earlier in the general conversation I'd made the fatal mistake of mentioning how much I'd enjoyed learning about music theory and taking my exams, so under the misconception that my knowledge must be fairly extensive, he launched into a totally incomprehensible discourse, producing by way of illustration scraps of paper on which he feverishly drew numerous staves and scribbled complex notation at incredible speed. If only I'd made it clear from the outset that I'd progressed no further than Grade 2 and could scarcely remember what a treble clef looked like I could have saved him a lot of effort, but it was too late and he was totally immersed. I, on the other hand, was completely out of my depth and so desperately tired that it took an iron will to prevent myself from sliding under the table. He was a veritable walking encyclopaedia of music whose enthusiasm knew no bounds, and on a future occasion at a different hostelry in Wiesbaden he was to quote every musical reference he could remember from Shakespeare's sonnets.

My first visit to Schweinfurt was in October 2002, where my main objective, apart from the recital, was to see the Georg Schäfer Museum, about which I'd read great things. Named after the late ball bearing tycoon who brought prosperity to Schweinfurt after the war, the recently built museum was a revelation. It contained Schäfer's lifetime collection of over a thousand works of art, but many of them were kept in storage. The paintings on display were mainly by 18th and 19th century German artists, with a central exhibition of endearingly humorous works by Carl Spitzweg. The building itself was a triumph of design, every detail worthy of as much attention as the paintings, and although an hour or so in most galleries was normally enough for me, I spent almost four enthralling hours there without so much as a glance at my watch.

My hotel's reception area was mostly unattended, but each time I approached, even on tiptoe, an enormous black dog called Max came flying out of a back room, rearing up on his hind legs and placing his front paws squarely on the reception desk, riveting me to the spot with gimlet eyes, his jaws agape and drooling. Thankfully he didn't actually bark, but he terrified me almost as much as the receptionist at the Steinengraben in Basel. At breakfast it became evident that the manageress was on a mission to discourage guests from the slightest temptation to overindulge, patrolling the buffet area at regular intervals. Despite the number of hopefuls seated at the tables she brought out ham and cheese just two or three transparent slices at a time. A single nursery portion of cereal occasionally found its way onto the table, and sometimes a solitary boiled egg. The only items in abundance were cartons of yoghurt well past their sell-by date. By chance I happened to be sitting at the table closest to the kitchen - the prime position from which to pounce on anything that escaped - and I persevered until sufficiently fortified to venture out into the wind and rain.

That evening, propelled along by frequent gusts and accompanied by showers of leaves and twigs, I scampered across to the Theater der Stadt, a dazzlingly lit state of the art building situated in a small central park. The howling gale outside seemed to wrap itself round the building and could be heard quite clearly above the sound of the piano, strangely contributing something to the atmosphere as Sokolov travelled through the works of Beethoven, Komitas and Prokofiev. There were also contributions from the audience in the shape of ringing mobiles, coughing and sneezing, a series of resounding hiccups and a whistling hearing aid in the front row. At least Sokolov had a fine piano to do justice to his artistry and it was a comfort to know that I would hear it all again very soon.

Travelling south to Tübingen, I found a historic and picturesque university town on the river Neckar, where the weather had calmed down nicely. In the small Tourist Office perched on the river bridge Sokolov stood browsing through the information leaflets but I chose not to disturb him. I booked a room in a hotel close to the university, which was convenient for the recital but far away from the centre. Lacking the energy or inclination to walk all the way back to town I spent a rather miserable evening watching a news channel on TV which was dominated by the havoc caused by extreme weather across Europe and gruesome happenings in Moscow.

I awoke feeling restored and wandered along the river, through the old part of town, a confusion of steep cobbled streets, brightly painted gabled houses dating back to the fifteenth century and quaint market squares, one of which was overlooked by a beautiful old town hall covered with decorative frescoes. Late in the afternoon I climbed the Osterberg for a view of the sun setting behind the hills and dusk descending over the rooftops and spires of the town.

At the concert hall I found my seat was so far over to the right side that I caught only the occasional glimpse of Sokolov's head as he came up for air, but after the interval I found an empty seat in the middle of the front row, which turned the evening around completely. The piano sounded marvellous at first but went out of tune rather quickly and necessitated an extended interval for it to receive attention. It held out for a while, but following the Prokofiev sonata and a blistering Ravel Toccata it was left sounding like something out of the Crazy Horse Saloon, which for me lent a poignant, home-spun quality to the Chopin mazurkas which ended the evening.

Afterwards I spoke to a lady who'd been attending Sokolov's recitals at the university since the seventies when she was a student there. "But you know" she said with regret, "I've never ever seen him smile." I took her with me to the artist's room, where he could be seen grinning and talking animatedly to a crowd of excited students. She stood at the back of the room, hardly able to contain her pleasure, and hinted that I must be very wealthy to hear him play so often. I explained the necessary economies, the endless search for cheap flights and accommodation, and when I mentioned that before setting out for the recital I'd eaten a four day old cheese sandwich I'd found at the bottom of my bag, she gave me her phone number, inviting me to stay with her next time I was in town. She felt no urge to speak to Sokolov; simply seeing him smile had been enough.

On my travels around Germany I received very many invitations to stay with people the next time I was in their vicinity, and although I knew the offers were genuine, I rarely plucked up the courage to dial their numbers a year or so later, afraid they might not remember who I was. As for the criticism directed at Sokolov by those who had never met him concerning his deadpan expression on stage and apparent lack of communication with his audience, over the years I explained to countless people that he was the most serious of communicators and a devout messenger. I pointed out that it should be more than enough to watch his fingers dance, to hear the piano sing. Every note was delivered with a generous heart and the music itself did all the smiling anyone could possibly need.

On a three hour train journey from Munich to Weiden an unwelcome diversion came in the shape of two overweight merrymakers who'd been evicted from the neighbouring compartment and taken up residence in the space between the carriages, along with an ample supply of alcohol and a ghetto blaster. Their choice of music, reminiscent of Turkish entries for Eurovision, was in itself not unpleasant, but after an hour of it the spasmodic vocal accompaniment became less tuneful and the frequent bursts of inexpert belly dancing rather distasteful, with far too much belly for my liking. It was a relief when a mass exodus at Regensburg enabled me to concentrate on the passing scenery.

Weiden didn't get a mention in any of the guide books I'd consulted. As far as I knew it might be a dull provincial town in a remote corner of Bavaria or just as easily an undiscovered gem. As we trundled through a pretty river valley and pulled into an immaculate railway station where a rack of post cards showed enticing views, I could see that Weiden would be a most agreeable place to rest my bones. Instead of lugging my bag into the centre I merely crossed the street and walked into the modest looking Gasthof Post which provided an inexpensive room with a balcony overlooking horse chestnuts in bloom and a view of distant hills.

The following day I strolled along the river and through the Max Reger Park with its vibrant flower displays, soothing fountains and endless tree-lined walks ringing with bird song. At lunchtime I sat contentedly under a tree in the market square, an expanse of cobbles with a maypole at its centre, an onion domed church at one end, an exquisitely decorated little town hall at the other, and on either side, rows of old houses painted in faded pastel colours. By three o'clock I'd explored every street and riverside footpath and taken a look at the sleek, modern Max Reger Halle, ten years old and named after the German composer who began his music studies in Weiden in the 1880s and became famous not only for his compositions, but also his rapacious consumption of alcohol, tobacco and food. He once famously asked a waiter to bring him two hours' worth of steak, and somewhat predictably expired at the age of forty-three.

Later, when I arrived at the hall and gave my name I was met with a blank stare. Finding an English speaker in this part of Bavaria took some time, but eventually someone called Elizabeth Schiffner came to my rescue and explained to the manager who I was, whereupon a ticket quickly materialised. I also admired a poster in the foyer and in a flash it was taken down, rolled up, secured with a rubber band and handed to me as if I'd just graduated. Elizabeth introduced me to her extraordinarily sparky eighty-three year old aunt, a one time operatic diva with a long and distinguished career behind her and now something of a local character. She'd sung leading Wagnerian roles at Bayreuth for many years and the two of them now attended the final rehearsal of every production there, as guests of Richard Wagner's grandson, Wolfgang.

The seats were unallocated so we made a dash for the third row and sat together. The aunt, who spoke no English, very nearly had a seizure when Elizabeth told her this was my 108th Sokolov performance in less than six years. Anyone would have thought poison had been administered as she stared wide-eyed and open mouthed, clutching theatrically at her throat with one hand and pointing at me with the other. At the interval she thrust a glass of champagne into my hand and dragged me round the foyer, introducing me to various friends of hers, some of whom assumed I must be staying at the Admira, Weiden's bit of five star hotel heaven, and looked horrified when they learned I was in the humble little gasthof opposite the station. As we settled down for the second half, Elizabeth told me that her grandfather had owned a butcher's shop in the town, and whenever Max Reger returned to Weiden he wrote a letter to the butcher in advance of his arrival, ordering vast quantities of his favourite sausages. These letters had been preserved and were now on display in the town museum.

The recital programme was Bach's Reincken Sonata, the Bach/Brahms Chaconne for the left hand followed by Beethoven Sonatas No.9 Op.14/1, No.10 Op.14/2 and No.15 Op.28. As I said goodbye to my companions, a lady with a broad smile introduced herself as the concert organiser, apologising for having arrived late with my ticket. She wore a traditional Bavarian outfit with long dirndl skirt and white puff sleeves. An amplitude of bosom strained to escape from the tightly gathered bodice, and I could easily imagine her weaving between the tables of a beer garden, foaming tankards held aloft, flashing her assets at the customers. Her smiling other half, clad in alpine huntsman's attire, completed the picture. On our way to the artist's room they invited me to join a small gathering at the house of a Mr Thomas, who was by all accounts a prominent figure in Weiden's cultural life. In her less than perfect but utterly charming English she asked, "You will like to come with us and we can make a drink there?" I imagined us sitting in Mr Thomas's kitchen, stirring mugs of cocoa and passing round the Hobnobs.

After a lengthy audience with Sokolov, five of us drove to Mr Thomas's house, where we were admitted by a tall, dignified housekeeper of about sixty who looked like a character from a nineteenth century novel, dressed in a long sleeved black ankle length dress and a starched white pinafore. In a spacious L-shaped room filled with books, abstract paintings and musical instruments, I was amazed to see three dining tables laid for supper, two of which were already occupied by a dozen or so people tucking into a hot meal. At the third table next to the grand piano at the far end of the room sat Mr Thomas, an elderly gentleman with a mischievous smile, waiting to greet us. It was now approaching midnight, I'd eaten nothing since lunchtime, and I could hardly believe my luck. Tender chunks of beef cooked in wine with mushrooms and a rich gravy were ladled onto my plate, which I mopped up with crusty bread and washed down with red wine. I was then directed by Mr Thomas to another table laden with cheeses and he followed me across the room to explain which region of which country each piece of cheese had come from. He spoke no English but we managed a few scraps of conversation in French. I asked if he played the piano but he shook his head and pointed at a cello parked in a corner.

Apart from our host and the concert organisers, my two remaining table companions were a piano technician who opened his mouth only for the purpose of inserting food and his girlfriend - a concert pianist from Moscow - who was talkative and friendly, handing me a copy of her latest CD to take home. At the end of the event a meticulously groomed couple were assigned the task of transporting Sokolov's English guest back to her hotel in their limousine, no doubt expecting to offload her outside the gleaming portals of the Admira. It must have been a novel experience for them to stand waiting while I rummaged in my handbag for the key to the night entrance, which was in the gasthof's back yard, right next to the wheelie bins. I did eventually get to see inside the Hotel Admira eight years later when I was again invited to a post-concert supper there. Sokolov was to be guest of honour and I was distracted throughout the recital, wishing I'd declined the invitation, but I should have known better than to worry; Sokolov was too tired to attend and sent his apologies so we all raised our glasses and toasted his empty chair at the head of the table.

Every summer from 1999 until 2019 I visited either Wiesbaden or Bad Kissingen, and sometimes it was possible to combine the two in one trip. In 2003 I began with Sokolov's performance of Bach/ Beethoven in the Christian Zais Saal in Wiesbaden, where my seat was on the right side, but I was content to settle for a view of Sokolov's face. The auditorium was a visual feast, flanked by sixteen Corinthian columns, the gilt mirrors behind the piano reflecting magnificent gold chandeliers. The combination of the music with all that gilt, crystal and gleaming black Steinway framing Sokolov's enraptured features was almost too much to bear. All I could do was take a mental photograph. (In 2006 the venue had switched again to the much larger and even more beautiful Friedrich von Thiersch Saal.)

Friedrich von Thiersch Saal, Wiesbaden

I felt too tired to socialise after the recital but nevertheless found myself leaving the Kurhaus in the company of the musicologist I'd met the previous year and his gang of musician friends. I dreaded a repeat of our last exchange when my lack of musical knowledge had come perilously close to discovery, but I was saved by one of the group who ran a successful Beatles tribute band and drew me aside to talk about his passion for anything connected with Liverpool. I'd been married to a scouser in the past and was well qualified to demonstrate the nuances of the accent and list all the Merseyside colloquialisms I could muster. It was a strange sort of task but much less risky than trying to bluff my way through a discussion on the overuse of rubato.

At one o'clock the musicologist rapped the table and announced to the assembled gathering that I knew absolutely everything there was to know about Sokolov and would be happy to answer any questions, whereupon I activated my "Goodness me, is that really the time?" routine, sidled towards the door English style and escaped into the night.

In Bad Kissingen the following day I found a peaceful, homely guest house in whose orchard chickens roamed, but it was a little too far away from the town centre for my liking, and although my room was bright and uplifting I felt lonely and dispirited. I wandered through the town looking for somewhere to eat, passing pavement cafés filled with cheerful diners enjoying the sunshine, and as I walked, every ounce of energy and enthusiasm began to ebb away, along with all interest in my surroundings and appetite for food, heralding the onset of a state of mind which had the nasty habit of creeping up on me from time to time. I made my way through a sea of tables and into an empty restaurant, sat in a corner, ordered a meal, put my head in my hands and wept. The waitress regarded me with concern, and without a word she quietly opened a drawer and took out a pile of paper napkins, placing them at my elbow. When the food arrived I picked at it with a fork in one hand and a succession of soggy napkins in the other, taking as long as possible over my meal before trudging back to my room, where I fell asleep instantly.

My unaccountable fit of melancholy seemed to have lifted the next morning and I ate breakfast in the cosy dining room, where I learned that the festival was showcasing the talents of a group of gifted young musicians from Russia. One such wunderkind was sitting at the table next to mine with his piano teacher, who treated him like a prized piece of Dresden china, fetching his food from the buffet table and even stirring his tea. At that time he appeared to be a painfully shy boy, but four years later his talent was to carry him through to the final stage of the prestigious Tchaikovsky Competition in Moscow, where he was awarded the Silver Medal.

Most of my day was spent sitting under the colonnades watching the townsfolk taking the air and the visitors queuing to sample the spa waters. There seemed to be any number of elderly widowers on the loose and I reckoned I could have landed a husband of sorts within a fortnight had I felt inclined. There was plenty of competition in the shape of ladies on the wrong side of seventy-five drifting around the rose garden and along the river promenade wearing cartwheel hats, pastel ensembles such as those favoured by the Queen Mother and daringly high heels. One lady in particular, whose clothes were of a more bohemian variety, wore a long auburn wig and heavy make-up with demonically arched eyebrows. The whole spectacle provided a much needed diversion and helped while away a long afternoon.

At seven I presented myself at the Regentenbau box office to find there was no ticket for me. I was shunted in the direction of Hilla Schütze, a charming lady who rectified matters in a flash and invited me to eat ice cream with her after the performance. In her youth she'd worked in Birmingham as an *au pair* and welcomed the opportunity to reminisce. Now a highly respected figure in the town, she was a writer, photographer, collector of antique toys and books and an authority on the history of Bad Kissingen.

The recital was an absolute sensation and I arrived in the artist's room to find it full of Russians. Once they'd dispersed the Germans invaded and it was chaos, but everyone had their moment with Sokolov. Unsurprisingly, by that time the ice cream parlour had closed so we dived into the nearest bar, and although I was concerned that such a place might not be to Hilla's liking, she ordered a pint of Guinness and downed it with enthusiasm.

On the morning of my departure I discovered that my B&B couldn't accept my newly acquired debit card and I was unable to get cash from a bank, so once again I left Germany owing money. This time it was to the tune of two nights' accommodation, a telephone call to England and a severely depleted minibar. On top of that I was worried that I might have a problem paying for the three trains required to get me back to Frankfurt Airport, but my hostess cheerfully handed over my fare and even insisted on driving me to the station, where she gave me a motherly hug and put a handful of sweets in my pocket for the journey. Once settled in a compartment I reached into my pocket and there among the sweets was my room key. I felt like the house guest from hell.

On arrival in Stuttgart late on an October evening in 2003 I headed straight for the Hotel Merit where I'd stayed two years before, situated in the red light district, next door to Winks Lap Dancing Club. The hotel had been swankily refurbished in the intervening period with a corresponding increase in room rates, but somehow I managed to get thirty euros knocked off the cost of a large double and retired to my bed feeling quite pleased with myself.

I went by train to Ulm the next morning, eager to explore fresh territory. The passing landscape was particularly beautiful with subtle autumn colours bathed in hazy sunlight. Divided in two by the Danube, one half of the city was in Baden-Württemberg, the other in Bavaria. My hotel was on the Bavarian side, close to the concert hall but a long walk out of the city centre. After a fifteen minute plod I asked a friendly looking man in his fifties if I was heading in the right direction. Within seconds he was ushering me into a silver Mercedes, introducing himself as a local lawyer and asking me how I came to be visiting the city for just one night. When I mentioned the recital he expressed a keen interest in attending and, having deposited me outside my hotel, hastened off in search of a ticket. My room overlooked the Danube, and on the opposite bank stood the Congress Centre where Sokolov would have been rehearsing. I spent the afternoon wandering along the river and photographing the ancient houses in the fishermen's quarter, then in the hotel restaurant I splashed out on a bowl of thick soup loaded with four different kinds of mushroom, in the middle of which sat an enormous potato dumpling. The hotel had its own brewery with huge copper vats bubbling away in the restaurant; the smell of hops permeated every corridor but the beer tasted wonderful.

At the Congress Centre my seat was in an enviable position and the performance of Bach's Reincken Sonata, the Bach/Brahms Chaconne for the left hand, Beethoven's Sonatas No.11 Op.22 and No.32 Op.111 was of the highest order. At the interval I spotted my lawyer friend Helmut with an older male companion, both looking immensely impressed. They were beside themselves with excitement when I suggested they might care to visit the artist's room with me after the performance. When the time came, they conversed with Sokolov in German and emerged from his room looking completely overcome.

As the starry-eyed duo escorted me back to my hotel, Helmut looked distinguished and dashing in a flowing cashmere overcoat and wide-brimmed hat, but unfortunately the sole and upper of one of his shoes had parted company during the evening, which rather spoiled the effect. I was wearing flimsy shoes myself and could do little more than hobble along the river bank, with Helmut flapping along beside me and his friend trailing behind. We partook of a nightcap at the hotel, discussed the performance and it felt good to have introduced two more newbies to the magic of Sokolov. I flew home the following evening, and from the aircraft window the small towns and villages of rural Germany glinted like dozens of tiny jewelled islands in a limitless black sea: another amazing sight to store away in my mental scrap book.

A few weeks later I travelled from Zürich to Lake Konstanz for a return visit to the island of Lindau, but was in no great hurry to get there so I lingered in the station buffet and drank tea. A dishevelled young man wandered in and left a small battered suitcase bound with silver tape on the table next to mine and disappeared. After ten minutes I'd convinced myself the case must contain some sort of explosive device, and my initial impulse was to drink up and get going. But then I began to consider the possible advantages of being blown sky high. The short term discomfort of a solitary couple of days on the island before the next concert was bad enough, but the long term prospect of continuing in a job I'd grown to detest combined with the probability of eventually running out of cash and being unable to follow Sokolov, not to mention the spectre of old age and infirmity, would all be resolved in a flash. I decided to sit tight and wait for the big bang.

The young man returned, opened the case, took out an exercise book and began writing, so it was after all my destiny to travel to Lindau. At St.Gallen I transferred to a regional rattlebox which trundled across the causeway connecting the island to the mainland and into Lindau's tiny station. It was two in the afternoon and I rambled round the cobbled streets for almost an hour before taking up residence at a hotel in the main shopping area. To avoid the feel-bad factor if at all possible I needed to fill the hours with positive thoughts and activities. Tea and cake seemed like a good start, followed by a glance at the yuletide window displays, one of which consisted entirely of different types of caviar. Finally I wandered along the lakeside to take what I hoped would be atmospheric photographs in the fading light.

Returning to a bistro I'd discovered on my last visit, I ate a delicious meal very slowly. By the time I emerged, the town was aglow with Christmas lights and a shuddering peal of bells rang out across the island. I was drawn towards the Münster, wondering if there might be an evening service I could attend, and found a poster on the door announcing that a free concert for Advent was about to begin. The interior of the church was gloriously over the top baroque, adorned with masses of greenery and blazing candles. Ninety minutes of seasonal music-making began with a group of musicians in Bavarian costume playing folk tunes on guitar, double bass, harp, zither and a traditional stringed instrument called a hackbrett. A group of girls sang pieces *a cappella,* a father and daughter from Bregenz played flugelhorn duets and a choir sang German carols from the organ gallery. As the final notes died away, the church bells rang out again and I came away feeling happy to have taken part in Lindau's pre-Christmas festivities.

The day of the recital was easily taken care of with a walk round the island. At the Stadttheater Sokolov played with astonishing abandon and my seat was satisfyingly close to the platform. The next morning the lake presented a spectacle crying out to be photographed. The water shone like glass and the snow-covered mountains were sharply defined against a sky streaked with silver. By the time I'd raced to the station to buy a new film for my camera the sun had broken through the veil of cloud and the entire scene was obscured by mist. The mountains didn't reappear until I was in a railway carriage on my way back across the causeway, but as the lake and town receded I dwelt upon the good things that I would have missed had I been blown to smithereens in Zürich railway station.

On arrival in Wiesloch a fortnight later I swiftly concluded that turning up in a small German town on a Wednesday afternoon in December with no room reservation was not a good idea. The station ticket office was closed, as were most of the shops, and no tourist information was available anywhere. I felt at a bit of a loss but made the right choice when I asked a woman browsing through some books outside a shop if she knew of any budget accommodation. With steely resolve she marched me round to the town hall, barged into the council offices and read the riot act about the lack of information for visitors, demanding that a member of staff find me a town map and a list of accommodation. Armed with the information I needed I urged her to return to her shopping, but she persuaded someone else to ring round the cheaper hotels on my behalf. They were all full, but a vacancy was found at a small guest house, with a warning that the rooms might be of a low standard. My rescuer, Heidi, looked doubtful, snatched up my bag and led me to her car so that we could inspect the room together, insisting that if it wasn't good enough I could stay at her house fifteen kilometres away, and she would willingly drive me to and from the recital.

The room was basic and charmless with just a small skylight, but I assured Heidi it was fine. She left me there reluctantly, handing me her phone number in case I felt lonely or encountered any problems when I moved on to Darmstadt the following day. Although the bed looked uninviting and I suspected the sheets weren't clean, I drifted off for a couple of hours with the television turned down to a murmur and the radiator up to full blast. When I went downstairs later I was given directions to the concert venue and the times of morning trains to Darmstadt, along with an assurance that the manageress would be driving me to the station, all of which must have been organised by the resolute Heidi.

It took five minutes to reach the Palatin, whose auditorium provided amazingly comfortable seats and generous leg room. The brightest jewel in the programme, Beethoven's Op.111, was deeply moving, the final movement loaded with emotion and ending with sustained trills, fading to nothing, by which time Sokolov's face was practically resting on the keyboard, the audience holding its breath until he raised his head. An elderly gentleman in the front row chose that exact moment to leave his seat, totter a few steps and collapse onto the wooden floor with an almighty thud, emitting sounds one could only imagine might be his last. This caused something of a stir in the orchestra stalls, and while Sokolov received a riotous ovation the poor old chap was scooped up and carted off to the nearest krankenhaus. Outside the artist's room stood the musicologist I'd met in Wiesbaden, who said, "I think the trills must have been too much for that old man, but honestly, he *could* have waited!"

In Darmstadt the next day there was an abundance of seasonal goings on, with the aroma of sausages, fried potatoes and glühwein wafting round every corner. I took a brisk walk to the Prince George

Palace and through the sixteenth century Herrngärten where pollarded trees guarded symmetrical beds full of standard roses and curly-leafed king-sized cabbages dusted with frost. Darmstadt seemed to have much more to offer than Wiesloch, but I had little time to investigate.

Sokolov had performed in Darmstadt with an orchestra on two consecutive evenings earlier in the week, and as a result the recital was completely sold out. Numerous ticketless individuals stood in the foyer holding up placards in the hope of waylaying any returns before they reached the cash desk. Mine was a dream ticket in the third row and the ladies on either side of me were ecstatic throughout. One of them was a friend of the conductor who'd led the orchestral performances, and she hinted, without going into detail, that he'd found working with Sokolov quite an experience.

In January 2004 I visited the city of Mainz, whose architecturally rich historic quarter occupied my free time to the full. I found a room in a central hotel just a minute away from the Frankfurter Hof, the city's concert hall in the heart of the Altstadt. The hotel occupied a creaky half timbered building overshadowed by the massive sandstone Kaiserdom, and was sufficiently attractive externally to feature on many of the local postcards. The jolly proprietor showed me three rooms: a gloomy cell with just a bed and washbasin, a much brighter option with a shower which emitted a strong whiff of rotting vegetation, and the gold standard room equipped with all facilities for which I settled, despite the small window overlooking what appeared to be a potting shed. The area outside the window was described rather ambitiously in the fire instructions as 'The Terrasse', and sported a substantial collection of dead plants, half used bags of compost, oddments of garden paraphernalia and miscellaneous household items, all carelessly abandoned to the elements.

It was almost dark and well below zero by the time I ventured outside, walking through the area surrounding the Dom and diving smartly into the warmth of an elegant café for a glass of tea. The luscious cakes were outrageously expensive, but I decided this would be my local watering hole: a place where I could hang up my coat and settle down in a corner for an unhurried interlude with a book or writing pad. The only entertainment on offer in Mainz that evening was a rock gig by an outfit called Montezuma's Revenge, so I called it a night and collected a bag of fries from McDonald's to enliven the cheese sandwiches waiting in my room.

By budget hotel standards, the breakfast on offer the next morning was nothing short of a banquet. The proprietor stood behind his little counter, surveying with pride the array of items he'd assembled, which filled three large tables. "It is all for you", he announced. "Take whatever you want!" The first thing I wanted to take was a photograph. There was no evidence of other guests, the food looked undisturbed and I was alone in the dining room for over an hour. I did wonder how many times some of the items might have been out on display, but duty bound to do justice to it all I paced myself, chose carefully and ate to bursting point. I couldn't imagine Sokolov doing much better at the Mainz Hilton International.

Setting out to explore in five layers of clothing, I encountered a contented looking Sokolov strolling towards the Frankfurter Hof for his communion with the piano. One of my main objectives was to see the Church of St.Stephan, an otherwise unremarkable Gothic building with the distinction of having nine gorgeous stained glass windows designed by Marc Chagall and finished in 1984 when he was in his nineties. In every conceivable shade of blue, they were stunning. Next on my list was the Church of St.Ignaz, a rococo gem where by the happiest of coincidences the organ was being played as I crept inside. A magnificent piece was drawing to a close, and as I sat down to listen to whatever came next, I looked up to see the organist gathering her music together and making ready to leave. I waited for her to descend the stairs so that I could find out what she'd been playing and she told me it was an organ sonata by Alexandre Guilmant. Fuelled by my interest in the piece she invited me up into the organ gallery, sat me down, unlocked the keyboard and played the final movement again. The combination of the church interior viewed from above and such a soaring piece of music being played especially for my benefit gave me goosebumps.

A plump little woman with tiny hands, she played with great sensitivity but was also able to meet the more robust challenges of the music. In the powerful passages, the wide ranging pedal work and multiple stop pulling required a certain amount of athleticism on her part, and as she lunged back and forth, occasionally leaving her seat in order to apply maximum strength to the really big chords, she came treacherously close to losing her trousers. Pieces by Bach and Handel followed, and eventually she went through the entire score of the Guilmant sonata, demonstrating the most interesting and dramatic passages. We talked at length about music, travel, God and Sokolov, and she seemed in no hurry to bring our meeting to an end. As we left the building almost two hours later she told me I'd been listening to the oldest church organ in Germany.

A brisk walk along the Rhine rounded off my afternoon and I returned to my room, where I found an English speaking television programme to accompany my teatime sandwiches. As soon as I realised I was watching a reality TV challenge in which a contestant had been charged with the task of finding the filthiest lavatory in South Korea I switched off and turned my thoughts to the more edifying prospect of the evening ahead.

Sandwiched between a supermarket and a gents' outfitters, the Frankfurter Hof's unpromising frontage suggested that of a fleapit cinema, but inside it was a different story. The impish impresario I met occasionally appeared in the foyer, where we compared tickets and discovered we were sitting together. His penchant for attractive young women undimmed by recent illness, he gazed approvingly at every good looking female under the age of twenty-five, largely because he couldn't help himself but in part to make it clear to everyone present that he and I were definitely not an item. Our seats were on the far right hand side with no view of the keyboard or indeed any part of Sokolov. "This seat suits me perfectly", he declared. "I can listen without distraction. *You're* not going to like it of course, because you won't see his hands. You won't see his face either, so for once in your life you'll be here for the f***ing music!"

Looking more well upholstered than ever, he told me this was going to be a year in which he would look after his health above all else. "I need to lose about ten kilos, which shouldn't be too difficult", he mused. Through gritted teeth I asked if he'd attended the afternoon rehearsal. "Oh yes", he purred. "But I had to leave before the end because it was much too beautiful." At the interval he and I agreed that the Bach/Brahms Chaconne and Beethoven's Op.111 had been the best ever. At the end of the evening, by the time I'd weathered the stampede for the cloakroom, the queue for the artist's room had dwindled down to the last few. Looking a little peevish, my concert companion stood outside in the corridor next to a table laden with baskets of fruit, chocolate and other goodies provided for Sokolov and his guests. "I've just been invited to a meal at the festival director's favourite Italian restaurant. I'm not going of course and he's very disappointed. In any case I can't eat at this time of night", he grumbled, wolfing down a handful of nuts and stuffing a Mars Bar into his pocket.

We went in to see Sokolov together and a period of light banter ensued until a glamorous female well known to my companion appeared in the doorway, at which point I knew my number was up. Had he spotted her earlier in the evening no doubt he would have suggested she and I swap seats, ostensibly to give me a better view of the keyboard.

After most performances it was customary to find folk wandering the streets surrounding the concert hall in a dazed but happy condition, having spent the evening on planet Sokolov. Outside, I struck up a conversation with the last two people to emerge from the artists' entrance. Horst Schrader and his friend Helmut invited me to join them for a bite to eat before they began their three hundred kilometre drive back to Tübingen. We found a table in a dimly lit old restaurant of the kind that simply didn't exist in my part of the world: smoke-filled and alive with conversation, every table host to intelligent argument, the exchange of ideas, the airing of profound thought. My companions were happy to discuss Sokolov *ad infinitum* which suited me perfectly. Horst, an earnest, intense and much travelled individual, did most of the talking, while Helmut, a big teddy bear of a man with an uncomplicated demeanour and kindly expression, did plenty of amiable nodding whilst tackling a bucket-sized helping of potato soup. By one thirty we'd run out of steam but were certain we would meet again.

Six months later, after a train journey through the unusually sun-scorched countryside between Frankfurt and Bad Kissingen, I ambled contentedly along Kissingen's flower-laden river promenade and through the rose garden, where more than fifty different types of rose were vying for attention. The town was representing Germany in a Europe in Bloom competition, and every conceivable opportunity to display flowers had been explored. It was business as usual in

Kissingen: residents and visitors gathering in the Kurpark for the outdoor concert, a lively tea dance in progress in the Kurhaus restaurant, and along the promenade the sound of birdsong, the rustle of foliage and the gentle plash of fountains.

Kurgarten Bad Kissingen

At seven o'clock I spotted Hilla Schütze in the concert hall foyer and she introduced me to a regular visitor to Kissingen's festival, Baron Brenn von Bibra, currently living in Los Angeles but with a family home in rural Franconia where he and his close relatives converged each summer. Hilla disappeared on an errand for Sokolov, leaving us to chat. The baron was a true gentleman and so knowledgeable about music that I feared I might be pushed into a conversational corner with regard to orchestras, unfamiliar conductors and soloists, but he wanted to talk opera, which was much safer ground for me. Hilla was soon bounding back across the foyer, mission accomplished, just as the festival's director made an entrance in one of her famous hats. These creations, sometimes frothy, often wide-brimmed, were said to remain firmly in place throughout performances, and she routinely posed in them for photographs with the most celebrated visiting artists for inclusion in the following season's glossy festival brochure. I'm not sure whether Sokolov ever featured in one of these photographs, but I could well imagine him being a dab hand at dodging any such arrangements.

Hilla strode forward to greet her, introducing me as she did so and explaining that I'd travelled from Birmingham especially for this particular recital. As the director continued her stately progress towards the auditorium she asked if I'd made time to attend any of the other festival performances and I told her I preferred to concentrate expressly on Sokolov. Looking back over her shoulder, eyebrows raised, she observed drily, "Well now, lucky him".

I accepted an invitation from Hilla to eat ice cream at the end of the evening on the understanding that I would pay this time. The baron was also invited and we ended up in what seemed like quite an expensive restaurant, where they ordered coffees and bowls of ice cream in various flavours, while I compromised with an iced coffee topped with cream. Our conversation was largely of a musical nature and I was keen to discover who the baron's favourite opera singer might be. I would have put money on Callas but he had no hesitation in nominating Dame Janet Baker. He told us he'd once driven three hundred and eighty miles from Los Angeles to San Francisco to hear her sing and driven straight back afterwards, which had taken him all night. He then pressed me on the subject of hotels, imagining I might be able to recommend a few attractive establishments that he could jot down for future reference. I couldn't think what to say, but Hilla had already heard about a few of the dumps I'd slept in and laughingly recounted what she could remember of my escapades in the grubby back streets of numerous European cities, leaving the baron hastily tucking away his notebook and pencil. As I surreptitiously fingered the menu to try and estimate the damage, the baron ordered a second bowl of ice cream. He did offer to pay the bill but I wouldn't hear of it, casually handing over an alarming number of euros and a wildly generous tip to a beaming waiter, as if my resources were limitless.

Later in July 2004 I heard Sokolov's Beethoven sonata Op.111 for the last time in Wiesbaden. The recital was a roaring success, CDs and DVDs sold briskly and an unusually long queue formed to get them signed. When everyone had gone, including a deputation from Tokyo who were hoping to persuade Sokolov to consider a recital tour of Japan, I told him this was the most painful time of year for me. "Yes, I know", he said. "It's because the programme is changing, but next time there will be Chopin". He went on to tell me the details, and confided that his recording company at the time were insisting on the release of a new CD before Christmas. He was now committed to ploughing through dozens of live recordings made since his last CD release in 1998 which would take up much of the precious time he needed to spend on preparing his new programme.

In November I squeezed three German recitals into the space of a week, starting in Münster, where the concert took place in the University's Hörsaal. I checked out the building earlier in the day and it looked like a typical school entrance hall with rows of coat pegs at one end, a few wooden benches and little else, so I figured there would be many students in attendance and little need to dress up for the occasion. On arrival that evening, however, I found the entrance hall had been transformed with tastefully draped tables for the sale of programmes, CDs, drinks and savouries. Sleekly attired attendees stood about sipping champagne and I felt conspicuous as I edged my way through the crush wearing jeans, a sloppy sweater and carrying a small rucksack.

The auditorium served as a lecture theatre during the daytime, with drop leaf tables fixed to the back of the seats, which many of the audience used as programme holders. As I sat down I was horrified to see that the young woman making for the seat directly in front of mine was carrying an infant still in nappies who was clutching with ferocious concentration a half eaten crust of bread. This unwelcome arrival, along with a man on my left who sniffed every ten seconds and a lady on my right who appeared to be in the throes of a significant nose bleed, didn't bode well, but thankfully the nose bleed subsided and the little mite in front uttered not a sound. The sniffing persisted for the entire duration and from time to time a tiny fist held aloft the crust for all to admire, but it was a largely uneventful evening on my side of the footlights. On the other side Sokolov went like a train and the piano responded magnificently.

The next day I moved on to Hamburg, where a friend, the formidable Dorothea, in whose cellar I would be sleeping on a glorified bean bag, announced that she'd decided to attend the recital with me. I stressed the importance of arriving early so that I could claim my ticket and she could buy one if any were available, but she allowed insufficient time and we got caught up in torrential rain and appalling traffic congestion, resulting in a frightful last minute dash. I had to disturb half a row of people to get to my seat but they seemed good natured enough - the lady on my right helping me off with my coat, the one on my left offering a sweet, and both of them thrusting their programmes in my direction in case I'd not had time to buy one. It was such a far cry from my customary early arrival with time to leave my coat in the cloakroom, saunter round the building, drink in the ambience and savour the moment. I vowed never again to depend on someone else to get me to a performance on time.

Laeiszhalle Hamburg

The blue and gold interior of the Musikhalle was spectacular and the recital thrilling beyond description, receiving an amazingly enthusiastic reception. I'd been told that Hamburg audiences were renowned for their reticence, but this lot were beside themselves. Dorothea preferred not to meet Sokolov and waited outside for me, but although I pushed my way along the crowded corridor and made a genuine attempt to be quick, I was waylaid by Franco Panozzo and had an unusually long conversation with him, which was such a rare occurrence that I was unwilling to forgo the pleasure. Dorothea took a dim view of being kept waiting, and to make matters worse it was a long walk back to the multi-storey car park. As we descended from the sixth level and gathered speed towards the bottom she drove into a concrete pillar, destroying a wing mirror and scratching her paintwork. She spoke not a word on the journey home and any attempts I made to commiserate were rebuffed so I retreated into silent recollection of the beautiful hall, the glorious music and my conversation with Franco. The night in the cellar with just the bean bag for company felt like some sort of punishment, but the next morning Dorothea was in a better humour and conceded that she'd greatly enjoyed the recital.

Three days later I visited the unappealing industrial city of Ludwigshafen, where I discovered the concert hall was a long way out of the centre and difficult to reach by public transport. My hotel was shabby and unwholesome but the price was right and the service friendly. I went by taxi to the BASF Feierabendhaus and noticed the dapper figure of my musicologist friend flitting about in the balcony. We collided at the interval and he invited me to join him for a drink afterwards. As a consequence, I made sure my time in the artist's room was brief, but he was keen to discuss Chopin's manuscripts with Sokolov and numerous other aspects of the programme. Sokolov became totally absorbed and after what seemed like about half an hour, those remaining in the room began consulting their watches. I retreated to the corridor outside, consoling myself that at least a lift back to my hotel was assured.

On our way to the bar, my companion indicated that he didn't think much of Ludwigshafen, an unsurprising observation from someone who lived amid the historic splendour of Mainz. As he was finishing his second beer and ordering a third I glanced at my watch, noted it was almost one o'clock and wondered aloud if my hotel had a twenty-four hour reception. The barmaid overheard me and offered to telephone the hotel to check - the kind of gesture I'd become accustomed to receiving in Germany but hard to imagine happening in Birmingham. It took several circuits of the city centre to locate Bahnhofstrasse and we found ourselves at the wrong end of a very long one-way street. Instead of driving round the block, my chauffeur slipped into reverse and careered the entire length of Bahnhofstrasse, ending up on the pavement outside the hotel, where a bemused night porter stood watching at the window.

In the dining room the next morning I found a dozen leather jacketed workmen from eastern Europe engaged in lively banter, lounging back in their chairs and smoking like bonfires, the wreckage of their breakfasts strewn across the tables. Retreating to a dim corner away from the harsh glare of the fluorescent lighting I took delivery of a basket of bread and a selection of spreadables in individual pots, many of which had already been opened and partly used. Not the classiest breakfast I'd ever eaten but strangely preferable to some of the uncomfortably upmarket ones I'd strayed into over the years.

One morning in February 2005 I left an icebound UK and flew to Frankfurt, where similar conditions prevailed. The train journey to Heilbronn through the beautiful Neckar valley was a delight. Under a mantle of snow, the stately villas of Heidelberg, the scattered villages, vineyards, orchards and fir plantations looked magical. In Heilbronn I met up with Horst Schrader, who'd braved treacherous driving conditions all the way from Tübingen. Abandoning our sightseeing plans we retreated into the fragrant warmth of a ritzy teashop to while away what was left of the afternoon. At the concert hall the new Schubert Sonata D959 sounded just about perfect to me and rendered Horst more emotional than I'd imagined possible.

The next day I began the five and a half hour journey to Osnabrück. From the train window I saw dozens of mouthwatering winter landscapes I wanted to capture on camera and for much of the journey an unbroken expanse of white stretched as far as the horizon, etched here and there with just a few skeletal trees. The glare of the snow kept me awake, the stretches of road I glimpsed looked fearsome and I wondered how long it would take Sokolov and his driver to complete the same journey by car.

Comfortably settled in the Dom Hotel where I'd stayed seven years earlier, I spent the following day walking in the Heger Holz forest, where I saw almost no one yet felt perfectly safe. My thoughts turned to the evening ahead and whether I would have the courage to search out and speak to someone Horst had mentioned many times and who sounded like something of a challenge. Horst had described a certain Herr Lechner as an aloof character, a lecturer in philosophy at Düsseldorf University who spent much of his time creating high quality recordings of European radio broadcasts, mostly of pianists and of Sokolov in particular. Herr Lechner was going to be in

Osnabrück, but Horst discouraged me from approaching him, telling me that he was not a social animal and would have little interest in meeting me. I was hoping I might prove Horst wrong.

My only clue to identifying Herr Lechner was that he was exceptionally tall and slim, and there were two possible candidates in the Stadthalle foyer. The first, who wore a cream suit, puffed on a cheroot and flirted with two glamorous women, was eliminated immediately. The second, a more soberly dressed and studious looking man, stood with his ear clamped firmly to the crack in the double doors of the auditorium, behind which Sokolov was rehearsing. There seemed little doubt that this was my quarry, so I ventured across and introduced myself. Contrary to Horst's prediction, Herr Lechner seemed quite pleased to be spoken to, and he told me he'd been attending Sokolov's performances since 1978 and spent many hours working on recordings and listening to music. The seat next to mine was unoccupied in the first half, so he joined me for the second, contentedly stretching his immensely long legs out into the aisle. Horst would have been dumbfounded had he seen us sitting there, so relaxed in each other's company.

Afterwards Herr Lechner asked if I knew how to get to meet Sokolov and I approached the manager of the hall, whereupon we were ushered onto the platform and straight through to the backstage area. Herr Lechner had never before gained access to the artist's room in such a way and was suitably impressed. After our respective audiences with the Maestro he loped off to catch his train and I walked back to my hotel feeling as if I'd passed some sort of test. Little did I know at the time that Dr Jochen Lechner was to become a valued lifelong friend and I would in the future spend many happy hours listening to music with him at his home in Düsseldorf.

An hour away by train was my final destination, Bielefeld, a city which was said to house one of Sokolov's favourite Steinways. I soon learned that three business conferences were in progress in the city and affordable accommodation was non-existent. Offered the choice of a dormitory bed in a youth hostel or a gasthof in a neighbouring village, I settled reluctantly for a last minute cancellation at the Mövenpick, a large chain hotel with stratospheric room rates and an extra charge for breakfast. On arrival the receptionist asked if I wanted breakfast and I confided that I could barely afford the room, let alone anything to eat. She handed me a breakfast pass free of charge and rustled up a complimentary pot of tea to keep me going until my room was ready.

A mountainous flight of steps led up to the rather forbidding Rudolf Oetker Halle. Grandly austere, it looked better suited to some kind of dictatorial address than to an evening of artistic enrichment, and the graceful interior of the auditorium was marred by a complex stage layout intended for some other event taking place that week which looked more like the setting for a rock concert. A constellation of spotlights glared down from above and the platform was cluttered with a series of floor to ceiling metal constructions resembling electricity pylons, in the midst of which stood the piano. The performance was wonderful but there was a wearisome amount of coughing from one person in particular, who barked like a sea lion. As the Chopin Polonaise-Fantasie got under way someone in the front row suffered a seizure and had to be hauled out of the nearest exit, but Sokolov, well accustomed to such occurrences, pressed on regardless towards an almighty finale.

In May 2005 Sokolov was scheduled to play in the Rokoko Theater in Schwetzingen, but as I walked through the gates to the schloss I could see there had been a change of venue and people were being redirected towards the recital rooms. Sokolov was happily hammering away in the Langer Saal, a disproportionately long and narrow room where most of the audience were to end up sitting much further away from the piano than they'd anticipated. Those who'd booked the first tier of boxes in the theatre were now sitting in at least row twenty, and as for the poor souls in the upper circle, they were right at the very back in rows thirty to forty. A squadron of staff had the unenviable task of intercepting ticket holders and reallocating places, placating those who weren't happy and getting everyone seated by eight o'clock. I was near the front with a clear passage through to the keyboard and I sat in a state of pure joy as Schubert's Sonata D959 flooded the room with heavenly sounds. At the end of the second half, a lady sprang from her seat and handed Sokolov a gift of chocolates which he tucked neatly under one arm as he made his way to the nearest exit, necessitating a descent from the platform into the central aisle and a long walk past the first twenty rows of seats to a side door half way along the hall. It was reminiscent of a wedding ceremony as everyone craned to watch his exits and entrances.

At the time of the 7th July suicide bombings in London in 2005 I was on my way to Bad Kissingen, and Hilla Schütze looked relieved to see me walk into the Max-Littmann-Saal. Across the foyer, the elegant figure of Brenn von Bibra drifted towards me, eager to introduce me to, amongst others, a local music critic and a Steinway technician who told me he loved working with Sokolov because he knew more about pianos than any other artist. I also met a formidable looking pianist whom I assumed to be somewhere in her fifties, who was of dramatic appearance and seemed considerably less interested in meeting me than the other people I was introduced to that evening, managing only a reluctant approximation of a smile. I found her rather intimidating and was relieved when she moved away in search of more worthy encounters, but alarmed a short time later to discover I was sitting next to her in the auditorium.

Towards the end of the first half I was seized with a terrific urge to cough. I could have left my seat easily and slipped outside but it would have been impossible to regain admittance before the interval, so I sat tight. The last few minutes of the Schubert sonata were agonising but I managed to contain myself, almost bursting a blood vessel in the process. Luckily the eventual volcanic fit of coughing rounded off by an almighty sneeze coincided with the final burst of applause, but at the interval my neighbour swept past and regarded me as she might a pile of excrement left unattended. I did my best to adopt an apologetic expression, and although I was quite sure she must have been a highly accomplished musician, I had to resist the childish impulse to observe that she probably couldn't play the piano for toffee.

Hilla persuaded me to stay over for an extra day instead of moving on to my next destination so that she could show me something of the surrounding area. We drove along forest roads, climbing to a viewpoint overlooking the town - the rose garden and fountain clearly visible, the copper roof of the Regentenbau gleaming in the sun - and beyond, the forests and hills of rural Franconia. We spent the afternoon in the Schloss Aschach Museum, dined in a garden restaurant where I sampled thickly sliced fried potato dumplings, and rounded off the afternoon in a hilltop café where we drank tea amid the scent of pines, ate generous slices of cake and Hilla told me something of her early life and fascinating family history.

The next day I travelled north to the starkly contrasting city of Essen, where I met up with Jochen Lechner. The hall had recently been modernised and the original chandelier lighting replaced by a galaxy of tiny spotlights scattered across the ceiling. Evidently Sokolov had requested the spotlights be extinguished while he was playing but as they cooled, they gave off sharp staccato ticking noises which created a serious distraction for the first fifteen minutes of each half of the programme. I didn't plan to speak to him afterwards, but Jochen expressed a wish to do so. We met with robust resistance, but as soon as Jochen mentioned my name we were ushered into the artist's room. I told Sokolov I was planning to be in Finland four weeks hence but he was concerned that one of the recitals would be in a church and he had no idea what the acoustic would be like. I assured him I was willing to take the risk.

One of the objectives during my trip to Munich in February 2006 was to visit the concentration camp museum at Dachau so I joined a small group comprising seven Americans, two Israelis and our Russian guide Ella, who spoke fluent English and Hebrew. We took the underground to Dachau, the only town in Germany bearing the name of a concentration camp. Ella said that few Germans were prepared to live there and it was inhabited mostly by Russians and other nationals, but prices were low and many Germans came to Dachau to do their shopping.

A short bus ride took us to the camp entrance, and once inside we stood in a ferociously cold wind while Ella described the admission procedure for prisoners. I tried to imagine what it must have felt like to be stripped of one's clothing and forced to stand outside for hours in such conditions. The horrendous details of how prisoners were transported by rail directly into the camp enclosure, lined up and brutalised before they even got inside were distressing in the extreme. The lucky ones didn't survive the journey; most of those who did were subjected to punishments, experimentation and torture on a grand scale. The rooms and equipment used for some of these activities formed part of the museum, along with a waiting room, gas chamber, ovens and prison cells, some of them 'standing' cells with no room to lie down, kneel or sit. The waiting room bore a notice concerning personal hygiene and the gas chamber was fitted with dummy shower heads. A cyanide-based insecticide, Zyklon B, would be poured into small chutes in one wall and the warm air pumped in from the opposite side produced the deadly combination.

Still displayed on the iron gates leading to the barracks were the infamous words: "Arbeit Macht Frei" (Freedom through Work) and there was a photograph of the building as it looked originally, with large letters painted across the roof which read: "There is one path to freedom. Its milestones are: Obedience, Honesty, Cleanliness, Sobriety, Diligence, Orderliness, Sacrifice, Truthfulness, Love of the Fatherland". Each of the barracks was built to accommodate two hundred prisoners but towards the end of the war as many as two thousand were crammed inside.

Ella particularised disturbing procedures involved in the experimentation programme, but the one example which had a lasting effect on me was a series of photographs taken of a man being used in an experiment to determine the order in which vital organs would fail if a pilot was forced to ditch into the sea. Those images haunted me for a very long time. The first picture showed him being helped into a Luftwaffe uniform complete with leather helmet; in another he was being lowered into a tank of ice cold water, and his expression of bewilderment was heartbreaking. In the final picture he was floating face up, presumably unconscious or already dead. It was compulsory for German schoolchildren to visit a concentration camp and I saw several groups on my way round. They were showing little interest, but for me it felt like something I needed to do. Remembering victims of the Holocaust whilst sitting at home or in a cinema was one thing, but paying one's respects in a place where so many of them perished was quite another and seemed wholly worthwhile.

The Herkulessaal was full to overflowing that evening and extra chairs had been placed directly behind the piano. I was unsure whether I liked the new Bach French Suite but the Beethoven 'Tempest' Sonata No.17 Op.31/2 was simply thrilling. I tried throughout the recital not to think about the man in the Luftwaffe uniform, but afterwards I reflected that visiting Dachau had brought my own life into perspective and I realised how fortunate I was to be able to live it as I wished.

Another trip to Bad Kissingen rolled round in July 2006 and I arrived on a fiercely hot afternoon, during which Sokolov had been obliged to try out no less than four piano stools before he found one that didn't squeak. A harsh sounding piano and a persistent foot tapper threatened to sabotage the evening, but what Sokolov did with Bach, Beethoven and Schumann was incredible. After the concert, a group of us embarked upon what was to become an annual event, walking from the Regentenbau to a small traditional restaurant/wine bar along the river promenade where beers were ordered along with helpings of the house speciality - a Franconian wine soup topped with whipped cream and cinnamon croutons. With characteristic lack of adventure I ordered a pot of tea and a ham sandwich, which came on a huge wooden platter containing a slice of rye bread heaped with thick chunks of ham, surrounded by pickled pumpkin, gherkins and onions. Hilla Schütze ordered something similar with camembert but neither of us could cope, so our platters were passed round the table for everyone to pick at until they were clean.

Hilla accompanied me to Würzburg the next day, where we visited the bishops' palace, whose most striking feature was a grand staircase with the largest ceiling fresco in the world by the great Venetian artist, Tiepolo, depicting four continents. Beneath the palace were vast wine cellars, and the surrounding hillsides were blanketed with vineyards. Moving on to the fortress overlooking the city, we strolled through sun-baked courtyards, climbed to the picturesque Prince's Garden and ate a late lunch in the fortress restaurant seated at a window overlooking the river Main flowing through the city and onwards between steep vine-clad hillsides, whose wondrous carpet of Autumn colour I saw on a later visit. We ordered sausages, which came in abundance – eight each – smothered in thick, salty gravy laced with onions and scraps of bacon. We were already thirsty, so this ill-chosen repast made matters even worse. I'd bought a cheap ticket to hear the Bamberg Symphony Orchestra that evening, but on arrival at the Regentenbau I found Brenn von Bibra standing at the entrance. He was holding two tickets in case I'd been unable to get one and insisted I take the one he'd bought, which was in a much better position.

With another full day and night to spend in Kissingen, I took a coach trip the next morning to Rothenburg, a perfectly preserved medieval town encircled by a high wall three kilometres in length which could be walked in its entirety along a covered wooden walkway. Its reputation as the most visited small town in Germany was borne out by the number of coaches in the car park, and the streets were heaving with trippers. Without them it would have been a photographer's paradise.

Initially I'd ruled out that evening's concert because it was simply too expensive: the Chinese Philharmonic Orchestra were playing the Brahms Violin Concerto with one of Germany's leading violinists, Frank Peter Zimmerman, but I decided at the last minute to try for a return, with forty euros as my upper limit, As soon as Brenn caught sight of me and I told him what was in my mind, he darted across to the ticket office, snapped up a seat in the front row and handed it to me. "Take it", he said. "It's a gift. Enjoy yourself." I tried to give him the forty euros but he wouldn't hear of it. The concerto was wonderful and Zimmerman played a stunning Bach encore.

Bad Kissingen 2013

In the late Autumn of 2006 I visited Düsseldorf Tonhalle, a former planetarium converted into an unusual and spectacular concert venue. Covered by an immense domed ceiling lined with metal gauze panels, the roof of the auditorium glowed deep blue like the night sky and was randomly scattered with tiny white lights. It was almost like sitting out in the open beneath a canopy of stars, and the combination of this amazing spectacle with a performance of heroic proportions was pure magic. It was Jochen Lechner's first experience of the new Scriabin programme and it made such an impression on him that instead of heading for the nearest tram stop at the end of the evening, he ordered a bottle of champagne in a nearby restaurant, where we toasted Scriabin and the genius of Sokolov.

Rising at four o'clock on a raw February morning in 2007 wasn't an easy start to my first trip of the year. It was so foggy over Düsseldorf that an automatic landing was necessary and when it was announced I was filled with terror, but it turned out to be one of the smoothest landings I'd ever experienced. It was then just a short train ride to Dortmund, and in the city's immaculate Konzerthaus the Scriabin programme now fitted Sokolov like a second skin. As for the new Schubert sonata, I went in with preconceived ideas about how he would play it but unsurprisingly he exceeded my expectations by a mile. In Dortmund the following year Sokolov played Mozart sonatas and Chopin preludes. He looked apprehensive as he walked on stage, as if he'd been sent out to wrestle with a lion for public entertainment with little hope of survival. Two and a half hours later, with six meticulously executed encores and numerous standing ovations under his belt, he left the platform triumphant, the lion well and truly vanquished.

In the spring of 2007 I found my way to Neumarkt in Bavaria, where Sokolov performed in the historic Reitstadel, a 14th century building originally intended for the storage of grain and later for ammunition, which had hosted a music festival for the past twenty-five years. Dozens of world class soloists and orchestras had performed there, tickets were always at a premium and I felt lucky to be there at all, let alone sitting in the third row. Sokolov's Schubert/ Scriabin recital was nothing short of apocalyptic; the comparatively small space could scarcely contain the power he generated. It felt as if the walls might disintegrate around us and at the very least I could imagine the sounds Sokolov produced ringing around the Reitstadel's timbers long after we had left the building. At the interval I spoke to the festival organisers, who gave me a copy of a glossy book which had been produced to celebrate the twenty-fifth anniversary of the festival, containing a history of the building along with photographs and personal messages from singers, musicians and conductors who had performed there over the years, including Sokolov.

A further trip to the Schwetzingen Festival was on the cards in May 2007 but my alarm clock failed to wake me and I slept on for a further hour, finally awoke, re-booked my cab, flew into my clothes, and arrived at the airport with face unwashed, teeth uncleaned and hair uncombed. With no queue at check-in I just scraped onto the flight and spent the rest of the morning in shock. By midday I was in Schwetzingen and setting off for an afternoon walk round the schlossgarten, passing the Mozartsaal but hearing no evidence of Sokolov's presence. I spent a long time in the outer regions of the gardens where wild flowers were allowed to run riot and all the usual amazing things happened. A red squirrel scampered up to me along a woodland path, a huge gleaming golden carp leapt out of a pool as I passed, an elegant heron took to the air in slow motion just feet away.

That evening the organisers had crammed as many seats into the Mozartsaal as they dared. With such a tightly packed audience the heat was intense and Sokolov was hemmed in on three sides by rows of seats. With daylight flooding in through uncovered windows, the glare of the candelabras, sudden bursts of birdsong penetrating the building and flies zipping around, conditions were far from ideal. He looked uncomfortable as he emerged from the doors behind the tiny platform into an explosion of flash photography, climbed two steep steps up to the piano and sat down, but as soon as his fingers touched the keyboard the transformation was instant. The Scriabin programme was played with such passionate abandon that the audience reacted with a deluge of cheering at the end of 'Vers la Flamme'. When I thought about what I would have missed had I failed to catch my flight that morning, my blood ran cold.

Ludwigsburg provided me with some fresh territory in July 2007. I travelled there from Essen, a five hour journey which included a beautiful stretch of the Rhine between Koblenz and Bingen where the river wound majestically between terraced hillsides, passing the famous castles perched on their crags. Picturesque towns and villages were scattered along the valley and on the river huge barges ploughed back and forth. I reached Ludwigsburg at three and settled into a dreary weinstube where I later discovered my room was positioned directly above a billiard room and an old-fashioned bowling alley. I figured I might just about tolerate the gentle click of billiard balls, but the thunderous roll of heavy wooden bowling balls and the clatter of falling skittles was going to be a challenge.

Wishing to escape the weinstube for the evening I bought a ticket for a chamber concert by students from the Ludwigsburger Akademie playing baroque instruments. It took place in the royal palace's Ordenshalle, originally a throne room full of rococo ostentation with a bombastic ceiling occupied by oversized cherubs and billowing clouds. The programme included pieces by Bach, Vivaldi and Frescobaldi and it was an excellent way to spend the evening. The audience took interval drinks out onto a terrace overlooking the baroque garden and a tree-lined grassy ride which led to the distant Schloss Favorite, built in the early 1700s as a gathering place for Duke Ludwig and his hunting parties.

The skittle alley was going full pelt when I got back, but mercifully it closed at eleven. After a predictably basic breakfast accompanied by a tepid drink I emerged into a bright morning and the clamour of market stalls, spending much of the day in the schloss complex which contained themed areas, formal gardens and woodland walks. In addition to Japanese and Sicilian gardens there was an aviary, a vineyard, a collection of historic fairground rides and a children's garden covering a stretch of hillside, with miniature castles and caverns, a gingerbread house, Snow White's forest clearing complete with woodland creatures, Little Red Riding Hood's grandmother's cottage, Ali Baba's cave and countless other fairytale settings .

At the Forum am Park Sokolov was in fine fettle and in his room afterwards he was lively, expansive and happy to chat. We talked about his forthcoming performances of Prokofiev's 1st concerto in Denmark and I reminded him that the last time he'd played that concerto in Finland back in 1999 his manager had urged me to go there, but I'd told him it was too far to travel for a concerto lasting only fifteen minutes. Ever the stickler for detail, Sokolov pointed out that when *he* played it, it lasted for *eighteen* minutes, so I of course replied that if I'd only known that, it would have made all the difference. As it turned out, I believe those orchestral performances in Denmark never took place.

In more recent times, whenever Sokolov was in Berlin he would perform in the Great Hall of the Philharmonie, whose almost 2,500 seats were snapped up each year as soon as they went on sale. Back in 2008 I heard him in the comparatively cosy Kammermusiksaal, where the surprisingly small platform was surrounded by blocks of raked seating and the bowl effect provided an exceptionally good acoustic. As I looked across at the rapt expressions on the faces opposite, I felt like part of a large extended family gathered round the piano to share the moment. Sokolov was playing the Chopin Op.28 Preludes, and at the close of the Chopin D flat major prelude (an emotional journey in itself and worth so much more than the sum of its seven sublime minutes) there was an audible collective murmur of approval from the audience. Expressed in Sokolov's language, many of these preludes took on a whole new meaning for me. He'd recorded them sixteen years earlier, but these precious live performances carried even more weight and meaning.

I'd never known an audience try so hard to persuade Sokolov to play a seventh encore as they did that night in Berlin. At the end of the sixth the applause was so intense that he returned again and again to acknowledge it. When it finally died away, just two people persisted for a few moments, and gradually everyone joined in again until the place was once more a tumult of clapping and stamping. By this time Sokolov was far away in his room, unaware that the audience were still clamouring for more. A few minutes later the manager appeared, shook his head and placed a cover over the piano, leaving us in no doubt that the show really was over.

Bad Kreuznach, another of Germany's myriad spa towns and a place of old style charm, welcomed Sokolov in the summer of 2008. I stayed in an antique building on the river bank, just two minutes away from the tiny concert hall. At the modest 200 seat Haus des Gastes I was introduced to the director of Kreuznach Klassic Concerts, who seemed rather taken with the idea of a visitor from far away. A speech was made to the assembled throng, reminding everyone how fortunate they were to have Sokolov in their midst, and ending with a welcome directed at me, which felt good. Franco Panozzo murmured, "You are famous at last, Barbara."

Sokolov looked exposed on the tiny platform and I prayed for a trouble-free passage for him. The Mozart Sonatas K280 and K332 flowed handsomely and the Chopin Op.28 Preludes were expertly tailored to suit his surroundings, producing a perfectly judged performance. The encores were cut short after three with the arrival on stage of a frail old gentleman whose sponsorship enabled such events to take place. Climbing the steps with some difficulty, he disappeared into the wings and reappeared with Sokolov in tow, turning to place his hands on Sokolov's shoulders in a semi-embrace and delivering an affectionate little speech which was acknowledged with a broad smile.

My first experience of the famous Gewandhaus in Leipzig was a memorable one. Its strong connections with Bach, Mendelssohn and Schumann made it a source of great pride, and music seemed to be the dominant feature of the city. The current building, opened in 1981 to replace its two predecessors, had a certain austerity, but the design and seating layout were perfect, giving everyone a clear view of the platform. The two Mozart sonatas which took up the first half of the programme were full of delicacy and wit and the Chopin preludes were everything I'd hoped for and more, infused with so much love. This was Sokolov's first recital in Leipzig, and consequently only 650 of the 1,900 seats had been sold, but such was the welcome he received that it was impossible to imagine he wouldn't be invited to perform there again. The combination of a marvellous acoustic, a seemingly faultless and highly responsive piano which produced gorgeous sounds, together with Sokolov at his very best, ensured a night to remember. A Gewandhaus regular told me that in his experience, no one – not even the greatest conductors - had ever received such an enthusiastic response.

Another iconic German concert destination was Bayreuth, a refined and elegant place which made an enormous impression on me, although it was November and I had insufficient time to explore. I did go inside the Margravial Opera House, a baroque confection of mindblowing splendour, and sat through an atmospheric presentation explaining the history of the building. When I arrived at the Stadthalle in the evening I was disappointed to find I'd been given the worst possible seat, on the far right of the front row. As soon as the doors closed I slipped into the middle of the third row and held my breath until the lights went down. The performance was stupendous, as was the reception; the excited audience's speciality appeared to be stamping and the place rocked between each of the five encores.

The Stadttheater in Fürth was yet another revelation. Despite being so close to Nuremberg it seemed a small and insignificant place to possess such an imposing concert hall. Inside this grandiose building I found a dazzlingly sumptuous little auditorium with 700 seats, reminiscent of the older Italian theatres. I was warned that the public were normally rather reserved and so I doubted Sokolov would generate the kind of unbridled enthusiasm I so often saw, and wondered how many encores the audience would demand. Although the three year old piano showed signs of fatigue towards the end of the evening, it started out with the best of intentions, responding to Sokolov's every demand throughout a gloriously fluid and fleet of foot Bach Partita No.1. He played Beethoven's Sonata No.7 Op.10/3 as if he had all the time in the world to say everything he wanted, and it was like being suspended in time and space as this masterpiece unfolded. Contrary to expectations the applause following the partita was immense and the responses intensified as the evening progressed. By the end of the sixth encore the audience had stepped right out of character and were up on their feet hollering for more. This had been Sokolov at his most persuasive, and someone in the artist's room summed it up when she remarked that you always came away from his concerts feeling like a better human being. With the characteristic absence of any contact with his audience by way of word, smile or gesture, it was a measure of the sheer power of his artistry that he could so captivate his audiences and even transform lives.

I was always fearful that I might arrive at a concert destination to find the performance had been cancelled at the last moment, and this happened to me twice. The first time was in Leeds, where Sokolov was taken ill during his rehearsal on the afternoon of the recital. On the second occasion I travelled all the way to Friedrichshafen on the northern shore of Lake Konstanz, spent a night in a hotel there and received a message the next morning to say that Sokolov would not be performing that evening. I felt devastated at the prospect of spending a chill November day wandering the streets and shoreline with no performance to look forward to, but luckily I bumped into Regina

Kunrath, whom I'd encountered before at several recitals, and we spent the day together. A warm long-term friendship developed with Regina and we shared countless unforgettable concert experiences in the ensuing years. Six months later I returned to Friedrichshafen to hear the re-scheduled recital in the Ludwig-Durr-Saal of the Graf Zeppelin Haus, a small venue with perhaps 400 people in attendance. Here, Sokolov produced another flawless performance of Rameau's Suite in D, Mozart's Sonata KV310 and Brahms' Handel Variations. Each time I heard the Rameau suite, some new treasure would reveal itself. Between the ravishingly beautiful slow trill two minutes or so into 'Les Tendres Plaintes' and the rustic charm of 'Le Lardon' so many wonderful things happened, and despite a raw sounding piano it was well worth the return visit.

In March 2012 Sokolov gave the opening recital at the first festival organised by the Emil Gilels Foundation at the Hochschule für Musik in Freiburg. The occasion prompted me to picture the young Sokolov attending all of Gilels' performances in St.Petersburg from the age of seven. I imagined him sitting in the Great Philharmonic Hall listening eagerly to his idol, little realising that half a century later he would be giving his own recital in Gilels' memory. How appropriate it was that Sokolov should be chosen to perform this task, and later in the week Martha Argerich, Lilya Zilberstein and Evgeny Kissin would make their own contributions. The festival was expertly organised with an interesting collection of photographs and memorabilia from the Gilels archive on display in the foyer. It was a celebratory evening before a discriminating audience containing many musicians. On the platform beside the piano was a huge photographic reminder of who we were remembering, and it was a touching moment when Sokolov, having received his flowers, laid them at the foot of Gilels' portrait.

Later that year Beethoven's Hammerklavier sonata was introduced and I remember in particular a performance in Leipzig in November. The audience were so silent and immobile I could have closed my eyes and imagined I was the only listener. It was as if everyone else had been hypnotised, and my own concentration was so deep and uninterrupted that I'd never before felt so completely taken over by the music. The Hammerklavier was masterly: robust, boldly punctuated, slow paced, and I relished the prospect of where Sokolov would take us in the following months.

In 2010 as I walked towards Frankfurt's Alte Oper it looked like a huge floodlit relic among the city's skyscrapers, and little did I realise what an especially uplifting musical experience it was going to be. The acoustic in my part of the hall was perfect and the indescribably beautiful sounds Sokolov extracted from the piano might have come directly from heaven. He took us on a celestial journey through Bach's Partita No.2, beginning with a grand flourish and ending with a celebration, and in those twenty blessed minutes my heart soared up into the firmament. Amidst the purity of sound and Sokolov's wondrous articulation I swear I could hear ethereal choirs, sacred instruments, the whisper of angels' wings.

Four months later in Essen's Philharmonie, Sokolov was awarded the 2010 Klavier-Festival-Ruhr Prize immediately before his recital began. During the presentation speech he stood listening patiently, arms at his sides, motionless apart from fluttering fingers - the only evidence that he was keen to get started. He went on to deliver a sparkling Bach Partita No.2, and from the stately unfolding of the Praeludium right through to the final gathering rush towards the climax of Schumann's Sonata No.3 Op.14 there was so much to savour, and a deeply searching performance of Brahms Op.116 was yet to follow. Whatever Sokolov played, the tiniest variations and subtleties of tone and colour revealed themselves one by one as he freely explored every possibility open to him within the boundaries set by the score. There were certain special evenings where the audience formed a kind of fellowship, where connections were made between complete strangers, where there was no need to know your neighbour, no necessity to speak the same language, where simply an exchanged glance said everything. This was just such an evening.

Recitals in Leverkusen and Wuppertal took place on consecutive dates in the late Autumn of 2010, both organised by the Bayer pharmaceutical company. The atmosphere in the Erholungshaus in Leverkusen felt intimate despite an audience of almost 800, and the public's exceptional concentration coupled with a full-blooded high energy performance of riveting intensity made this one of those ultimate experiences which I couldn't imagine being repeated the next evening. I therefore anticipated an anticlimax in Wuppertal's grandiose Mendelssohn Saal, but how mistaken I was. This spacious and beautiful concert salon had fewer than 400 seats, the sound was huge and the impact monumental. Sokolov's reading of Schumann's Humoreske in particular produced a performance of unbelievable magnitude. As for the Op.32 pieces by Schumann, I'd hitherto found very little to like about them, and when I learned Sokolov would play them after Humoreske I thought they would make a dull conclusion to the evening, but as usual he knew best and transformed these pieces into something utterly intriguing.

Later in November 2010 I visited the imposing Gothic town of Landshut in southern Bavaria, where Sokolov performed in the Rathaus's historic Prunksaal. Walking into the auditorium gave me a tremendous lift: it was one of the most amazing interiors I'd ever seen, resembling a medieval banqueting hall with dark wooden seats and flooring, an elaborately fashioned timber roof from which huge circular wooden chandeliers were suspended, and a high minstrels' gallery. The walls were decorated with a painted mural in rich colours, depicting 'The Landshut Wedding', a historic and significant event dating back to 1475 when the son of the Duke of Bavaria married a Polish princess. Details of the ceremony and subsequent festivities, including what was worn and precisely what was eaten, were so well documented at the time that every four years during the summer Landshut gave itself over to a lavish pageant and re-enactment of the wedding, performed by over two thousand townsfolk in authentic costume.

It was my first time in Landshut but Sokolov's third, and from the ease and freedom of his performance it was evident that he enjoyed playing there. A studious and highly appreciative audience silently absorbed the music, and again Sokolov launched into Schumann's Humoreske with an exhilarating degree of impulsiveness, taking the wildest passages to the very edge. The whole programme was flawless and I sat back, already more than satisfied, anticipating the usual string of encores with which I'd become so familiar. I almost shot out of my seat when Sokolov began playing something new, astonishing, and unknown to me. 'Le Rappel des Oiseaux', a mini-masterpiece by Rameau, came as a glorious gift, evoking the chatter of birdsong, the flutter of feathers, the rustle of leaves. Sokolov's lightness and deftness left this piece hanging in the air, and I scarcely noticed the two Chopin preludes which followed. As for the town itself I only managed a conducted tour of the Residenz building, which was chiefly about ceilings and did nothing for my vertigo, but nevertheless Landshut left a lasting impression.

In Mannheim, at the Rosengarten's Mozartsaal both piano and acoustic were marvellous and Sokolov was at his best, but I'd already been warned that the audience would disappear very quickly after the performance, so it came as no surprise when after just two Rameau encores everyone left at great speed as if the building was on fire. Apparently the underground car park took an age to empty so the aim of the mass exodus was to see who could be first to escape the resultant petrol fumes. The German couple who were accommodating me that night (Gudrun and Peter Schmitz-Jacobi, whom I'd met at a previous recital in Ludwigshafen and who had become close friends) felt embarrassed by the swift exit and explained the reason to Sokolov, who countered that there were surely other car parks in Mannheim that people could have used.

Over the years numerous impediments threatened to wreck my travel plans. Flight delays, rail strikes, general strikes, extreme weather events, industrial action by pilots, cabin crew, baggage handlers, airport staff, concert hall staff, as well as the SARS virus, bird flu, swine flu, foot and mouth disease, terrorist threats and volcanic ash had all played their part, but in June 2011 the humble bean sprout was believed to have triggered an outbreak of e-coli in Germany. I very nearly cancelled my trip to the Schwetzingen Festival but as soon as I was sure Sokolov was on his way I decided to throw caution to the winds, and in any case my friends the Schmitz-Jacobis were waiting to provide me with a safe haven.

It was my fourth visit to Schwetzingen but the first time I'd heard Sokolov perform in the lovely 500 seat Rokokotheater overlooking the palace gardens: the perfect venue for a summer evening. The front section of the platform had been removed to accommodate five extra rows of seats, so the piano was positioned further back in a kind of recess, from which it seemed that only a fraction of Sokolov's monumental effort was being projected effectively. The following evening I attended a recital by another pianist in the same venue, and as a result of fewer tickets being sold, the extra seats were removed and the piano came forward onto the open platform, where it sang out freely.

Rokoko Theater Schwetzingen

Later that month in Passau the recital took place in the city's resplendent Rathaussaal, where the piano was positioned at the side of the room on a shallow platform in front of two illuminated stained glass windows. It was Sokolov's first performance in Passau and the reaction he was to draw from the 400 people gathered there was huge. Firstly the director of the festival gave a long speech cataloguing Sokolov's musical credentials, and finally the man himself emerged from a room at the rear and walked between rows of seats towards the platform. Despite several interruptions, including a mobile ringing in the front row and a medical emergency in the third, Sokolov remained unperturbed. The first half of the recital was greeted with prolonged and profuse appreciation and the audience seemed stunned by what they'd heard. The whole performance carried something extra that night; an almost unprecedented degree of intensity, a wildly passionate Schumann in particular. This was Maestro on a mission; it was much more than heart and soul, and it seemed there were no boundaries he would not cross. The distance he was required to travel between the anteroom and the platform, combined with the audience's unfamiliarity with his tendency to play many encores, resulted in only two before the applause died away, but this fortunate gathering left the Rathaussaal with more than enough to dwell upon.

Sokolov was travelling on to another venue the next day in preparation for a performance the day after that. I asked him if there would be somewhere he could practise when he got there and he told me he had no idea what time he would arrive but in any case the only piano available was small, old and out of tune. I pulled a face. "Yes, all of it together", he said. "So I think I will rest and sleep". Pointing at my head I said, "And practise in here?" "Yes", he smiled.

Schumann was replaced by Rameau's Suite in D, which I heard for the first time in Ludwigshafen in February 2012. At first I found it less interesting than the Suite in G from 1997/98 but I was delighted that Sokolov had returned to Rameau, a field of repertoire in which he seemed so at home. Along with Mozart's Sonata KV310 he continued to deliver each of the Brahms Handel Variations with the appropriate lightness of touch, singing sweetness, surging energy and powerful attack, creating an atmosphere of mounting excitement which could not fail to engage the listener. Two weeks later in Frankfurt's Alte Oper, increasing familiarity highlighted the richness of many of the Rameau pieces and I began to realise that my initial assessment of the Suite in D had been way off the mark.

In March I sat in the balcony of Bremen's Die Glocke and was rewarded with an astonishingly clear, perfectly balanced diamond cut sound. The new programme was now in full bloom, each part of the Suite in D having taken on its own special character. During one of the quiet passages, a long, loud snore emanated from somewhere in the parterre which I hoped Sokolov didn't hear, but it caused the inevitable flurry of indignation amongst the audience which caused an even greater disturbance. At the interval, however, he left the stage with the floorboards thundering reassuringly in his ears, and by the end of the evening the storm of applause and stamping might well have been heard out in the street.

In the summer of 2013 I travelled directly from a concert in Barcelona to Berlin, whose Philharmonie provided none of the Palau de la Música Catalana's colourful distractions but simply Sokolov's mesmerising presence, boundless energy and poetic expression. On this occasion he had moved on from the Kammermusiksaal to the main hall, where all 2,440 seats had been sold. My seat was far, far away from the platform, in the back row of one of the uppermost sections, but when I closed my eyes the amazing acoustic could have fooled me into believing I was much closer. Everything came together in perfect unison that night: conditions just about ideal, audience holding its breath and Sokolov intent on setting the place alight. After the interval I lost my way in the complex labyrinth of corridors and found all the doors to the auditorium closed. In a state of panic I barged through the nearest entrance, which gave access to a section much closer to the platform, just as Sokolov was sitting down to resume. I crept forward in the darkness and fortuitously an empty aisle seat presented itself, as a result of which the second half was even more thrilling than the first. The reception Sokolov received was remarkable, and if anyone had strayed into the foyer of the Philharmonie at that moment and heard the screaming they might have been forgiven for assuming a rock concert was drawing to a close.

Heidelberg 2015

Summer 2015 took me back to Dortmund, where a modest fifty or so extra seats were positioned strategically to the left side of the platform, ensuring no one sat within Sokolov's field of vision. There was room for many more, but on this occasion the artist's comfort seemed to have taken precedence over the drive for maximum revenue. This sensible arrangement was a relief to me, for I'd often watched with mounting anxiety as members of the public seated on stage directly beside the keyboard repeatedly crossed their legs, dangled a shoe from the end of a toe, fanned themselves with their programmes, exchanged whispered remarks, handed small children items to fiddle with, and occasionally those children had sat right next to the artist, swinging their legs back and forth like clockwork until they drifted off to sleep.

This discriminating festival audience knew exactly what to expect and sat in enthralled concentration. Sometimes I'd had a problem with the acoustic in Dortmund depending on where I sat, and in certain areas it was rather like being in an indoor swimming pool. On this occasion the acoustic worked in my favour and I enjoyed a perfectly balanced sound. There were so many wonderful moments during Bach's Partita No.1: I swear I heard an extra ornament or two, and in the courante that impish dancing left hand of Sokolov's had me spellbound. The gigue appeared to be gaining in velocity with each performance and this one began at a suicidal speed, but he emerged unscathed.

Returning to the platform following the partita Sokolov was greeted like a conquering hero. The first movement of Beethoven's Sonata No.7 Op.10/3 arrived with a delicious amount of bite; the largo was overwhelming, and despite the broad tempo the whole sonata reached its scurrying conclusion all too soon. After the interval the rightful occupant of my seat showed up so I was obliged to move to a less favourable position, but this did little to reduce the impact of Schubert's Sonata D784. The climax was greeted with a bombardment of bravos, and not until the end of the sixth encore was Sokolov able to convince this delirious audience that his job was done.

A couple of weeks later I was in Leer, a north German town in Ostfriesland, close to the Dutch border, where the Theater an der Blinke possessed a creditable acoustic and the resident piano withstood a vigorous workout under Sokolov's hands. A freewheeling Bach partita got things off to a great start, and the audience soon realised how fortunate they were to have an artist of Sokolov's calibre in their comparatively remote neck of the woods. There was a real sense of mounting excitement as the evening progressed, and the opening notes of the Chopin Prelude Op.28/15 generated an audible ripple of anticipation. It was good to see a provincial theatre with such a sizeable audience, and Sokolov was left in no doubt that he'd made his mark.

The next day I moved on to Kiel for Sokolov's annual contribution to the Schleswig-Holstein Festival, where the Kieler Schloss audience simmered with expectation. With a marvellous acoustic and a piano with a more refined tone than the one in Leer, Sokolov was well equipped to deliver a gold standard performance. The Bach gigue was nothing short of kamikaze (but then no one could ever accuse Sokolov of playing safe) and as for the Beethoven, for me the whole sonata radiated a golden aura. There were no microphones at either venue, so both performances disappeared without trace but for the fragments that lingered in the minds of those who were lucky enough to be there.

Baden-Baden's resplendent Festspielhaus was reputedly Europe's second largest opera house and concert hall and claimed to have exceptional acoustics. The first time I was there it was also Sokolov's first recital in Baden-Baden, and although only 700 seats were occupied, the reception was rousing enough for a full house. The artistic director was stunned by Sokolov's performance and told me she had learned more about pianos that day than she ever expected to learn in a lifetime. She added, "I'll make sure he's invited back here if it's the last thing I do".

Sokolov very soon became a regular at the Festspielhaus and in the autumn of 2015 I sat close enough to study those dexterous hands once more. The craftsmanship that went into every phrase was already legendary, and to watch the whole process in close-up was a singular pleasure. The Chopin Nocturnes Op.32/1 & 2 gained greater stature with each performance and seemed to be every bit as personal to Sokolov as the mazurkas which had featured in his 2000/01 programme. He'd continued to play the mazurkas regularly as encores for many years, sometimes putting them into storage for a few seasons and then bringing them back for another airing. In Baden-Baden the piano didn't react well to Chopin's 2nd Sonata, and after the desperate turmoil of the first movement it produced a noticeable metallic resonance and a few other strange sounds during the seismic funeral march. But Sokolov threw everything at it, and with the final hammer blow he snatched his hands from the keyboard and his backside from the piano stool as if to say, "That's it. I did my best. Take it or leave it!" The barrage of applause made it clear we were more than happy to take it.

A few weeks later in the Alte Oper Frankfurt, the Steinway met the challenge of the Schubert and Chopin sonatas with the utmost resilience and beauty of tone. I'd become so accustomed to sitting close to the piano in recent weeks that it seemed strange to find myself in the fourteenth row, but as Sokolov addressed the sombre opening bars of the Schubert sonata it was like stepping back from the close proximity of a painting, where I was able to observe the performance from a different perspective and appreciate the whole. Sokolov now wore the first half of the programme like a much loved old overcoat, but there was nothing shabby or threadbare about this performance. There were no standing ovations either until the end of the recital, but where applause was called for, the pieces were firstly allowed to die away while those around me exchanged meaningful glances, sighed with contentment, shook their heads in wonder. Sokolov's Chopin sonata was not for the faint-hearted. At the end of a staggeringly powerful first movement I marvelled that the piano was still intact, and from that moment on I listened with a mixture of anxiety and elation. Intense applause greeted the final fleeting presto and as Sokolov walked away it was as if a great force of nature had left the platform.

Spring 2016 brought two German recitals on consecutive evenings, firstly in Hanover's NDR Sendesaal, where Sokolov was performing Schumann's Arabeske and Fantasy and Chopin's Nocturnes Op.32 along with the 2nd Sonata. It was such a powerful programme that to sit virtually next to Sokolov firing on all cylinders and playing as if it was his last night on earth was indescribably thrilling. The hands were lifted perilously high, the feet threw a party of their own as he lunged and stamped, his heels smacking against the wooden floor. By the end of a sublime Schumann Fantasy I was in a kind of trance, and my companion, who'd travelled from Israel expressly to hear Sokolov, said that his enjoyment of the first half had been so complete, he could have gone home there and then, totally satisfied. Personally I would have been happy to skip going home and simply die on the spot. An incendiary Chopin sonata followed and I knew I would find no words to describe an evening of such gripping intensity. The same could be said for the following evening in Braunschweig's vast

Stadthalle. The sheer physicality and fierce concentration required to perform this demanding programme at such a stratospheric level must have used an enormous amount of energy. Knowing nothing of Sokolov's eating habits, I could only imagine the internal motor which drove him was fuelled mostly by love.

My 400th Sokolov performance was in Munich's Herkulessaal in April 2016, and I remember that as the lights were dimmed, those seated behind the piano receded into darkness, and the only prominent features on stage were Sokolov's hands and his silver halo of hair. One of my favourite younger generation pianists, Yulianna Avdeeva, whom I knew to be a Sokolov admirer, sat close by and was visibly moved. The evening was everything I'd hoped for, with no indiscriminate clapping, only minimal coughing and a blessed reverential hush between each movement. Sokolov asserted his authority in the second movement, creating vivid imagery in my mind's eye. A spectacle of colour and pageantry marched across Schumann's landscape with Sokolov cast as the fearsome Commander-in-Chief, whipping the troops into shape, leading them into battle, spurring them on to death and glory. He transformed the Herkulessaal into a place of intense concentration, and at the interval many in the audience left their seats as if recently released from a hypnotic trance. Some shook their heads in amazement; one or two wept. There was no mistaking we now had two monuments: Schumann and Chopin side by side. From the vast ocean of possibilities Sokolov had come up with many hidden gems over the years, but more recently he'd turned familiar works into rediscovered treasures, and for me the Schumann Fantasy was much closer to the Holy Grail. Easing us into the second half with two immaculate Chopin nocturnes, Sokolov went on to send shock waves through the building with a tectonic 2nd Sonata, by the end of which the audience were totally enraptured. One solitary slip in the final encore reminded us again that Sokolov was also human. It put me in mind of an accomplished high wire act allowing itself one precarious wobble towards the end to demonstrate just how difficult and dangerous it really was.

The 2016 midsummer recital in Bad Kissingen coincided with Sokolov's twentieth appearance at the festival, and a video recording was arranged. The audience were requested, in the nicest possible way, to switch off devices and keep quiet – and again I wondered why this was not standard practice at every performance. For someone like Sokolov, who had never in his life exhibited the slightest inclination to show off, I imagined that the presence of cameras might induce a certain amount of pressure, but not only did he rise to the occasion, he soared above it on gilded wings, with an aerobatic display of his own special brand of fearless attack counterbalanced with an amplitude of tenderness. The Schumann Arabeske flowed effortlessly and once more I admired the beauty of the closing bars, where Sokolov lingered, as if, one by one, he was hanging out the notes to dry. He threw every part of himself into the Fantasy and maintained a dizzying momentum until the final notes. At the emotionally charged conclusion he returned to the platform several times, and then, at the moment when there was usually a stampede for the bar or people began exchanging comments with their neighbours, there was simply a stunned silence. No one in the hall stirred for several seconds, as if the first person to speak or move might be accused of committing an act of sacrilege. It was quite extraordinary.

Later that year in the vast and striking Meistersingerhalle in Nuremberg with its widespread seating area, initially I was dismayed to hear a very thin sound struggling to find its way towards my part of the hall as Sokolov began playing, but within a few bars of the first movement of Mozart's Sonata K545 I became acclimatised, realising that Sokolov's choice of this sonata to start the programme was a stroke of genius. As much as I'd adored the previous season's Schumann/Chopin extravaganza, it had presented the audience with a massive emotional upheaval followed by an even greater one, whereas now we had a comparatively easy to digest first half followed by a mightily substantial main event, ending with a series of extra sweet delights to tempt us to stick around a while longer. With the Mozart programme now firmly established, Sokolov had reached the point, after almost sixty performances of the Schumann Fantasy - with the final one just a matter of weeks away – where he would deepen his excavation of the Fantasy even further before leaving it behind. As he held the audience captive during the final movement it seemed that he, of all pianists, had made this piece his own. An elderly gentleman whom I understood to be the 90 year old founder of the Hörtnagel Concert Series, appeared on stage at the end of the evening. Old enough to be Sokolov's father, he handed him a bouquet of flowers and held him in a cheek to cheek embrace, as if congratulating his very own infant prodigy.

In November at the Festspielhaus in Baden-Baden the piano stood before a black backdrop decorated with bold slashes of red and orange: a suitably demonic setting for maybe Scriabin's Vers la Flamme or Poème Satanique, but an unlikely environment for the playroom innocence of Mozart's K545. Nevertheless it was a joy, and the K475 Fantasy was infused with such theatricality that the entire Mozart programme effervesced. The blazing inferno stage set was more than justified in the second half when Sokolov threw himself headlong into an especially impassioned Schumann Fantasy. After the aching sentiment of the third movement I was left feeling that this could never be bettered, but two evenings later he poured out his heart once more in Schweinfurt's Stadttheater. Mozart's angel bells rang out at the start of the evening and the closing bars of Sonata K457 swept in like a whirlwind with a devilishly cutting climax. I cast my mind back to the beginning of the season, before I'd heard the Mozart programme for the first time in Oslo, when I'd held the view that Mozart's keyboard works were cold, devoid of true feeling; music I could never relate to. Now I knew better.

In the spring of 2017 the piano in Hamburg's Laeiszhalle was a real beauty and it seemed that Beethoven's Op.111 would never be in safer hands. Oceanic in its scope and depth, it became a towering edifice, the first devastating movement delivered with titanic strength and the second imbued with a sense of weightlessness, as if we were drifting amongst galaxies of stars. It was a pity that between each of the six encores, members of the audience exited the hall but then decided to barge back in again when they realised there was more music to be had. There was frequent banging as the doors closed, shafts of light as they were re-opened and general commotion as people scrambled back into empty seats. My concert companion, a Laeiszhalle regular, said he'd never seen anything like it before. For most of us it was quite simple: if you wanted to leave, you left. If you were hoping for more, you remained seated and exercised a little patience.

In April that same year Cologne's huge Philharmonie was filled to the brim and the Mozart opener exhibited a captivating freshness, with the smoothest velvety runs imaginable. The second movement was played with indescribable delicacy, the opening bars light and airy as thistledown. Beethoven's splendid Op.90 sonata had long been in full flight with its multitude of colours and variety of moods. Under Sokolov's deft command its moments of urgency seemed unhurried yet lost no impact and the lilting melody in the second movement danced effortlessly in perfect preparation for Op.111, whose opening movement began with ferocious roars and fearsome leaps. Soon the slow deep base trill heralded the beginning of a diverse narrative in which Sokolov explored the finely drawn anatomy of this miraculous sonata. As the first movement drew to a close I waited, as always, for those final thirty sublime seconds when I imagined myself borne aloft by angels. Sokolov articulated each of the sonata's many facets with singular skill, from the frenetic, the explosive, the daring, to the cosmic wonderment of the arietta, which began at a more funereal pace than I could ever remember, gradually drawing listeners towards a greater view of the universe and ultimately of themselves, ascending to a point where the audience was suspended in time and space amid a galactic panorama of shining planets. Then of course there were the sustained trills which dominated the latter part of the second movement – so intense they could have been made of flesh and blood.

Throughout the following three years I crossed and re-crossed Germany, paying regular visits to familiar venues and discovering new ones. In Saarbrucken I attended Sokolov's first performance there and the Beethoven programme produced a riotous standing ovation. It was thrilling to witness such a wholehearted reaction in a hall where for many people Sokolov had been an unknown quantity until that night. There were no subscription seats, but the prime places were reserved for sponsors and they were some of the first to be on their feet, which was good to see. In the past I'd often watched resentfully as sponsors drifted in and out of sleep whilst occupying premium seats.

The piano survived the rigours of the evening apart from one or two twinges towards the end. I often looked at pianos Sokolov had just finished playing as they stood alone on stage, their duties discharged, wondering how much remedial work would be necessary to restore them to their former state of health. The evening in Saarbrucken ended in a happy commotion of excited exchanges and a huge crowd of exhilarated souls, some of whom were already aware of Sokolov's greatness, others newly converted, clamoured to enter the artist's room for a brief moment in the presence of the gentle colossus who had held them spellbound for the past two and a half hours.

Church acoustics may not have been everyone's cup of tea but I firmly believed that hearing Sokolov perform in a church was an experience not to be missed. On a summer evening in 2017 I returned to the picturesque Bavarian town of Passau where his recital took place amid the Italian baroque splendour of the Church of St.Michael. Overlooked by an extravagance of angels and a great golden sunburst above the altar, the piano looked magnificent as it stood waiting for Sokolov to step out and take charge. Such a lavish setting could have been a distraction but in fact it greatly enriched what was for me another life-enhancing event. The sounds Sokolov produced seemed to take on an added lustre, and with nothing to confine it, the music was set free to rise above the altar where angels and cherubim gathered, and drift out across the area where we lesser mortals sat in rapt silence. I found that I was scarcely breathing, such was the quality of the performance and the glory of the sound created by the confluence of artist, instrument and architecture.

In Bad Kissingen that summer the platform of the Max-Littmann-Saal had been given a new look by way of red, gold and green floodlights trained onto the crystal lanterns suspended at intervals around the stage backdrop, reflecting onto the inlaid wooden panels behind the piano. With the hall's lighting at normal level the colours were pleasantly muted, but when the main lights were dimmed the effect was to heavily accentuate the colours, leaving artist and instrument in dark and dramatic foreground silhouette. This new arrangement didn't meet with universal approval, some likening the spectacle to, amongst other things, a fun fair or a house of ill repute, but I rather enjoyed the air of theatricality it brought to the performance. Sokolov swept all before him on his steadfast mission to illustrate and illuminate, from the delicate transparency of Mozart's K545 to the unfathomable density of Beethoven's final sonata. Not for a moment could he be accused of skimming the surface of the music. Every note had been meticulously weighed, carefully considered and given its own individual value. Every nuance of Beethoven's Op.90 was explored to the full and the whole sonata was driven with delicious momentum, its final sweet notes hovering in the air as if to sprinkle the audience with fairy dust.

Sokolov gave the final performance for the Klavier Festival Ruhr in July 2017 in the 1,745 seat Mercatorhalle in Duisburg. His masterly account of the Mozart programme showed every facet of his formidable technique and powers of expression. Sokolov and the piano formed a perfect partnership and he simply went like a train – maybe a miniature one to begin with, but we were soon travelling with the grown-ups, gathering momentum towards the end until the mighty locomotive that was Sokolov came to a standstill. The first half was received with immense enthusiasm, but when it came to the Beethoven the entire audience stood to acknowledge what they'd heard, and when Sokolov reappeared a stupendous roar swept towards him. The inexhaustible array of sounds he produced from the piano had been amazing. One minute we were staring into the abyss and the next floating, weightless, contemplating the vastness of the universe, dazzled by imagery of inexplicable beauty. The wide ranging encores by Schubert, Chopin, Rameau, Schumann, Griboyedov and Debussy produced some melting pianissimi and at the end of the more profound pieces Sokolov slowly removed his hands from the keys, allowed them to rest in his lap and kept his head inclined towards the keyboard for several seconds. The audience understood, and waited.

From Duisburg I travelled to Kieler Schloss, where a single light at each exit and a handful of muted spotlights directed towards the piano rendered the audience invisible, creating a powerful image and an intimate atmosphere. All day long the wind and rain had been relentless, the sky a uniform grey. Much of Germany was suffering inclement weather, but inside Kieler Schloss Sokolov had taken control of the elements and his Mozart K545 promised eternal sunlight whilst even Beethoven's storm clouds were edged with silver. Sokolov's life-affirming performances of Beethoven's Op.111 mirrored such a wealth of human emotion, it was impossible to walk away unmoved. No doubt he would have insisted the credit be placed entirely at the feet of the composer, but the relationship between himself and the repertoire was so intimate that one could almost imagine he'd had a hand in its creation.

In Baden-Baden's Festspielhaus it was as if a kindly uncle had settled down to tell us a story when Sokolov began Haydn's Sonata No.32 in G minor. Haydn's music was a succession of stories and Sokolov had a spellbinding facility to tell them. The feather-light touch, the delicacy, the vivacity I'd heard in Stockholm the week before were all there, but underpinned with something much more robust. Humour was never far away in these sonatas, yet there was also substance and seriousness. The piano sang out with enormous power but developed a resonating edge during the Beethoven programme, and by the fourth encore it sounded quite raw, but far from being a problem it somehow reflected the rigours of the great journey we had embarked upon. It was thrilling to be part of the unbridled elation at the end of the performance and I walked away from the Festspielhaus feeling as if a whole lifetime had been compressed into three precious hours.

My next trip to Germany took me back to Frankfurt's Alte Oper, where the most prized bells in Christendom could not have produced sweeter sounds. Sokolov's unique brand of pianism brought Haydn's inventive trio of sonatas to life so vividly that a whole cast of characters from the virtuous to the downright ridiculous took shape in my imagination. Some years earlier, there had been an online discussion about Sokolov's sense of humour - an Italian critic having described him as 'glacial' - and I'd argued that where humour was present or implied in the music Sokolov was perfectly capable of expressing it well. Indeed I went further and said that he had a positive gift for highlighting the comic element and whatever was required he delivered with a true sense of fun.

After the intermission he embarked upon the mighty Beethoven pieces, taking all manner of risks but paying no penalties, the audience hanging on to his coat tails every step of the way. There was almost always a deathly hush as Sokolov communed with the stars, as if the public were hoping to catch the crackle of meteor dust in the atmosphere, but in Frankfurt this breathless silence prevailed throughout the entire sonata. Unlike the piano in Baden-Baden which had handed in its notice long before the conclusion of the programme, this one remained compliant to the very end.

The final performance of 2017 was in the Bavarian city of Regensburg, in the university campus's Auditorium Maximum. I'd been warned that it wasn't a purpose built venue and the acoustics were awful, so my expectations were non-existent. The building was constructed of vast expanses of concrete and the deafening echo of voices in the entrance hall filled me with apprehension. I could do little but anticipate the worst, so I geared up for disappointment and took my seat. As Sokolov began the first Haydn sonata the contours of the music sounded blurred, indistinct, but thanks to the mysteries of the human ear I adapted within minutes and the sound soon became one of pleasing resonance and perfect clarity. After the final airy notes of Beethoven's Op.90 had fluttered around us like scraps of confetti Sokolov unleashed upon his audience the most extraordinary torrent of power and emotion, drawing us inexorably into Beethoven's Op.111 turmoil. The first movement was visceral in its intensity, but as Sokolov reached the last few bars, heaven came close and we were soon communing with the angels. It seemed strange that such an unlikely location should produce what was arguably Sokolov's greatest Op.111 to date, and what an education it was to watch him at work. At times his fingers seemed so deeply embedded in the keyboard that one wondered how he could possibly prepare himself for whatever came next. And I vowed never again to pre-judge a concert venue, certainly not when Sokolov was in residence.

In March 2018 it felt good to be back in Bremen's splendid art deco concert hall Die Glocke, where the auditorium was packed to the rafters and the first class resident Steinway had not only been polished lovingly by someone with an eye for detail (occasionally the piano was covered in fingermarks and I longed to go in search of a duster), but produced luscious sounds of astonishing immediacy. As soon as the lights were dimmed, out stepped Sokolov with Papa Haydn at his heels; an old friend who sounded fresh and revitalized. Each of Haydn's colourful characters came to vivid life and from the beginning of the evening's first whimsical journey we were blessed with the nimblest of runs, the lightest of trills, all perfectly paced for the greatest effect. The scene changes came thick and fast: in the daintily drawn B minor Menuett the notes danced like blossom on the breeze, the middle section was deliciously subdued and the lumbering cloak and dagger theatricality of the C sharp minor first movement was endearingly expressed.

Initially, the announcement of the new second half comprising Schubert Impromptus Op.142 had been a disappointment. I'd hoped for another mind-blowing sonata in which to sink my teeth, but I was soon embarking upon a voyage of beautiful discoveries. Amid the first impromptu's rippling melodies I was becalmed on a silvery sea, but dark and turbulent waters seethed just beyond the horizon.

Schubert and Sokolov combined to turn the simplest themes into something profound: a potent and penetrating collection of narratives which transformed the audience from mere observers into virtual participants. In the second piece there was might and majesty, in the fourth sorcery and mischief. The finale was a fleet-fingered *tour de force,* after which Sokolov leapt from the piano stool the second his hands left the keyboard.

A week or so later I was back beneath Düsseldorf Tonhalle's starry blue dome to hear Sokolov following in Haydn's nimble footsteps, breezing through the first movement of the B minor sonata with unhurried ease and delivering the second with delicacy and refinement. The tempo of the third movement enabled the listener to digest every detail and the comic grandiosity of the C sharp minor first movement was wonderfully described. The second half of the recital quickly gathered me into the inescapable thrall of the Schubert programme. With these impromptus Sokolov laid before us a dense tapestry depicting four diverse landscapes, from the shimmering radiance of the first piece and the exquisite softening of certain chords in the emphatic declaration of the second impromptu's opening theme, to the final piece where we were taken on a tantalizing excursion into a world of supernatural powers and magic spells, inhabited by mischievous goblins and woodland sprites.

In Freiburg Sokolov gave the opening recital at the 4th Emil Gilels Festival in the Wolfgang-Hoffmann-Saal at the Hochschule für Musik. Waiting for Sokolov to appear, the audience sat in a reverent silence which was to prevail until the very end of this remarkable evening. It was a venue where Sokolov's approaching footsteps could be heard long before he reached the platform, and as he walked towards the piano he looked weary, but the moment he made contact with the keyboard it was as if he'd plugged himself into the mains.

Supporting and sustaining him were a first class acoustic and a lovely Steinway of mellow and creamy tone. Conditions could not have been more favourable and the performance was nothing short of superhuman. Each piece was executed with what seemed like a fresh approach, renewed attack, reconsidered application. From the cascading notes in the first movement of Haydn's G minor sonata right through to the interval the audience were totally engaged, and after the break they were disarmed by a ravishingly beautiful account of the Schubert programme. The first impromptu was accompanied by the most graceful hand movements and those gorgeous bass notes were never far away. In the second, the muted chords sounded more lustrous than ever and I was elated to discover that the third impromptu which I'd struggled to come to terms with was increasing in value by leaps and bounds, leaving me wondering how I'd ever found it a problem. (Strangely, whenever I needed to work hard to engage with a piece I often grew to love it all the more.) The fourth was a complete marvel where Sokolov created a magical atmosphere in which there was all manner of mischievous behaviour in Schubert's fairy kingdom. I glanced occasionally at the portrait of Gilels beside the piano, as if seeking some sort of reaction from him, and as the audience burst into rapturous applause I visualised a jubilant Gilels thumbing his nose at all who doubted his wisdom in championing young Grisha Sokolov at the Tchaikovsky Competition in 1966.

After an unusually long and dreary UK winter it was a delight to be in blossom-laden Heidelberg in the spring of 2018 for Sokolov's Haydn/Schubert programme, where he bowled along with an almighty spring in his step, seemingly determined to give his audience more bounce, more bite, a touch of extra swagger, along with even greater delicacy and depth of feeling. The Haydn programme was a model of lightness and precision, providing an agreeable contrast to the richness and diversity of Schubert's impromptus. The earnestness and honesty with which Sokolov played the first piece made my heart ache, and the riches just kept coming. He brought a dignified and modest grandeur to the second, and in the third he touched on a wealth of colours and textures from delightfully coquettish trills to graveside solemnity. In the bewitching fourth Sokolov was cast as the sorcerer, commanding all around him in an imaginary sylvan glade where elves and fairies gathered to do his bidding.

In Munich's Herkulessaal he gave an affectionate reading of the three Haydn sonatas and then, amid the faded tapestries, his endless store of sound colours flooded the auditorium as Schubert's impromptus sang out, the first of which propelled me upwards through a gap in the clouds where there was perpetual sunlight and limitless blue. The second piece was played with nobility, those mighty triple chords melting at the edges, the bass trills rolling like thunder. From Munich I travelled to Nuremberg and sat in the front row of the Meistersingerhalle, where the volume was immense. At times during the Schubert impromptus the music flowed like molten lava and the bass notes roared thrillingly. After the emotionally draining works of recent times, in particular Chopin's 2nd Sonata, the Schumann Fantasy and Beethoven's Op.111, I now found myself walking away from recitals with a feeling that I'd not suffered nearly enough and had enjoyed myself far too much. But even with no monumental sonata that season I was happy. Not only did Sokolov transmit his richly detailed pageant using every power at his disposal, he portrayed lovingly every scrap of humanity behind the music, in all its strengths and frailties.

On a Friday evening in May 2018, with a marvellous instrument at his fingertips, Sokolov set about demonstrating the much prized sound quality in Bielefeld's Rudolf-Oetker-Halle, releasing the glories of Haydn to dance among the lofty pillars. The sonatas were finely etched, exquisitely articulated and at the heart of the three pieces lay the B minor jewel which Sokolov delivered with elegance and understatement, the presto executed with modest panache; nothing flashy, nothing thrown in purely for effect, just sheer musical integrity. The clarity of sound enabled small hitherto unnoticed details to emerge, and at the interval an exemplary audience showed its appreciation, offering generous applause and a gentle drumming of the floorboards. I didn't notice whether the piano required any adjustment during the interval, but it maintained its mellifluous voice to the final chord. Some passages were played so deliciously they were almost edible. The opening bars of the first impromptu raised a theatrical curtain to reveal the multiplicity of scenes in Schubert's dramatic spectacle. How I savoured that luminous bass note which heralded the real start of our journey, as Sokolov embarked upon his voyage into the heart of the piece like a majestic vessel slicing through the ocean. The second impromptu evolved into something more lingeringly profound each time I heard it and here again there was no artifice, no over-sentimentality. Sokolov offered nothing but his lifelong stock-in-trade: absolute sincerity.

The following evening in Münster University we were lucky to have the same splendid piano. The acoustic was entirely different and the sound resultantly less rounded, but Sokolov could always be relied upon to engineer the best possible outcome, whatever the conditions.

The final scampering notes of the fourth impromptu produced an explosive reaction from the audience, and as Sokolov worked his way through encores by Schubert, Rameau, Chopin and Griboyedov I was struck more forcibly than ever by the seriousness with which he regarded every encore, cherishing each one as if it might be the last piece he would ever play in this life.

On to Cologne, where he presided over the Haydn sonatas with regal authority, each driven along with resolute momentum but with no sign of haste, even in the skilfully executed B minor sonata which received its very own prolonged round of applause. No other artist could better express Haydn's punctuation marks, from the smallest hesitations to the most exclamatory underscoring. As always, however, the Schubert impromptus stole the show.

In Passau's spectacular Grosser Rathaussaal, a handsome salon within the city's Town Hall accessed via a 15th century staircase, we had reached the blessed midsummer moment when artist and music were hand in glove, yet Sokolov's fathomless reservoir of ideas was far from exhausted and there was always something new to discover. At either end of the room were wall paintings depicting momentous civic events in Passau's history. For some, the pictorial splendour of the concert salon may have been a distraction from the music, but for me it created an appealing sense of pomp and pageantry. After a very hot day the stifling temperature in the room was a challenge for the audience and an even greater one for Sokolov, who was sandwiched between two clusters of spotlights mounted on stands and trained in his direction. To perform in such sweltering heat must have felt close to torture, but with his mind fixed firmly on the job in hand he maintained a cool exterior and gave us an impeccable account of his deeply satisfying Haydn/Schubert programme. This was another enthralling journey into Sokolov's unique sound world where every visit to the lower end of the keyboard was especially penetrating, each bass trill giving out a volcanic rumble. The penultimate passage in the fourth impromptu gave the distinct impression of a ticking clock, as if time was running out, the minute hand moving inexorably towards the moment the elemental spirits from Schubert's land of fantasy galloped away into the distance as fast as their fairy feet would carry them.

After the voluminous sound in Passau, the piano in Bad Kissingen two evenings later had a more streamlined, silvery tone, and I was in a position to be able to study the mesmerising fluidity with which Sokolov's hands moved over the keyboard. Watching them in action was quite extraordinary - they floated, they fluttered, they hovered and then plunged like birds of prey – and during the first Schubert impromptu they were as graceful as a prima ballerina's. Six exquisitely crafted encores followed; additional gifts that were an integral part of what happened at a Sokolov recital, all of them equally valuable, but on each occasion one in particular would take precedence. That night I walked away with the melancholy beauty of Schubert's Hungarian Melody ringing in my ears. With the end of the season in sight I reflected that the most recent Haydn programme had been an education. But since my discovery of Sokolov he had enhanced my appreciation of music in general a thousandfold and shown me how to listen in the truest sense of the word.

At the end of a grey November day with no sun to enliven the late Autumn colours, Sokolov walked out into Leipzig's darkened Grosser Saal, took his place at the piano, touched the keys – and suddenly it was springtime. With the opening of Beethoven's early Sonata No.3 Op.2/3 the music blossomed as Sokolov portrayed the reckless enthusiasms of youth. The contrasting gravity of the second movement was eloquently expressed and after the whirling scherzo which followed, the music waltzed off into the distance, preparing the way for the quicksilver finale, the sheer audacity of which prompted warm and prolonged applause. The accompanying Bagatelles Op.119 which Beethoven had dedicated to Haydn, began with an engaging lightness of step. At first hearing, the bagatelles seemed no more than a motley assortment of random ideas, some more complex than others, but soon revealed a wealth of varying moods and unexpected rhythmic shifts condensed into a fascinating fifteen minutes.

In Mannheim's Rosengarten Congress Centre in the spring of 2019 the Beethoven was crisply articulated and delivered with a dazzling display of agility. The Brahms Op.118/Op.119 programme was a lustrously beautiful voyage through a multi-layered emotional and visual landscape where at times, especially during Op.118/3, I felt as if I were airborne, skimming across the earth's surface at great velocity, crossing continents and shining oceans. I was reminded of those high speed film sequences where time was condensed and the sun rose and set in the space of a few short minutes; where light and shadow altered the landscape as clouds constantly re-assembled. Listening to this mesmerising odyssey over the coming nine months was going to be the greatest gift.

In April I approached Stuttgart's Liederhalle complex with mixed feelings, having visited the Beethovensaal on three previous occasions and been disappointed with the sound quality and the sprawling dimensions of the auditorium. This time, however, the piano sang out sweet and clear, heralding what was to become an immensely pleasurable event. At this venue it all depended on where you sat, and on that particular evening I must have found the perfect spot. The audience followed Sokolov through the Beethoven sonata and bagatelles in mute admiration and the Brahms pieces generated much excitement, covering so much ground, from the intensely personal storms of the heart and mind to the wider world and its countless marvels. Not only did Sokolov describe bold and dramatic panoramas, he lovingly outlined the most exquisite miniatures. The lyrical interlude in the Op.118/5 Romance suggested a secluded pool in which beautiful fish swam beneath the surface, occasional ripples catching the sunlight. In my imagination water lilies lay resplendent amongst the lily pads and above them iridescent winged insects hovered. Sokolov handled this sequence with touching delicacy before meeting with darker and more muscular challenges.

The six encores were all undisputed gems, but for me the most prized jewel was the Rachmaninoff prelude. As I listened to Sokolov's incisive account of this quintessentially Russian piece I gave thanks that I'd already set foot on Russian soil in 2006, walking the corridors of the Conservatory in St.Petersburg in a state of reverential awe and visiting the School for Specially Gifted Children where Sokolov attended as a young boy. Without this experience stored away in my memory bank, hearing this evocative piece would surely have prompted me to visit Russia without delay.

I moved on to Freiburg's handsome Konzerthaus where I had the rare opportunity to sit in the front row directly at Sokolov's feet. For me it was an occasional necessity not only to listen but to watch feet and fingers in mutual harmony, to attempt to grasp the magnitude of what he achieved, the thought processes involved in his preparation, the phenomenal concentration required, the emotional and physical energy he expended during a performance. The piano was an admirable specimen too; in fact as fine a piano as one could ever hope to hear: robust, richly toned and utterly steadfast until the final mysterious conclusion of the Debussy prelude.

The Brahms programme was by turns achingly tender and colossally powerful. I loved the finale of Op.119 which burst onto the scene rather like the final act in one of the more cheerful operas or ballets, or maybe a Shakespearean comedy where the major players paraded around the stage, each tying up their individual loose ends. There was a tumultuous outpouring from the audience and as the encores ensued there was complete uproar, as if Sokolov had taken us to the moon and back, shown us the seven wonders of the world, and just for good measure thrown in the secret of the universe, all in the space of less than three wonderful hours. How enriching was the experience of spending an evening travelling with him, entering his infinite world, crossing borders with no need of luggage or a passport. For the mere cost of a concert ticket anyone whose heart was open to such a possibility might easily catch a glimpse of heaven.

Sokolov's sell-out recital for the Klavier Festival Ruhr took place in June 2019 in the Historische Stadthalle in Wuppertal, a stately building with handsome reception rooms and a magnificent auditorium of ornate refinement. These sumptuous surroundings provided an ideal backdrop not only for the concert itself but for the cameras and microphones set up to record the event. The recital attracted a discriminating capacity audience who were reminded beforehand of the importance of keeping disturbances to the minimum for the sake of the recording, and they dutifully played their part. Sokolov's commitment was never in doubt, but any number of outside agents from technical glitches to audience-generated irritations could easily ruin the most scrupulously planned enterprise. I was especially anxious that all would run smoothly and the recording might appear on the market at some point so that I would have an enduring reminder of my 500th Sokolov performance.

The Beethoven sonata was delivered with youthful vigour. At the playful conclusion of the final movement with its impish trills and tantalizing hesitations, the applause came in abundance and there was still a subdued ripple of appreciation hanging in the air as

Sokolov began the Op.119 bagatelles, steering his course through this whimsical pick-and-mix, deftly illustrating their strange miscellany of moods, from picture book simplicity to manic confusion, finally drifting into the ether on a note of reflective tranquillity. In the second half he faithfully transmitted each of Brahms' creations to a rapt audience and the extraordinary qualities which set him apart from his contemporaries were much in evidence; qualities not only confined to his absolute command of any piece of music he turned his attention to but also as a dignified individual who seemed to possess not the smallest trace of self-importance.

A beguiling combination of encores rolled out, comprising Schubert's Op.142/2, Rameau's Les Sauvages, Brahms' Op.117/2, Rameau's Le Rappel des Oiseaux, Rachmaninoff's Op.32/12 and Debussy's Des pas sur la Neige. All six offerings were painstakingly presented as individual works of art, the grandeur of the pianism was more than a match for the elegant setting, and my sense of enslavement to the music was total. Throughout the Brahms programme I contemplated how difficult it was going to be to say goodbye to these living wonders at the end of the year, but reminded myself that next season Sokolov would most likely produce something equally compelling.

Bad Kissingen beckoned once more in July 2019, and as I sat in the Max-Littmann-Saal quite close to the piano I found myself admiring its sleek lines and gleaming surfaces, likening it to a treasure chest waiting to be unlocked. In anticipation of the myriad sounds it would soon produce under Sokolov's masterly direction, I felt blessed to be there at the start of another conducted tour of the inner worlds of Beethoven and Brahms as seen through the eyes and mind of Sokolov and transmitted through his heart and hands. As those sounds began to spill out across the auditorium it felt as if notes were raining down on me like confetti; a strange and wonderful sensation. But of course it was only Sokolov, weaving his magic.

An excellent acoustic was assured by virtue of the hall's cherry wood lining, a splendid piano was on hand and Sokolov was in great shape. The other vital ingredient to complete the formula was the audience, and rarely had I witnessed such a disciplined gathering. It was clear they knew Sokolov and his preferences, paying due respect to his need for continuity. The articulation of the Beethoven sonata's many voices was stunning and at the conclusion there was a comfortable silence during which Sokolov was free to turn his attention to Beethoven's engaging and unpredictable collection of bagatelles which were allowed to unfold without interruption. With artist, instrument, acoustic and audience in complete accord, the result was transcendental.

It might have been assumed that by midsummer Sokolov's programme had advanced from work in progress to finished product, but no – he could always shed fresh light on even the smallest detail. In the second half I was transfixed by the passion and intensity of the Op.118 A minor intermezzo, the hypnotic lyricism of the A major. Every one of those Brahms pieces had a special meaning for me and I believed no one could illustrate their beauty more eloquently. So often I walked away from a performance thinking I would never hear anything like it again, ever, and so many times he came back to prove me wrong.

That same month I heard Sokolov's contribution to the Schleswig-Holstein Musik Festival in the Kieler Schloss Konzertsaal, where he was able to obtain minimal lighting. His passage from the wings to the piano was illuminated, but the light was extinguished as soon as he was safely seated and from then on he occupied his own private circle of light. From the outset, quite apart from the unsurpassable quality of the playing, I was struck by the amazing beauty and clarity of sound. The Beethoven I experienced in Kiel stopped me in my tracks and I almost felt as if I were listening to the sonata afresh. The piano was one of the finest I'd heard in a long time and it felt as though a multitude of exotic birds might have been released into the auditorium to circle above us, forever in silent flight, their colourful plumage echoing the sumptuousness of the music. There was a sense of completeness about that performance, as if the final word had been spoken, and it brought to mind the words of an American music critic many years ago who expressed the wish that his last day on earth might be spent listening to Sokolov playing Beethoven.

At the end of the sonata a thin scattering of applause was quickly stifled and the bagatelles began their relatively short but fascinating journey, peppered with expertly negotiated gear changes, veering from nursery to nightmare, each one stamped with Sokolov's exceptional gift for telling a tale, whether it be part of the grandest sonata or the flimsiest trifle. Here was an artist in control of his craft, in companionable collaboration with his instrument. The glorious singing tone prevailed throughout the second half and I learned later that Sokolov had been guiding this fledgling instrument through its first appearance on the concert platform. He and the piano had given the impression of being old and trusted friends, but apparently this was the first time the piano had been played in public, and it seemed to have passed its initial test with top marks.

In November 2019 a Lufthansa cabin crew strike prevented me from travelling to Würzburg which was disappointing, but within days I was approaching the illuminated facade of the Festspielhaus in Baden-Baden with the familiar surge of expectation. There was never any doubt that Sokolov would deliver, but other factors played a vital part too. In Baden-Baden everything was as it should be, with a dependable piano and an essentially peaceful but super-enthusiastic audience whose uproarious reaction at the end of the evening almost blew the roof off.

Sokolov's excursion into three diverse works by Mozart became increasingly fascinating and although each had a different character, he wasted no time in addressing the keyboard to begin the next piece so that they flowed from one to another leaving no opportunity for interruption. The Prelude (Fantasie) & Fugue KV394 was something of an oddity. Had I entered a room with no prior knowledge and heard it being played I would not necessarily have assumed I was listening to Mozart, but then I was no expert. I'd read some criticism of the Prelude in particular from a musician's point of view, but as a mere listener I rather enjoyed its sheer athleticism and also the voluminousness of the Fugue. Each time I heard the Sonata KV331 which followed I found more to admire in its delicately etched variations and I was happy that Sokolov didn't take the alla Turca at breakneck speed. I'd often heard it performed as a kind of showpiece, but Sokolov never chose to indulge in such tactics.

I could never have imagined it possible that a Mozart composition would take me prisoner, but the Rondo KV511 did exactly that. The inexplicable melancholy of the opening theme was revisited at intervals and sounded as old as the hills and from far, far away. I treasured the softly spoken chords delivered with melting tenderness half way through this piece and was comforted that its captivating beauty would carry me contentedly into the next season, softening the impact of losing my beloved Brahms. But I had no way of knowing that I would not be setting foot in Germany again for a very long time.

§

The discovery of Sokolov's existence enriched my life beyond description, but everything came to a standstill with the arrival of the pandemic, and at the time of writing this book it has been two and a half years since I attended a recital. He no longer performs in the UK, so I must continue marking time until it's safe and I can summon the courage to fly again. Each recital has its own character and flavour, and whenever I listen to Sokolov he has a way of convincing me that this really is the only thing in the world worth doing. I live in hope that one day I can return to my old life and take my seat in a European concert hall. Once there, I know that in the moment before he begins casting his spell, as the audience retreats into silence and the lights are dimmed, if I listen very carefully I may hear his footsteps as he approaches the side of the platform. Even before he comes into view, for me the music will have already begun.

ACKNOWLEDGEMENTS

I met the following people either at Sokolov performances, through the Sokolov Facebook Group or on my travels, all of whom offered me their assistance, encouragement and in some cases their hospitality and lasting friendship. I would like to thank them for whatever part they played along the way.

Erik Haugan Aasland, Michael & Marina Berner, Brenn von Bibra, Willem Boone, Sonja & Johanna Brenner, Anne Catuogno, Yossi and Julie Chajes, Letizia Colombo, Wiebke Dannehl, Ineke Eldering, Filippo Furlan, Antonio Giancotti and Maria-Rosa, Hubert Giziewski, Leander Hotaki, John and Beth Hutchings, Alex Kirsch, Alina and Robert Kisiel, Marie, Mohamed and Paloma Kouider, Emile and Zitha Kraemer, Robert and Friedl Kruijswijk, Regina Kunrath, Dr Jochen Lechner, Barbara Leubner, Evgeny Lykhin, Elizabeth Marschan, Vladimir and Valerija fa Milic, Harald and Marlis Muehlhausen, Franco Panozzo, Franco Perretta, Dina Pruzhansky, Béatrice Reuflet and Jean-Francois Renard, Klaus and Heide Rupf, Waltraut Schenke, Gudrun and Peter Schmitz-Jacobi, Horst Schrader, Hilla Schuetze, Isabel Serra and Quim, Lyudmila Sinyagovskaya, Pete and Angie Taylor, Barbara Troeger & Patricia Pfaff, Holger True, Nadia Zhdanova and many more.

Special thanks to Christine Deahl for her proof-reading skills, and to Pete Taylor and Jochen Lechner for their technical help and advice.

Since the completion of this book I have resumed European travel and attended several of Sokolov's recitals, the first of which, in Paris's Théâtre des Champs-Elysées in May 2022, felt like a long-awaited homecoming.

Printed in Poland
by Amazon Fulfillment
Poland Sp. z o.o., Wrocław

29686964R00177